'I would read/listen to anything that Paul Brady has to say. A voice of our times.'

Harry Belafonte

'A troubadour, an honest man, fearless and true, an inspiration to anyone who would like to be a storyteller ... And all that's without trying to describe the way he sings and plays, that's beyond me ...'

Eric Clapton

'Paul Brady is strong stuff ... more real and more honest than most people would even try for ... a genuine voice speaking from the heart but with a brain still attached ... I love his work and always have.'

David Crosby

'People get too famous too fast these days and it destroys them. Some guys got it down – Leonard Cohen, Paul Brady, Lou Reed – secret heroes.'

Bob Dylan

'This is the story of a youngster in love with the music he heard on the radio in Ireland, teaching himself piano and guitar before finding his own voice and becoming a leading international singer-songwriter.'

Mark Knopfler

'Like so many of his songs and his presentation of them, *Crazy Dreams* is a work of art at once driving and delicate, gritty and graceful.'

Paul Muldoon

'Few can write, sing and play with more gorgeous melody, virtuosity and soulful lyrics than Paul Brady. He's written some of the most powerful and beloved songs I sing and will always be one of my favorite artists.'

Bonnie Raitt

'There is no limit to Paul's scope in music, going from the re-statement of Paddy Tunney's great songs (and other traditional music) to his thoughtful compositions about the darkness and joy of living in the modern world.'

Stephen Rea

To my wife, Mary Elliott

PART ONE

Crazy Dreams

Paul Brady

MERRION
PRESS

First published in 2022 by
Merrion Press
10 George's Street
Newbridge
Co. Kildare
www.merrionpress.ie

© Paul Brady, 2022

978 1 78537 429 6 (Paper)
978 1 78537 430 2 (Ebook)

A CIP catalogue record for this book is available from the British Library.

Typeset in Sabon LT Pro 11.5/17.5

Front cover image: Paul Brady in Rhode Island, 1973 © Eva Rubinstein
Back cover image: Paul Brady, taken by Kate Horgan

Cover design by Fiachra McCarthy

Unless otherwise credited, all internal images courtesy of the author.
Image on page 159 © Colm Henry

Merrion Press is a member of Publishing Ireland.

CONTENTS

PART TWO

FOREWORD

The date was Friday, 18 February 1977. The venue was St Mary's School Hall in Irvinestown. It was an evening that featured James Simmons, Frank Ormsby and myself reading a few poems, with Paul Brady and Artie McGlynn providing the music. There were 500 people in the hall, each of whom had paid a pound sterling for the privilege of being there. There was absolutely no doubt as to what had brought them out on a chilly evening in a time of even more chilling sectarian violence. They were there to see Paul Brady.

Like so many great artists, the young Paul Brady had shown a capacity, both eerie and unerring, to steep himself in a range of traditions and then combine them into something we hadn't quite seen or heard before. Though he hadn't so publicly embraced the rock and roll that would be foregrounded in his solo career, he was every bit as informed by the showmanship of Chuck Berry as any Child ballad or the plangencies of Cathal Buí.

At a mere thirty years of age, he was already an alum of The Johnstons, a band he'd joined ten years earlier. He had been a member of Planxty, a group that already enjoyed a legendary status. He was still in the midst of his landmark collaboration with Andy Irvine. Even in 1977, Paul Brady's command of an audience was breathtaking. He was clearly a force to be reckoned with.

In the intervening forty-five years, I've had the privilege of getting to know Paul Brady and to develop a deeper sense of his commitment to the idea that his remarkable success has had to do less with his own 'command', or his own being a 'force', than with the idea of his being at the service of a power beyond himself. I have often heard him speak of his being possessed by a 'beast' when he performs. This dedication to the notion that he has made himself an instrument of the song is one that he shares with many great artists, including Bob Dylan, who has so tellingly asserted: 'It's not me. It's the songs. I'm just the postman. I deliver the songs.'

I suspect that this humility may have had Paul Brady occasionally question the appropriateness of writing a memoir, a genre that might at first blush seem to smack of solipsism and self-regard. The reality is that a memoir is compelling precisely because it is based on selflessness, giving us a sense not only of the individual but, more significantly, the individual in society. Paul Brady's story is fascinating, but it fascinates above all as a getting down of a very specific time and place. As another Northern Irish boy whose mother was a teacher, who was the beneficiary of the 1947 Education Act and attended an excellent grammar school where he studied Irish, English, French and Latin, and who ended up being somewhat blasé about the opportunity afforded him at university, I've been struck again and again by Paul Brady's constant illumination of the society in which we were raised. Like so many of his songs and his presentation of them, *Crazy Dreams* is a work of art, at once driving and delicate, gritty and graceful.

Paul Muldoon

1

STRABANE 1950

Leafy green wallpaper from a bygone time. This is the first thing to register. A small room with, from a three-year old's viewpoint, a high ceiling; one bare light bulb glaring down; a black cast-iron range at one end. Musty, fusty coaly smells, someone whistling a popular tune, strangers coming and going, carting in beds, chairs and tables from the cold, dark outside into the living room of an unfamiliar house ...

Strabane, County Tyrone, Northern Ireland. The year is 1950 and the Brady family have just moved from Barrack Street, where there are no longer barracks, to Church Street where there is no longer a church – though an ancient, forgotten graveyard remains.

Home at the time to around 6,000 living souls, Strabane is an old town, crucible of unrest in the past and soon to be in the future. Situated at the confluence of three rivers, the Mourne, the Finn and the Foyle, historically the border between counties Tyrone and Donegal since the twelfth century, many a skirmish, night of rape and plunder would have taken place between the O'Neill and O'Donnell clans long before the English and Scottish planters arrived in the late sixteenth century. And since 1921, fewer than thirty years before the Bradys arrive in Church Street, it is also a border town between Northern Ireland and the Irish Republic, or the Free State, as locals call it.

The child Paul – myself – is at the time the youngest of Sean and Mollie Brady. My sister Anne, three years older, is the firstborn. My brother, Barry, will arrive five years later. There is talk of a miscarriage in between, which took its toll.

My parents have arrived in the area six years before the move to Church Street, not long after getting married. Blow-ins the pair. Sean, a 'Wesht of Ireland man', a Free State man, Sligo born and bred. Mollie, a North of Ireland girl, from the other end of Tyrone where it bordered County Fermanagh. Temperamentally, two very different people.

Both were primary school teachers. Sean qualified in De La Salle training college in far-off Waterford under the Republic's education system. Republic of Ireland schools followed the Free State ethos where the Irish language, the influence of the Catholic Church, and a heroic version of the struggle for Irish independence underpinned the standard three Rs.

Mollie qualified in St Mary's in Belfast under the new state of Northern Ireland's education system, with schools following the British model, where Irish history was still too present and contro-versial to form part of the curriculum.

Both intended to work after marriage and children, so a border town was their only practical option. When they moved to Stra-bane, they took up positions in schools three miles from each other, a short distance as the crow flies, but poles apart in cultural and political terms.

Sean's school, Murlog National School, was across the river on the outskirts of Lifford, in County Donegal, in the Irish Republic. Despite being in the Republic, the school was in the diocese of Derry, now a Northern Ireland city. Ancient diocesan boundaries long predated the carving up of the country in 1922. Accordingly, teaching positions and promotions in County Donegal remained at the pleasure of the Bishop of Derry.

Mollie's school, Sion Mills Primary Elementary, was three miles south of Strabane and in Northern Ireland. It was, by Northern Ireland standards, unusual. Founded in the mid-nineteenth century by local linen mill owners, the Herdman family, to educate the children of their factory workers, its charter from day one, based on their Quaker philosophy, was to mix gender and religion. It was now under the control of the Northern Ireland Education Authority of the day and students were subject to all the required examinations up until the 11-plus, an examination taken at the age of eleven to twelve in UK- and Northern Ireland-governed schools to determine the type of secondary school a child should enter.

Most education in the North was and still is controlled by the Churches, Catholic and Protestant going to separate schools, confirming each in ignorance of the other and fuelling the prejudice and bigotry that inevitably follows. Pupils at Sion Mills were spared that early indoctrination. To this day I feel I benefited from the climate of tolerance and freedom of association that came with this early integrated education.

Soon after the family moved to Church Street, and before school age, I accompanied my mother to her school where she taught Senior Infants. Child minders were not an option on a teacher's annual salary of £150. We had no extended family of grandparents, uncles and aunts close by to take up the slack. I remember sitting in the corner of her classroom at my own little desk playing with crayons and building-blocks while the rest of the class got on with their lessons.

2

EARLY SCHOOLDAYS

In time, I too started at my mother's school. Why there, as opposed to my father's in Lifford? Well, our home was, after all, in Northern Ireland and it made administrative sense to stay within that system. Unusually, for a young woman in those parts at the time and seen as 'modern', Mollie owned a car, even before her marriage – a dark-blue new Morris 8 that she bought in Omagh in 1939.

Socially independent, driving far and wide in the North and even once to Dublin to visit friends, she used the car for the three-mile daily journey to Sion Mills School while Sean cycled the shorter distance to Lifford, just across the bridge that straddled the border.

One downside of not going to the school around the corner in Strabane was that I never really integrated into the local school-age social or recreational scene or had childhood friends in the town beyond the kids of our immediate neighbours.

This 'outsider' feeling, coupled with the subtle background experience of neither parent being natives of the town left me with a sense of dislocation, of 'not-quite-belonging', that has lasted all my life.

School holidays in autumn and winter saw frequent trips to aunts, uncles and cousins in Omagh, Enniskillen and Irvinestown. In summer, we spent long periods in the Donegal seaside resort, Bundoran, where many of these same relations congregated. Mollie came from a close-knit family of nine. Sean had two sisters and a younger brother, Colm, who was to pass away in tragic circumstances in 1955.* With up to thirty first cousins around our own age, our childhood focus was more on extended family than on hometown friends. The seasonal absences from home increased the sense of dislocation.

Sion Mills School in the early 1950s, while officially integrated in religion and gender and outwardly tolerant and respectful of difference, was nonetheless reflective of the official culture at large in Northern Ireland. The unionist, Protestant people were dominant and the nationalist Catholic population at best compliant and good neighbours but not really to be trusted politically or with responsibility. The school principal was always Protestant. Religious instruction was taught separately and with equal emphasis, but the overall ethos was unionist.

The main sport was cricket. Sion Mills always had, and still has, a good cricket team (though my only foray onto the cricket pitch resulted in being 'bowled for a duck'). On the school sports day in 1953 – the year of Queen Elizabeth's coronation (I was six) – the prizes were silver spoons with the Queen's head at the top of the handle in little presentation boxes with a Union Jack design. I was excited when I got one for being 'placed' in the three-legged race and then heard my mother saying in the car on the way home, 'Don't show that to your father!' The implication was that Sean might be annoyed at the presumption of loyalty to the Crown. Mollie might have been voicing her own prejudices. Apart from Sean's belief that the ruling class was stupid to persist in discriminating against, and

---

* Colm had joined the British Army during the Second World War and had been captured by the Japanese and imprisoned in Burma. After the war he stayed in the army and was stationed in Germany. In an accident he was thrown out of an open-top jeep and killed instantly. I can still remember the phone call telling my father the news and the feeling that permeated the house for days afterwards.

denying power to, the Catholic minority – *If they'd only given an inch none of all this [the later violence] would have happened* – he was disinterested in day-to-day political goings on and let little of it bother him.

Still, I didn't show my queenie spoon to him.

The outbreak of that phase of IRA violence in the North between 1956 and 1962 reinforced the cultural tensions. Strabane was not immune to the political unrest and was divided in terms of allegiances. In 1956, aged nine, I saw the odd sight of armoured cars in desert-sand yellow camouflage parked in the Bowling Green outside Strabane's Police Barracks. Rushed back from Cyprus (the other hot spot of dwindling empire of the moment) to deal with the sudden IRA campaign, the British Army hadn't had time to repaint them. The picture of them patrolling Tyrone's verdant hedgerow-bordered back roads was indeed bizarre. When my local friends and I hovered in awe around them I heard our Protestant neighbour's children grumbling that we Catholics were spying on them and giving information to the IRA. How ridiculous. I knew nobody in the IRA. But that was what they had been raised to believe.

In fact, there existed an unspoken ambivalence in my own household about the 1950s IRA campaign – a stopping short of outright support, but a clear understanding of why it was happening. My mother's stories about her family's experience of ethnic bullying by the B-Specials in rural Fermanagh in the 1930s and 1940s, inculcated in us a visceral sympathy with the notion of fighting back.

Now, due to these recent Troubles, we were often stopped by patrols at night when travelling home from visits to relations and subjected to intimidating interrogations and searches. As soon as my father gave his obviously Catholic name, the tone would become supercilious and threatening. It was scary and left me in no doubt as to where we stood in the political pecking order at the time. This ambivalence was something I struggled with for years until I finally sorted my own head and heart out in the mid-1980s with my song 'The Island'.

Whatever about the cultural ethos of Sion Mills school, my memory tells me I was happy there. Though music didn't form part of the curriculum, I found out I was good at art. Naturally ambidextrous, I drew all the time and all over everything: copybooks, textbooks, desktops even.

I fondly remember boys like Gwynn Elliott, Brian Allison and Gregory Donaghy. Gregory, like me, went on to be a musician and singer, and at one time was a vocalist with the nationally famous Cadets Showband. Towards the end of my last year at primary school we had a sing-song in the class. Just the previous Christmas, Gregory and I had got guitars from Santa and we brought them in that morning. Straightaway we set about reinventing the current Elvis hit 'All Shook Up', the Everly Brothers 'Wake Up Little Suzie' and 'Cumberland Gap', Lonnie Donegan's recent hit. The class sang along raucously. Somehow an advance on just singing to family and friends at parties, this new experience imparted a fledgling sense of the power that performing gives access to. Of course, with power comes expectations. Gregory already knew three more guitar chords than me. The pressure was on at age eleven.

3

MOTHER'S AND FATHER'S PEOPLE

My mother Mollie McElholm's people originated in County Donegal. Family oral history talks of J.J. McElholm, a blacksmith from Ardara at the turn of the nineteenth century. He married a woman from Lettermacaward and they had twelve children. He also ran one of the many illegal hedge schools throughout the country where he taught Catholics to read and write. For this he was arrested and sentenced to six months hard labour in Sligo Gaol but was released on foot of Catholic emancipation, namely the Roman Catholic Relief Act 1829.

Three of their children went to America. Two came to County Tyrone early in the nineteenth century, one to Drumbinnion, which is our direct line. The other seven died during the Great Famine in the mid-1840s, as did J.J. and his wife. The Drumbinnion son was a shoemaker and had a great reputation for making shoes for clubfeet. His son, John James, was my great-grandfather and, in 1869, was the first Catholic to be *paid* for teaching. He taught in the townland of Feglish in County Tyrone for the princely sum of £8 per annum.

Next in line, my grandfather James Joseph McElholm, known as Josie, trained as a teacher in De La Salle College, Waterford, as did his brothers: Dan, Willie, Alfie and Sam, and as my father did. Teaching was in the bloodline, on both sides of the family.

Given how poor and disadvantaged these families were, how were my forbears able to afford this training, not to mention the accommodation and living expenses that went with it? I found out that in the mid-nineteenth century there was such a shortage of primary level teachers throughout the United Kingdom of Britain and Ireland (as it was then), that a scholarship scheme was launched called the Queen's (later the King's) scholarship.

Gifted pupils from the age of thirteen onwards could be apprenticed to a teacher and known as monitors. If they showed promise they were offered the chance to take up official teacher training at one of a half-dozen venues in Ireland. Their training, accommodation and living expenses were paid for by the state. The course would last maybe one or two years, and no doubt the living conditions were basic. But this is what seems to have enabled my family forbears, and in turn my parents, to get onto the education high road.

Josie married Brigid Colton in 1911 and they rented rooms in a townland called Kinine (from the Irish *ceann eidhneán*, ivy-clad hillock) in a farmhouse of the same name owned by a local bank manager. Over time came nine children with my mother Mollie (Mary Ellen) the firstborn in 1912. The banker and his family moved out at some point leaving Josie and Brigid to rent Kinine and the attached 30 acres themselves. Josie, however, had his heart set on *buying* the house and farm. He finally achieved his dream for £105.

There was fierce jealousy amongst some locals over this. Josie was Catholic; the bankers who sold the house were Protestant. In football parlance it was 'against the run of play'. Mollie told us that Josie and Brigid never used the water from the well on the farm as it was said to have been poisoned by embittered neighbours! Despite this, Josie seems to have been popular and well-loved in the locality. He had a great reputation for helping out neighbours in difficulty and was called 'the Master' (schoolmaster) by all, a sign of respect.

My mother and father both being teachers meant education was not only valued but worth putting above other dreams, perhaps. My parents' teaching careers enabled us kids to have a comfortable childhood – there was little spare money around, but neither were we poor or considered so.

On my father's side, the Bradys, there was in fact a connection to Lifford and Strabane back the line. Although my great-grandfather John Brady was from the midlands (born in 1836 in Clonbroney, County Longford) when he came of age, he joined the army, as many young Irishmen of the time did. This was the British Army at the time since Ireland was still part of the United Kingdom.

John was initially posted in the Curragh Camp, County Kildare – one of the biggest garrisons in the south-east of the country. There he met Mary McNally, a young woman from the nearby town of Naas, and they married in November 1873. John was soon transferred to the garrison at Lifford, County Donegal. John and Mary Brady had three children born and baptised in Lifford.

The eldest was Edward Hugh who emigrated to Australia. Next was Mary, and finally my grandmother, Oonagh Brady (b. 1879). Sadly, John died in the 1880s and Mary Brady (née McNally) remarried Pat Bohan, a shopkeeper from Ballymote, County Sligo; she moved there and practiced as a midwife. This ended the family's Lifford connection for now.

Mary and Pat Bohan had four children of their own: Kathleen (who drowned on nearby Strandhill beach), Mary Agnes or 'Doty' as she was called, Sarah and Elizabeth, known as 'Baby'. These were Granny Oonagh's half-sisters – my half grandaunts.

In the late 1950s and 1960s, twice a year, we journeyed to Ballymote to visit Doty and Baby, by then getting on in years. The first sights of the Ox Mountains in South County Sligo gave me the feeling I was now in a different and magical part of Ireland. The Bohan sisters were in themselves quite mysterious. There was a fascinating history surrounding them that we children knew little about at the time. It was to do with the relatively undocumented involvement of women in the Irish Rising, the following War of Independence and the ensuing Irish Civil War. Even in the 1970s, when I visited them with my wife Mary and our infant daughter Sarah, I never thought to ask them directly about their interesting pasts. I regret not having asked.

To put it in context, the first two decades of the twentieth century witnessed a hugely dramatic time in Ireland, politically, culturally and socially. The Bohan girls and their half-sister Oonagh (my grandmother) were very close and they grew into their teens surrounded by agitation and excitement of all kinds. The demands for Home Rule, the serious urban labour unrest of 1913, the First World War, in which thousands of young Irishmen of all persuasions fought and died, and the existence and increasing militancy of hard-line republican organisations like the Irish Republican Brotherhood (IRB) and James Connolly's Irish Citizen's Army (ICA) all ratcheted up the emotional mood in the country.

The 1916 Rising brought things to a head. A 'glorious failure', it was savagely put down by British forces. The leaders of the Rising were condemned to death by firing squad.

After the executions the mood of Ireland, initially confused, ambivalent, indeed in many instances hostile towards the revolution, changed. Sinn Féin, a previously ineffective republican party, took centre stage with seventy-five of its members elected to the British parliament on an abstentionist ticket in the general election of 1918. Abstentionist meant that although you were officially elected as a Member of Parliament, you refused to take your seat in protest at the political status quo.

One of the abstentionists was Éamon de Valera who now became president of Sinn Féin. Another was Countess Markievicz, one of the most interesting of the active participants in the fighting.

Born into an aristocratic Anglo-Irish landed family – the Gore-Booths, whose family seat was at Lissadell in County Sligo – after a life of privilege she rejected her class and threw her lot in with the Irish revolutionaries. She fought in the Easter Rising of 1916 and only avoided execution on account of her gender.

My grand-aunt, Baby Bohan, developed a friendship with Markievicz based on the women's shared politics and possibly too that they were both natives of County Sligo.

The Irish guerilla War of Independence (1919–21) and the Civil War (1922–3) that followed were heady times. Baby Bohan, like Markievicz, was a member of Cumann na mBan (the Irishwomen's Council, a paramilitary organisation in favour of armed rebellion). Baby was politically a radicalised young woman. Her association with Markievicz continued throughout the War of Independence. Although she never talked about those times when we visited as kids, a fascinating document, handwritten by Baby, was found by my sister Anne in papers she left behind.

Baby took the anti-treaty side in the subsequent Irish Civil War. Cumann na mBan was outlawed by the new Irish government and Baby's continued involvement in the organisation led to her arrest in 1923 on foot of a warrant signed by the new Irish Free State's defence minister, Richard Mulcahy. This in turn led to her and several other women going on hunger strike for thirty days in the North Dublin Union where she was imprisoned.

Markievicz was later arrested because of disturbances caused when she had been speaking publicly on behalf of the prisoners. She too joined the hunger strike towards the latter end of it. Baby was close to death when the hunger strike was called off. She was nursed back to health by Markievicz herself.

The immediate years after the Civil War were a nightmare for the losing side. There was discrimination if not brutal exclusion of those who fought against the treaty. You could say goodbye to a career in public service if your name was on one of the blacklists at the time.

The last straw for the anti-treaty side, however, came in 1926 when de Valera decided that 'abstentionism' as a Sinn Féin political tool was self-defeating. He left the abstentionists to form a new party, Fianna Fáil and took the 'oath of allegiance' to the British Crown.

To the Bohan girls and Oonagh it was like the Civil War had been fought in vain, as if the loss of life and disruption of society was a waste. Worse was the fact that family members disagreed with each other about de Valera's decision, and families were pitted against each other for generations. Some never got over the new status quo and spent a life in quiet (or sometimes not so quiet) rejection of it. Some left Ireland for good.

The scars ran so deep in the Bohan side of the family that in the late 1930s and early 1940s, when pensions were being given to those who took part in the War of Independence by de Valera's government, Baby and Doty refused to accept theirs.

So little is talked about all that now. So little was said about Baby and Doty's involvement in the pivotal events that shaped present-day Ireland. Even my father Sean, their nephew, didn't talk about those times. The politics of Ireland to this day is still influenced by the legacy of the Civil War.

My father's own immediate family had their ups and downs too. His mother Oonagh married Mick Brady, coincidentally with the same surname. They had four surviving children: Kathleen (known as Teaco), Mary Therese (known as Máirín), Sean (my father born in 1914) and Colm.

Grandad Mick had a business in Sligo with his brother JP selling bicycles built from scratch, cars, motorcycles, radios and the first cylinder record players. They were well-off for a while. They had a shop in the centre of Sligo town and an outlet in Dublin. The

IRISHMAN NOT WANTED.

It is true the British militarists have dismantled five motor cars on which myself and my family were entirely dependent for a living. They have given no reason for taking away in broad daylight, by armed forces, parts of my property thereby declaring that I (a mere Irishman) was not to be allowed to live in Ireland.

Now our Irish National Assurance Company has appointed me as the "National" Representative for Sligo and district, I appeal to every Irishman and woman to take out a Policy with this Company, because by so doing you are building up the Irish nation as no other act of yours can. These monies so collected will all be invested in Ireland to support Irish enterprise, and will not be given over to the foreigner for the one and only object of stealing our money, our property, and our living from us.

Still more to your interest you can get better value in insurance from the Irish National than from any foreign company.

Please let me explain to you.

A post card or wire will bring me to your door, or call on me at your convenience and we will talk the matter over.

My address is No. 5 LORD EDWARD ST., SLIGO.

M. F. BRADY,
Of the Suppressed Brady's Garage, Sligo.

two girls were sent to boarding school in Eccles Street Convent, Dublin, one of the most prestigious girls' schools in the country. The youngest boy, Colm, went as a boarder to Blackrock College, again one of Ireland's top boys' schools. There was a governess at home to educate and look after the children when they were young. Mick was the hands-on practical guy; JP was the business head and salesman of the business.

There was some disagreement between the brothers. JP opened his own shop in nearby Castlebar. He moved to Dublin, ending up in Clonmel in County Tipperary where over the next few decades his business thrived. Profiting from the petrol rationing during the Second World War, he anticipated a rise in demand for bicycles and motorcycles. He made a lot of money. He was also at the forefront of the sales drive of domestic radio sets with an ad campaign slogan 'Brady-O for Radio' that was known all over the south of Ireland.

My grandfather Mick was not as successful. He was less of a businessman, more of a gifted mechanic. He moved the family around to Birr, County Offaly, then to Limerick and later to Ballina in County Mayo. During the War of Independence his business suffered at the hands of the British military offshoot, the Black and Tans, who in 1919 'requisitioned' his cars – a Clyno, an Overland Tourer, a Model T Ford and a Calthorpe – with no compensation. This was a major financial setback and caused him to circularise a printed protest to try and rectify the situation, to no avail.

The brothers tried to stay in touch it seems, though by the time I came along, the two families had drifted apart. As kids we never heard of the JP side of the family's existence. Only in my generation was there a reconciliation. My sister Anne and I met the Clonmel Bradys. JP's daughter Mona had married Des Hanafin, a prominent local political figure and their daughter Mary, my newly discovered second cousin, was for a time deputy head of the Fianna Fáil political party and, among other senior positions, Minister of Education in the Irish government.

Despite my grandfather Mick's cars being requisitioned by the Black and Tans, finances improved throughout the 1920s. By the turn of the decade the family had around £2,000 in the bank (approximately £100,000 in today's money). But Mick's health deteriorated, leading to an early death in 1934 from spinal meningitis. The business collapsed, and this drastically affected the circumstances of the family.

I never knew my grandfather Mick, but I can picture the family set-up, my dad in the workshop watching his dad working miracles with engines. Stories passed down tell of Sean learning to drive as soon as his feet could reach the pedals. When Mick was about to leave Sligo for Dublin for business one day, the starting handle of the Model T Ford sprang back breaking his hand. Sean, aged twelve, drove to Dublin instead. He drove the entire 120 miles with his father Mick in the passenger seat.

Maybe we make it all fit in retrospect, that we inherit what we love from our ancestors; certainly, there was love of education on both sides of the family, a strong revolutionary pulse on the female Brady line – but music was there too.

As a young woman in her twenties and thirties Grandmother Oonagh Brady was, in fact, a celebrated singer in the Sligo locality. A participant in many Feiseanna Ceoil (music festivals) she was mentioned in local newspapers and periodicals. She even formed part of the opening act on a John McCormack concert in Sligo town. It was a love of music and more tellingly perhaps *performance* she passed on to her own son, Sean, my father. Either way Granny Oonagh was musical well into her late seventies – we children knew her as a jolly old lady who entertained us singing big dramatic patriotic Irish songs like 'The West's Awake' and 'Follow Me up to Carlow' whenever we visited her.

4

BEGINNINGS OF MUSIC

There was a love of music in our house and before long, a piano appeared in the front room. Both Sean and Mollie had musical talent and liked to pick out tunes, though neither had had any formal lessons. I remember evenings when we all sat by the fire and sang together.

Mollie loved singing sentimental old Irish songs like 'Eileen Aroon' and Percy French's 'The Pride of Petravore'. Sean, for reasons I never fully explored, favoured popular Latin American songs of the previous century like 'La Paloma', 'La Golondrina', both composed in the 1860s, as well as dramatic patriotic Irish songs that he would have learned from his mother.

Sean was also a talented actor who produced and appeared in several amateur dramatic revues and plays in the town. His speciality became the one-man show, in the form of a monologue. His favourites were 'The Face on the Barroom Floor' by Hugh Antoine d'Arcy, 'Laska' by Frank Desprez, Robert Service's 'The Shooting of Dan McGrew' and 'Little Rosa', a half-spoken country hit in 1956 for Webb Pierce and Red Sovine. While Robert Service's poems were common enough, the others were quite rare in Ireland and I never found out how he came across them.

When I say one-man show, it really was a show. The stories Sean picked were rife with drama. The monologue form was often the chosen party piece of the time by those with a yen for public speaking, but the usual style was a basic colourless sing-song drone with little personality in the delivery. Sean gave performances. He *lived* the parts, spoke in different voices according to character, dragged every emotional nuance out of the story. With his facial expressions and body language the effect was riveting. I remember him in Bundoran during our summer holidays holding entire rooms in the palm of his hand, leaving people in tears. Sometimes he would even shed a tear himself for effect while winking at us conspiratorially. He would be barely inside a hostelry when he'd be called upon. A local hero. I often wonder if, in a different era and in different circumstances, he might have become an actor rather than a schoolteacher – a job he was temperamentally unsuited to and never really liked.

My years of watching him in full flight shaped my own later performances of the great traditional ballads like 'Arthur McBride' and 'The Lakes of Pontchartrain'. Like him, I loved a story with strong characters and high drama. As I got older, I accompanied him on the piano as he sang his party pieces.

Unknown, outside our own locality of Northwest Ireland, in the mid-1960s, Sean uncharacteristically allowed himself to be persuaded by a few friends and admirers to enter the national Toastmasters competition in the Hibernian Hotel in Dublin's Dawson Street. How proud I was to be in the audience when he won it outright. Sean was later asked to represent Ireland in an international Toastmasters get together in Glasgow. He didn't win this time and the next day flew back home. His one and only brush with national prominence was over. Never again did he involve himself with public speaking competitions or dramatic productions.

There may have also been a certain tension at home surrounding Sean's love of performing and production. I think Mollie found that side of him a threat, something she had no experience of that was impossible to control. Was there a touch of jealousy? Was it that time spent having fun with others was time spent away from her, from home duties? She never actively encouraged him to keep his life in the world of drama alive. I still regret that he didn't reach a wider audience. He could have shown the theatre world a thing or two. He was also a talented artist and many of his paintings and drawings graced the walls of our home in Church Street.

As far back as I can remember I had an instinctive relationship with music. Music was the touchstone that gave me a sense of belonging to the world. If I was unhappy, isolated or under threat, music was an escape, a trusted friend; the sense of order inherent in a beautiful melody was instantly a comfort. To my surprise nobody in my immediate circle, child or adult, seemed to need music in the same way.

Tales I overheard as my mother and father did the 'my-kid-is-smarter-than-your-kid' waltz with their peers, told me that by eighteen months, I was la-la-ing the melody of 'Now is the Hour', an old Maori song that became a worldwide hit with English lyrics in the late 1940s. Still, however natural a part of me it was, and however musically gifted I was recognised to be, it would be twenty years before events would conspire to leave me with little option *but* to choose music as a career.

The perilous nature of a musical career was a preposterous idea to people of our societal status – the notion that you might presume to earn a living from something you enjoyed doing.

In the meantime, like many, I went to piano lessons around age six or seven to a dear old lady Miss Dillon who seemed ancient to me. Her piano stood in a darkened gas-lit room like something out of *Great Expectations*. I struggled through five-finger exercises, major and minor scales, and arpeggios. Miss Dillon herself had a bad shake in her hands which impacted on her ability to play or show me what to do. Since this is the dominant memory from my piano lessons it's fair to say I didn't learn a lot. It was not a happy time. I was discovering a great love of music, but the lessons had nothing to do with the stuff I wanted to learn. I would try and practise the scales but instead would wander round the keyboard finding ways to play the music I heard on the radio.

I was good at playing by ear. I spent hours in the front room working out how to play. I relied on my ear to pick out what sounded right or not. I found the whole business of reading music a chore, and still do. I never found not reading music a disadvantage, bar sight-reading exams at school later. In any case, I persuaded my parents to let me off the hook and I got out of the dreaded piano lessons till I started in boarding school at age eleven.

Our family grew in September 1955. My brother Barry had a difficult entry into the world. Mollie was rhesus negative and he was rhesus positive which meant that she developed antibodies which could enter his circulation and attack his blood. It was a serious condition at the time. The anti-D injection to combat the condition didn't arrive till 1967.

Initially Barry developed jaundice, but he also had to have a total blood transfusion because of the rhesus factor. This solved the problem but the experience deeply affected our mother psychologically. Barry remained in hospital for four weeks. Mollie became nervous about his health and in the first few months was protective, bordering on obsessive, imagining he had brain damage. The fact that a few years previously she'd had a miscarriage can't have helped. Back then a consultant had written to her to advise against having any more children 'with this husband' and this at a time there was no contraception. I can only imagine the pressures that must have introduced to the marriage. Mollie only relaxed after Barry got three straight As in his A-levels!

Eventually Barry thankfully recovered and came home. From

then on, Mollie (understandably) devoted most of her time, energy and focus to him. The dismay at being supplanted by a new and fussed-over arrival took its toll on me. Never a tactile mother at the best of times, hugs or cuddles with her first son became fewer, leaving me feeling increasingly left out and threatened. I was not above being jealous.

I retreated more and more into the only thing I could control – music. When not being 'shushed' by my parents, so the baby could have his daytime nap, I banged away at the piano to make them feel their decision to send me to Miss Dillon wasn't a waste of time and money. I'd resurrect some sheet music I'd long ago learned by heart and pretend to read it as I played. Making up my own hybrid versions of songs I heard on the radio was probably the beginning of my expressing myself in an individually artistic way. The music I was coming up with belonged to no one but me, and soon became the soundtrack to a newly discovered and safe inner world.

This was before the advent of Rock 'n' Roll, at least on the Irish and UK airwaves. Looking back, a lot of these hit songs seem, in a post Bob Dylan world, lyrically schmaltzy, corny even. But they were a true product of their time and had unforgettable melodies, arrangements and production. Singers like Nat King Cole, Ella Fitzgerald, Harry Belafonte, Frankie Laine, Eddie Fisher, Mario Lanza, Rosemary Clooney, Theresa Brewer, Slim Whitman, Johnny Ray, Bing Crosby and Frank Sinatra lit up the airwaves with their magic. I still feel a tug at my heart the rare times I might hear songs like 'Mary's Boy Child', 'Three Coins in a Fountain', 'Stranger in Paradise', 'Rose Marie', 'Oh My Papa', 'Because You're Mine', 'The Shrimp Boats', 'Someone to Watch Over Me' and 'Now Is the Hour'.

A recent Jamaican immigrant pianist to UK, Winifred Atwell, was regularly storming up the British charts with lively ragtime-based instrumentals like 'Let's Have Another Party', 'The Poor

People of Paris' and 'Coronation Rag'. I was immediately attracted to her exuberant style and developed simple but credible versions of my own, to the delight of my parents. I recently discovered that Winifred was also a huge influence on a young Reg Dwight, who went on to change his name to Elton John.

Another song that was a hit at the time was 'The Happy Wanderer', staying twenty-six weeks in the British charts in 1954. This I learned to play and sing, and it was possibly the first song I ever performed in front of people. 'Tom Dooley' by the Kingston Trio was another hit that I enjoyed performing. A friend, Danny Deeny, a doctor's son from the Bowling Green, was also beginning to play the piano and a good-natured rivalry developed between us and our respective parents as to who was better. But there was an empty space inside me waiting for music that would speak to me in a whole other way – music that would express thoughts and feelings that were still just beginning to stir. As if on cue, with a seismic jolt, in 1955 Rock 'n' Roll raised its beautiful head, changing the lives of a whole generation across the world.

While Bill Haley's 'Rock Around the Clock' is generally accepted as the first white Rock 'n' Roll hit, it kind of passed me by. I heard it, knew it was different to what had gone before, but it sounded contrived – Haley looked a bit like your dad and sounded like someone who didn't quite believe what he was singing.

Dean Martin and Frank Sinatra were still everywhere. Elvis arrived to threaten Sinatra, followed by the saccharine Pat Boone, but so had Buddy Holly, Eddie Cochran, Jerry Lee Lewis, Chuck Berry and yes, yes, yes, the greatest of them all – except that he was very black and outrageously gay (which wasn't talked about then) – Little Richard.

A host of British singers like Matt Monroe and Dickie Valentine, Tommy Steele and youngsters Cliff Richard and Adam Faith were clamouring for attention. There was a certain amount of 'new' music on the BBC and Radio Éireann (Irish Radio), but it was sporadic, uncommitted and stuffy.

My generation of pre-teens had discovered Radio Luxembourg, or the English-language branch of Radio Luxembourg. Set up in the 1920s as a commercial broadcaster, the parent station broadcast throughout Europe in French. The English-language version was designed to get around the UK legislation that gave the BBC, a non-commercial service, the sole right to broadcast within Britain. Its reach extended to Ireland. Over the war years the station was popular, but by the 1950s it was the dominant outlet for popular music in English-speaking Western Europe. Soon the trickle of 'new' music became a torrent with a multitude of new artists and records appearing every day, hosted by young, cool DJs with mid-Atlantic accents and wall-to-wall tunes hot off the press from America within days of release. Radio Luxembourg was where we kids spent hours basking in what would become the sound that defined our generation and separated us from the world of our parents.

5

WHERE IS IRISH MUSIC HIDING?

I'm often asked on foot of my success in the first big folk music era of the late 1960s and 1970s, what part Irish folk music and song played in my earliest years. The answer is: virtually none. When I look back now, I go … where was it hiding?

Firstly, a religiously integrated school in Northern Ireland was not the place to hear it. Nothing that would smack of favouring one side's culture over the other would be entertained. Secondly, Irish traditional music and song, as we know it now, was practically non-existent in the media of the day. This was understandable in Northern Ireland where the BBC held sway but bizarrely to me, in the Republic the only folk music on the airwaves in the 1950s was céilí music by Scottish bands like Jimmy Shand and Jim Cameron or the Irish yet similar sounding Gallowglass Ceili Band. The line-up would include fiddles, but the dominant sound was tenor saxophone and piano accordion with the lately arrived electric bass guitar beefing up the rhythm section. It was a rare thing to hear the uilleann pipes, the concert flute, the button accordion, the concertina or indeed the now ubiquitous bodhrán, which I don't recall hearing until the mid-1960s. As for traditional sean-nós singing or songs in Gaelic, they were only heard on sponsored music programmes like the Gael Linn programme, or the Walton's Music Shop programme, where you might just hear a reel or jig played on the fiddle or flute in between Willie Brady singing 'Come Back Paddy Reilly to Ballyjamesduff' or 'The Tipperary Tinker' by Charlie Magee ... *and his gay guitar*, as he was introduced.

The reasons for this would take a whole other book to explore but it has always fascinated me. Somewhere in the political and cultural tensions on the island of Ireland there existed a conundrum. Did the fact that the Protestant community in the North looked to Scotland and England for its heritage, that Scottish music was the folk dance music most often heard on the more established BBC (TV programmes like the White Heather Club which ran from 1958 for around ten years), mean that the powers that be in Radio Éireann and Dublin 4, in their rush to appear sophisticated and to follow the dominant cultural herd weren't ready to acknowledge the wealth of brilliant music on their own doorstep? Did it smack too much of the peasantry? Was it all too close to the 'pig in the parlour' for comfort? Was it all the more acceptable if it appeared in a dress shirt and kilt?

Was it that, until the arrival on the scene of Comhaltas Ceoltóirí Éireann, the society for the preservation and promotion of Irish traditional music in the early 1950s, our own native music was underground, disorganised as a cultural force and as a result unappreciated in popular social and intellectual circles?

I've been watching a lot of the recent timely and fascinating revisions of Irish history on television, in particular the portrayal of the new Irish State post-independence as being ultra conservative, in thrall to the Church and only really interested in the well-being of the moneyed classes. *Social issues must wait till the state is secure* was the mantra after the Irish Civil War. Poverty was rife and the poor were seen to be to blame for their condition. The horrors that took place against children in care were ignored in almost the same way as the ordinary German people turned a blind eye to the Holocaust later.

What has this to do with traditional music, you might wonder. But I believe that traditional Irish music, as played by the ordinary Irish people, was an embarrassment to the Irish Free State. The state and education system couldn't wait to distance itself from the plain people and their crude utterances.

Instead, Ireland was awash with popular songs of my parents' generation either from the pen of Thomas Moore, Percy French or John McCormack, 'Panis Angelicus', 'Hail Glorious St Patrick', or the sentimental songs written by countless Irish American composers or Irish music-hall writers of the previous hundred years that yes, were well-constructed and pleasant to listen to, but echoed of a time that was gone. Songs like 'The Mountains of Mourne', 'The Old Bog Road', 'Galway Bay', 'Are You Right There Michael?', 'Kathleen Mavourneen', 'The Rose of Tralee', 'Lovely Derry on the Banks of the Foyle' sung by a plethora of Irish tenors like Brendan O'Dowda, Patrick O'Hagan and Joseph Locke only touched me superficially. There were Gilbert and Sullivan tunes from the movie *Darby O'Gill and the Little People*, 'How Can You Buy Killarney' and 'If You're Oirish, Come Into the Parlour'; in fact, any form of 'Oirishness' so long as it was composed by the learned and better classes. Even the output of a Jewish songwriter from Brooklyn who had never been to Ireland was favoured over native traditional music.

I appreciated the beautiful melodies, if not always the sentimental lyrics. I knew where they had come from, why they were written and still sung: they were the product of songwriters who, while not always Irish, knew what it felt like to be an immigrant torn away from the homeland, perhaps never to see family again, who knew that the listener needed to wallow in a sentimental song as a tool to preserve a threatened identity. I have nothing against Thomas Moore or John McCormack. In fact, I adore John McCormack's voice, but had it any more cultural value or was it more 'Irish' than say, Darach Ó Catháin's voice? I don't think so. The Irish State would be over forty years old before the likes of Darach would be heard on the national airwaves, and even then, only on 'specialist' shows like the Gael Linn programme.

Perhaps too, because I lived on the border, hearing input from both BBC and Radio Éireann, and dealing daily with the subtle conflicting cultural signals in a mixed society, the overall picture was uniquely confusing and my memory plays tricks on me.

The mixed-up musical undercurrents of those days still strike a chord with me, heighten my sense of being an observer of two different worlds full of cultural certainties and assumptions. The result meant Irish music did not impact on me until the arrival of the Clancy Brothers in the early 1960s. It would be 1966 before I would fall under its spell.

6

HERE COMES SUMMER

Back in the mid-1950s these thoughts and reflections had yet to rise to the surface. With both parents being teachers, the family had long summer holidays at the seaside town of Bundoran in adjoining County Donegal. In the early years we stayed at Miss Sheerin's boarding house in the West End, later renting a cottage and finally investing in a mobile home permanently situated in a caravan park.

My extended family of first cousins and our friends, when we were not swimming or diving off the board at Roguey, were hanging around the new cafés that were springing up as people had more disposable income. In every café was a jukebox. Most of our pocket money ended up in playing our favourite songs. In one café, the Barbecue, there was even a dance floor. It was a magical time and further cemented my relationship with 'pop' music.

As a pre-teen in the late 1950s, Bundoran in summer was a great place to be. For a start, every day was a holiday in the true sense of the word. We'd sleep in (or not). After breakfast we'd meet at Shene Pool, an open-air seawater pool in the West End. My parents, aunts and uncles would congregate on the rocks and all us children would be together learning to swim, dive, horseplay, explore rock pools or just lie about.

My dad and Uncle Gerry were particularly good swimmers. Dad had been swimming since he was a teenager, jumping off corn boats in Sligo harbour in the 1920s. He had a beautiful, relaxed crawl and was a fearless diver. He and Uncle Gerry taught us to swim. It gave me a love for the water. I'm still a competent and confident swimmer now, swim two or three times a week and go scuba-diving in far-off climes as often as I can.

As we progressed through our teens, we learnt lifesaving and did exams that gave us badges we sewed on to our togs. Very competitive. Very cool. More badges, more interest from the opposite sex, we thought. Of course, there was an ongoing rivalry between our gang and the local boys. They resented our arrival every summer, taking over their place. It sometimes got close to getting physical. Once on the beach there was a sizeable set-to where the weapons of choice were stranded jellyfish. The sight of one flying towards you struck terror as you stood half-naked in your togs! But in time, each year, a truce was enacted and confrontations avoided. Indeed, several local boys played guitar and gradually that grew a bond between us.

And all the time there was this wonderful music as a backdrop. The amusement parks all around the beach had loudspeakers and played the big hits of the day, *all* day. Every outdoor activity was accompanied by the sound of Buddy Holly, Elvis, Hank Williams, Eddie Cochran, Duane Eddy, Cliff Richard, the Shadows, Helen Shapiro, Alma Cogan, Roy Orbison, Jim Reeves.

All the time too, we were far away from our home in Northern Ireland with all that tribal and religious tension and angst. I hated going back over the border to Strabane, the regular wake-up call being a roadblock manned by the B-Specials.

Back home with school looming, I managed to hold on to that summer seaside feeling by playing those songs we loved on our newly acquired record player, a little pink Dansette. Every household had to have one, from the modest, as we had, to actual pieces of freestanding furniture combining radio and record turntables called radiograms. Nor did we lack records to play on it. Mollie's sister, Auntie Frances, was married to Tommy Gannon, who had a couple of shops in Lisnaskea and Enniskillen that sold, among many other things, records. Their eldest son, my first cousin Adrian, and I were close in age and shared a love of music. I loved visiting the Gannons and picking up the newest releases from their shop. I remember coming home with two singles: 'Cathy's Clown' by the Everly Brothers and 'Good Timing' by Jimmy Jones. Before long, it was LPs – *The Shadows Greatest Hits* being the LP devoured, eking out every last drop of summer before school started.

7

ST COLUMB'S COLLEGE

The 11-plus was the big hurdle in Northern Ireland education in the 1950s. It was the first filtering of academic prowess on a national scale that children had to face. Prior to that were individual schools' periodic tests, which had a winnowing effect, but the 11-plus was the big bogey man of all tests.

Kids and parents feared an outcome that might determine whether or not a child should be encouraged to continue in education. Kids who passed were given free secondary education, thanks to the 1947 Northern Ireland Education Act. This post-war legislation, which broadened the social benefits of the welfare state, was a huge boon and incentive to previously disadvantaged communities, including a disproportionate number of Catholics.

The exam took place outside the school in a designated centre – in itself intimidating – and we were herded in with kids from different schools with many unfamiliar faces. Fortunately, I passed and found myself facing secondary education.

St Columb's in Derry's Bishop Street was one of the most highly regarded Catholic secondary schools in the north-west. Run by secular priests under the governance of the diocese of Derry, it had a reputation for excellence in academics and sports. Originally it was designed as a seminary for recruitment to the priesthood. The mainly clerical teaching staff was unsophisticated and a product of a philistine Catholic Church system with little appreciation of the importance of the arts. The college motto was 'Seek Ye First the Kingdom of God'.

Middle-class aspirations were relatively new for Catholics in Northern Ireland. Getting ahead was everything – especially getting into university. A good job for life and preferably a profession were the target.

My parents were anxious that I would gain entry and as a boarder, in spite of the cost. (The schooling itself was free, boarding was extra.) Following the required application procedure and vetting, I was accepted. The fact that Derry was only fourteen miles from Strabane, and that several boys from the town already attending the school travelled by bus as 'day boys', wasn't a consideration for Mollie or Sean.

The summer of 1958 was dominated by preparations. Down I went with my father to Danny McLoughlin's, the draper, to get my school uniform, blazer and blue and black striped tie, green and white football socks and old-style Gaelic football boots that laced up over the ankles.

Football? I knew nothing about Gaelic football or handball – the only two sports which were played in St Columb's. I wasn't sporty. Though I had good hand-eye coordination, my glasses left me feeling vulnerable. I was overcome with apprehension and excitement in equal measure.

The big day arrived. I was driven to Derry by Ma and Da and dropped off. I knew only a few Strabane boys: Philip Browne from my street and the Heverin brothers, Michael and John. Like me John was a first year (a 'yap' was the title) while Michael and Philip had already been there a year.

The first few days were a blur. Yap sleeping quarters were in a dormitory divided into cubicles with two boys in each. All yaps were on the same floor, while older boys were on the floor above. Senior students eventually had their own rooms with two boys sharing.

On the second or third day something was up. We were warned about 'the ducking', a ritual baptising of yaps. I stuck close to my friends and tried to find some level of invisibility while I figured out what was happening. After evening meal, a vibe careered around the dining hall. Whispers began: 'It's going to happen now.'

We were all let outside and, as if on a signal, everyone started running. Second and third years jumped on yaps and dragged them to the water taps outside the toilets, pushing and holding them under till they were soaked. If you struggled, you risked having your head banged against the wall. It became more and more violent, blows raining down and youngsters wailing. I was terrified.

The most bizarre aspect of it was the sight of several priests walking around the grounds reading their breviaries ignoring what was going on. Clearly the event was tacitly approved of, accepted as tradition, a way of 'making a man' of you. Overnight my world had come to feel very different. I felt abandoned and bereft. How could this be happening?

In the first year there was a constant jockeying for pecking order among students. Arguments took place. Accusations flew, 'You're a sneak, a liar, you think you're better than me!'

The slightest hint of a fight was leapt upon by 'the mob' who would taunt both parties and gleefully escalate the event so that the only way to avoid being permanently deemed a coward was to 'man up' and have it out physically.

My turn came after an innocent comment resulted in me being challenged by another boy, Bobby Burns, who also wore glasses. I think I'd made the mistake of saying I couldn't understand his South Derry accent. Things reached a pushing and shoving state and before long the mob had ushered and jostled the both of us to 'the jacks' (the outside toilet area) where all disputes were settled.

Our glasses were surrendered for safekeeping, and we tore into each other in a frenzy of punching. It was ridiculous and terrifying. The baying of the onlookers added fuel to the craziness and eventually with two bloody noses and floods of angry tears we were pulled apart by a prefect. It didn't solve anything. We two just avoided each other for the remainder of our time in school.

The violent episodes continued. Second-year boys who had the same done to them the previous year saw it as their right to continue the tradition. It wasn't personal. You were just a yap. There was a night-time visit to our dorm via the backstairs from the second-years' floor above. You woke up around midnight to the sound of running feet, roaring and shouting, screams of fear and cubicle partitions being battered with fists to instil more terror. A bar of soap in a football sock was the preferred weapon. In the pitch darkness all you could do was hide under the bedclothes with the pillow over your head and wait for the thumps that inevitably came as they moved along the dorm. Then, just as suddenly as it started, it ended as if on a signal, the lights went on and the dean appeared in a temper. There were of course no subsequent prosecutions. Take it like a man!

I never settled into St Columb's. It was a different world to me. Coming from a secular primary school with mixed religion and gender into an all-male Catholic boarding school run by priests was a shock. My unorthodox primary education hadn't prepared me for this. The nationalist ethos permeating the atmosphere, including the Irish language and Gaelic football, was unfamiliar. Most of St Columb's boarders came from either South County Derry or the Irish Republic in County Donegal – both areas strongly nationalist. They would have been familiar with Gaelic football and the republican political and cultural backdrop. It was a long way from my sports day prize of a teaspoon with the head of Queen Elizabeth II on it.

In later years, when the polarised communities descended into horrific violence, each certain of the purity of its cause, I appreciated that my earliest schooling, albeit part of a flawed and contentious system in need of major change, took place in an integrated environment. Right then, however, I felt exposed like an alien. A feeling of 'not fitting in' grew in me and, in time, that would form the dominant emotional backdrop to my life. In later struggles to find my place in the conflicting worlds of folk and pop music, and to steer my path through the assumptions and expectations accompanying the political upheavals to come, it would take decades to realise and accept that maybe I wasn't here to 'fit in'.

Eventually I learned how to keep out of trouble. I got on well academically. I liked Latin and French. My French teacher was the future Nobel Prize winner John Hume – yet to enter politics and become the force that was to be so positive and influential in the decades ahead. He was a natural teacher and inculcated in me a love of the French language I still have. He had, however, an appalling French accent as I recall.

Irish was more difficult, but I grew to love it and with a couple of visits to the Donegal Gaeltacht in my senior school years I became adept if not fluent. My da had Irish and in the school holidays would help me out. I grasped the language's grammar and architecture but, not regularly mixing with Irish speakers in later life, I've been left with the stunted vocabulary of a sixteen-year-old student. Having a keen musical ear, however, I learned to approximate the Donegal dialect, sparing me the attentions of one Irish teacher Hugh McKeown whose classic put-down was 'Boy, you speak Irish like a native ... of South Borneo!'

It remains one of the big regrets of my life that, along with the vast majority of my compatriots, I struggle with what *was* our native language. The colonists did a thorough job.

Of course, I studied music too. I took piano lessons and musical theory and did okay in exams but, though I learned how to play various Schubert impromptus and Beethoven piano concertos, I never took to classical music. A part of me appreciated the beauty in it, but there was a core part that wanted to make my own music.

In St Columb's, music was treated only as a GCE subject at O and A level, and music meant classical only. Few students took it up. The music teachers were not permanent staff, almost like 'we have to include music to qualify for funding but it's really not what we're into here'. I was refused permission to bring my newly acquired acoustic guitar to school. What were they thinking? Guitars meant pop music, I guess, and pop music was bad? That a student playing any kind of music for their own enjoyment might be a positive and enriching thing never seemed to enter their heads. There wasn't even an outlet for Irish folk music – surprising in a Catholic school in Northern Ireland. In all the years I was there I never heard one Irish song in Irish or English till I went to the Gaeltacht in my fifth year.[†]

Gilbert & Sullivan was okay, however. I appeared in a college opera in my third year, *The Yeomen of The Guard*, in which I shared the role of Dame Carruthers with another student. Was the school consciously avoiding Irish musical culture in case it might be seen as too nationalist or lending tacit support for the continuing IRA campaign of the late 1950s which the Catholic Church had distanced itself from? Possibly too, the overall artistic ethos, if it existed at all, mirrored the prevalent cultural cringe that was endemic throughout Ireland in the late 1950s. In reality,

---

[†] A Gaeltacht is an area where the main spoken language is Irish and students in their teens from all over the country were encouraged to spend a couple of weeks in the summer living with local families and improving their grasp of the spoken language. The only rule was that no English was spoken. By and large it was adhered to. Boys and girls sat together in the daily classes but there was plenty of time left to socialise. With teenage hormones running riot, many of us fell in puppy love for the first time in the Gaeltacht. *Ah mo Ghrá thú* (I Love You), the pain of it!

however, I believe the unspoken college values were petty, with lip service given to the concept of the arts – arts were just not what St Columb's was about.

Around my third year I attracted the attention of another student. There ensued a campaign of bullying and mental torture that deeply affected me. In classic bully behaviour I was diminished and humiliated at all times. He called me 'worm' and though it never became physical, the threat was always there. It was a strange combination of impulses and reactions. By this time, I was regularly playing pop tunes in the music rooms when the teachers were not around. I was getting good at Chuck Berry and Jerry Lee Lewis stuff and this boy liked what he heard. But then he would order me to play for him. It was always done with no one else around and this macabre dance began where I felt that if I didn't keep him happy, he would become even more abusive. It was like 'Worm, I'm impressed, I'm envious of you, but I want to destroy you.'

My instinct at St Columb's … to keep my head down, get on with things and not expect anything was well founded and, bullying aside, it was a successful survival tactic.

On a happier note, in my fifth year, I did get to experience literature and music on my own terms, albeit vicariously. In 1963, the St Columb's students' magazine appeared for the first time, edited by a progressive English teacher J.J. Keaveney. I had a poem published called (tellingly enough) 'And All for Music'. The poem recalled the first Beatles concert in Dublin's Adelphi theatre, which of course, I wasn't at!

'And all for "music"'

'When music sounds, gone is the earth I know …
… Rapt in strange dream burns each enchanted face …'
                                        (Walter de la Mare)

Helter skelter, down street and alley
Crowded, they run with hair flying wild;
They reach the hall.
Where mad with frenzy, screaming girls
And boys, their long locks in their eyes.
Augment the brawl.

Alas! Poor constables who strive
At first their pride, then peace to keep,
Go under foot;
And dubious type with eye intent
On wallet of his neighbour close
Escapes with loot.

The din increases – a small boy shouts –
'A car! – They come!' – he disappears –
O! Painful sight!
'Tis true indeed; amid the mob
A clarion sounds – a car draws near
With blinding light.

Four bashful youths, unkempt of hair,
From forth the ranks of many thousand
Fans do creep.
Toward the steps with officers
Of peace all round, they madly push
Oh! – for a peep.

'At last! Inside!' sighs one: toward
The dressing-rooms they quickly dash,
Shaggy of mien;
Outside, where but a while before
A ballad singer dejected stood,
Tumult doth reign.

MUSIC IN MY TEENS

Between the ages of eleven and sixteen, away from the tension in St Columb's, my enjoyment of school holidays intensified. I could get back to the guitar. Over those years I learned a lot. I was self-taught. I wasn't aware that books with guitar chord diagrams existed. I made up my own fingering and it was only later I realised there were easier ways to learn.

I spent hours learning the repertoire of the Shadows from *The Shadows Greatest Hits* album I'd got from my uncle's shop. I'd lift the needle on the Dansette at the difficult bits and drop it again and again, till I figured it out. I soon got on top of all the other hits like the Everly Brothers' 'Wake up Li'l Suzie', Buddy Holly's 'That'll Be the Day' and I threw a decent shape at Chuck Berry's 'Johnny B. Goode'.

Everything I liked off the radio I made a fist of in no time. As my peer group social circle expanded, I became a popular addition to parties in the town. Unsure as to whether my popularity was on foot of my 'dazzling personality' and 'hunkish physique' or whether it was because I was able to keep the party going, I remained wary. 'Hey Paul, we're having this great party next Saturday and uh, bring your guitar?' kinda thing. Yeah, right! At that age, what you want more than anything is to be desirable just as you are, not for how useful you are to others.

Things were hotting up in Bundoran too. The ancient rivalries between the townies and us summer imports began to dissolve as I'd hang with local musicians like Frankie McKiernan and Liam Travers and swap chords, tricks and licks. It was a thrill to feel I could not only hold my own but raise a few eyebrows too.

The Holyrood Hotel was one of several hotels in Bundoran my parents went to in the evenings. Bundoran was a summer Mecca for people from West Tyrone and Fermanagh and even further afield. When the Glasgow Fair was on in July, many Scots would arrive in the town, as would Belfast people of both religious persuasions. This was before the Troubles flared up again in 1969. The abortive Northern IRA campaign of the late 1950s was forgotten and the old status quo had returned.

With the exception of the Great Northern Hotel, where the yet-to-be-famous Derryman Phil Coulter had a pared-back band, few of the town's hotels featured organised entertainment in the early 1960s. The usual thing was a pianist in the background playing popular tunes till someone, emboldened with drink, would propose someone else to do a turn. The pianist would encourage the nominated performer who'd get up to the mic and usually begin a song without any care as to key or tempo. It was the pianist's job to keep up. Naturally, as most of those called upon were total amateurs, many's the train wreck happened. But it was all good fun.

All through these years, my dad was always asked up with his one-man show, always bringing the house down. Now that I was testing the waters as a performer, I watched every move he made. It was a learning curve in how to connect with an audience. When I came to write and perform myself years later, I subconsciously modelled myself on his style and delivery.

At first Sean was accompanied by the resident pianist. Then one night in the Holyrood Hotel, when I was fourteen, he asked me would I play 'La Paloma' with him. We'd done it at home a few times, so he knew I could handle it. It worked and I felt a rush of excitement and confidence as he acknowledged 'his son, Paul' to the crowd.

Eventually I was doing a turn myself on guitar singing a Burl Ives song, 'The Wayfaring Stranger' or Buddy Holly's 'Peggy Sue', or my mother's favourite 'Summertime' on piano. Even then I *still* hadn't heard much traditional Irish music except at Mollie's home-town, Irvinestown, where her brother Uncle Bernard played the fiddle. But that was music from another age – yet to capture my imagination.

By now I had become well-known around the Holyrood Hotel as a versatile musician, sitting in on guitar with the house band. It was fairly standard popular Irish fare, the clientele being for the most part middle-aged and of all persuasions. Anything that had become popular over the previous decades was likely to get an air-ing – a lot of Irish *come all ye's*; songs like 'The Boys From the County Armagh', 'Lovely Derry on the Banks of the Foyle', 'Lovely Leitrim' (a recent hit for Larry Cunningham) and for the Scottish visitors 'The Northern Lights of Old Aberdeen' or 'Annie Laurie'.

The resident hotel singer, Cormac McCready, was a fan of Tony Bennett and the Rat Pack: Frank Sinatra, Dean Martin and Sammy Davis Jr, so 'I Left My Heart in San Francisco' was on the list along with Bobby Darin's 'Mack the Knife' and 'Things We Used to Do'. 'Speedy Gonzales' was another fave.

The Clancy Brothers' US fame had finally made it to Ireland and 'The Holy Ground', 'The Bold O'Donohue' and 'The Leaving of Liverpool' were great crowd-pleasers. All of these songs sat together easily in my head, especially the Clancys' repertoire as our own folk music began to grab my attention.

Without realising it, I was becoming indispensable in the equa-tion of the night. I was part of the band, unpaid, but having fun and getting loads of experience. At the end of the summer of 1962, aged fifteen, I was asked by Sean and Cormac would I consider coming back the following summer as a fully-paid member of the band. I jumped at it. My parents were happy as it kept me under their watchful eye and anyway I'd been doing it already. So a deal was struck with old John McEniff, the owner, and for £4 a week plus full board I had landed my first paying job as a musician. I was thrilled.

The following year for the first two weeks of the school holidays, I went to the Gaeltacht in Rannafast in West Donegal. I was enjoying speaking Irish and one of the first things I did when I got there was to translate into Irish one of my favourite songs of that summer, Joe Brown's 'Picture of You'.

I brought my guitar with me and, by now a practised performer, I had been noticed at a couple of sing-songs and was asked to take part in a farewell concert the last night of our stay. A perfect opportunity for the first airing of my new translation 'An Pictiúr Sin Álainn Díot', perhaps not perfect grammar, but poetic license prevailed. It was well-received. I was getting used to applause.

For the rest of the summer I was in Bundoran, having the time of my life, swimming and hanging around with my mates all day and playing every night. The Holyrood 'show' was getting a reputation in the town and more and more people were dropping in for their night out which, of course, was the object of the exercise.

I was gaining in confidence and would take over the piano when the lads went on a break and I'd try my hand at MC-ing too. I got good at jumping in when someone from the audience would get up to the mic to do a turn. I'd have their key nailed and be right there with them until the inevitable key change came, and I'd pick them up again. It was a roller-coaster ride but I enjoyed the challenge and by the end of the summer I was accompanying anything in any key required.

By now the owner's son Brian McEniff had returned from Canada with his new wife, Catherine, to take over the business from the ageing John. The following year I was back in the Holyrood for £12 a week plus board. Just turned seventeen, I was an old hand, knowing all the tricks of the trade and was right on top of my gig as guitarist and occasional pianist with a few party pieces of my own. Brian, of course would go on to great things, winning the All-Ireland Football Championship in 1992 as manager of the Donegal team and becoming one of the hotel moguls of Ireland.

9

DUBLIN 1964

Things were changing fast. My final year in St Columb's boarding school was coming to an end. Thoughts of what to do next raised their heads. My strengths were languages: French, Irish, Latin and to a lesser degree English. Maths was a no-no. Science I was okay at but had no interest in it. Music, I knew meant studying classical music, which to me (then) was music by dead people. Nothing in the pantheon of classical greats really moved me as much as Little Richard, Hank Marvin or Chuck Berry.

I did reasonably well in the A-levels and like everyone else in the UK education system who achieved this, was offered a scholarship to university. My sister Anne and several of my cousins were already in Queen's University Belfast and it was presumed I would follow. I drifted into accepting this as an inevitability. Though what did this mean? No clear long-term vision of what I should aspire to be was presenting itself. Whenever I thought about it, which was rarely, I supposed I would become a teacher and work as a musician in the summer holidays. An arts degree, the dosser's choice as it was called, was obvious – 'When in doubt do arts.'

However, in the summer of 1964 there was evidently a surfeit of doubting dossers in Northern Ireland, for the arts faculty in Queen's University was overwhelmed with applications. To sort the problem, it was decided by the powers that be to apply an age criterion as well as an academic standard to the selection process. Students born before a certain date in 1947 would be eligible. Those born after that date would have to go back to school for another year. I fell into the latter division. This was a no-brainer for me. No way was I going back to repeat a year in St Columb's, even as a day boy. And that was how University College Dublin (UCD) came on the horizon.

A few students from St Columb's had gone to UCD, so there was a precedent. But for all I knew, Dublin might as well have been Shanghai. I had never been there in my life. Truth be told, I had never been further from Strabane than Ballymote in County Sligo to see my Bohan grandaunts – a distance of around eighty-five miles. I'd never even been to Belfast, apart from being born there, which didn't count. Life was moving fast and becoming very interesting indeed.

My application to the arts faculty of UCD was duly made and shortly after, accepted. Mother, father and son drove down to Dublin in the late summer of 1964 to find accommodation. After a bizarre day of traipsing around some god-awful kips we came upon a place in Synge Street, off the South Circular Road and within walking distance of Earlsfort Terrace, where most of UCD was housed at the time.

In a daze I was shown upstairs to a room of about 8m x 5m with six single beds, six matching bedside cupboards and a built-in wardrobe. Not a whole lot different from the boarding school I had just got rid of ... except I had my electric guitar and little amplifier shoved impotently under the bed waiting for I knew not what. I was quite freaked by the whole experience. This was only one of several rooms with as many beds again in each. The breakfast room in the basement had four tables and eighteen chairs. Big business.

For the first month I went to lectures. I knew hardly anyone except some day boys from St Columb's, and even then, only vaguely since I'd been a boarder. We never mixed. After classes, heading to Kirwan's or O'Dwyer's pub at the bottom of Leeson Street quickly became part of the routine. All the Derry boys stuck together. I tagged along putting up with the constant schoolboy slagging that they seemed to have brought with them. I had little option.

Musically it was a strange time too. I was mad to sing and play. The showband era was at its height in Ireland. In Bundoran the previous summer every night the Astoria Ballroom hosted the biggest bands in Ireland: the Royal, the Miami, the Cadets, the Capitol, the Clipper Carlton all came through town. As a regular playing in the Holyrood I knew the security guys on the Astoria door and after our gig was over, around half-eleven, we'd pop down the road to catch the end of the dance. Sometimes I had a girl in tow – a Ballyshannon babe who worked in the bar, or a daughter of a Scottish family staying in the Holyrood who showed interest in my guitar technique! All happy to tag along to the dance.

The Beatles, the Stones and the whole British blues scene had happened by then too. The Beatles had even appeared at the Adelphi in town the previous year, occasioning my aforementioned elegy in the St Columb's magazine. I was a fan of the Yardbirds and John Mayall's Bluesbreakers featuring Peter Green and Eric Clapton.

In my head I was already part of that world. Yet here I was. Stuck. In UCD. Under false pretences. Pretending to my parents, the college and myself that I was anything but a musician.

10

CHINK OF LIGHT

A couple of weeks after I arrived in Dublin, a poster jumped out at me from a hoarding.

Blues Extravaganza at the Crystal Ballroom
Bluesville. The Greenbeats. The Inmates. The Semitones

I had to look twice. Mentally I had written the idea of the blues out of my head in terms of ever seeing it live in Ireland. I mean, I was well into the British blues scene, but this was Ireland, land of Dickie Rock and Brendan Bowyer the lead singers of, respectively, the Miami and the Royal Showbands. I guess I imagined that's all it ever was going to be.

I could feel the anticipation and excitement rising in me. Where was the Crystal? Anne Street. Where was that? Off Grafton Street, someone I asked said. Just around the corner.

I went off like I was looking for the Holy Grail and, in a few minutes, amid the lunchtime office crowds, I was standing outside the place.

There among the posters for the Airchords Showband, the Ohio Showband, all the usual suspects of the era, was the blues extravaganza poster. Appearing next weekend.

I was going to be there.

The next few days passed snail-like. College wasn't making sense. I'd come in each morning from the digs and head downstairs to the 'canteen'. I was an outsider, way out of my depth and lonely. Everyone was focused on something, knew someone, had some reason to be there. Outside the library, a bevy of beautiful girls. I'd never seen girls like this, surrounded by lads who looked like they were rugby players or sons of millionaires, a panoply of superior beings who seemed to know exactly what to say and wear, what gesture to make and just how to pitch that perfect peal of laughter.

The mechanism of finding friends is a strange thing. You wraith around the outside watching, listening, getting a feel for so-and-so who's surrounded by breathless beauties, figuring out why. Who's throwing musical shapes, theatrical shapes, using cool language, an accent, a look. A guy called Brian seems to have what it takes. Long-haired and louche with a kind of West-Brit drawl and Mick Jagger-like body language. A succession of chinless wonders that seemed to be babe-magnets peppered the entrance hall.

But finally, the weekend arrived and I made my way into the Crystal. If the UCD scene felt exclusive, this was even more so. A different scene, again gorgeous girls … but somehow from a diffe-rent planet to the earnest young things of UCD. These were street-wise, heavily made-up with lots of black mascara and pink lipstick, some working, some college, some arty, all with a kind of raciness that said 'Come on … but not you, hopeless!' A looser kind of guy fraternity, clothes that bit more way-out and colourful, everyone letting their hair down.

Despite still being an outsider, I was a bit more at ease here. The lights, the stage, the sound of the roadies testing the gear, the amps, drum kits, all were what I was familiar with from Bundoran. The music was the kind I loved but never got to hear from the showbands who always covered current hits. I was mesmerised. It was cool

Dublin, but it was still just a dance. There were musicians coming on, they'd sing songs, people would get off on it and there was the overt feel of sex around. Academia, definitely not. I positioned myself, as was my style at the dances back home, up close to the stage but not too close to be noticed. Kind of to the side but where I'd miss nothing.

I hung around till the very end, not making any attempt to dance or get off with anyone but stuck by the side of the stage watching everything that the bands were doing. From the nights at the Astoria Ballroom in Bundoran I was used to going up and chatting to the guitarist in the band as they packed up after the dance and although I was out of my depth here, I ran up to the Inmates' lead guitarist, Brendan Bonass, whose playing really impressed me.

He was a *ciotóg* (left-handed person) and played his Watkins Rapier upside down! Very cool.

I was born ambidextrous, having equal facility with both hands, which was helpful when I was drawing and painting as a child, but soon I naturally gravitated to the dominant left hand. In a fit of societal paranoia in the mid-1950s, my parents, fearing future disadvantage, forced me, aged seven, to use my right hand, particularly when writing, with the tacit approval of the contemporary education system. By the time I got my first guitar at eleven, I was 'successfully' changed and began learning to play in the right-handed way. But it made the process more difficult. To this day my playing technique is unorthodox, my fingering and chord shapes all my own. I'm sure this is partly due to a residual confusion between the right and left brain as a result of being changed. I never came across a left-handed guitar until I saw Brendan Bonass playing one in Dublin in 1964. I often wonder how different my playing would be now if nature had been left to run its course.

Bonass was a great player with a sweet sound. I had nothing much to say beyond complimenting him in a sycophantic way and then I heard myself almost from a distance saying, 'Look, I'm just down from the North. I'm really good and I want to get into a band. Can you help me?'

He looked at me as if I'd crawled out from under a stone, and muttered something like, 'We're happy with our band thanks.'

But I kept pestering him and eventually asked him for his phone number which, generously but foolishly, he gave me. We parted company, permanently he probably hoped, and the world went on.

Instantly, and for the first time in my life, I knew that whatever the consequences, I had to become part of this thing I was witnessing. This was the moment I decided to make music my life.

I went off on a cloud that night and within a few days I called Brendan up. At first he tried to put me off but when he saw that wasn't going to be easy without being rude, gentleman that he was and still is, he suggested a meeting in the Bamboo coffee house in Dún Laoghaire later that week.

I'd never been that far out of town but I jumped aboard the No. 8 bus, got off where he said and met him and some other guys who I kinda recognised from the blues gig.

I was quizzed as to what I was into, what my experience was and what equipment I had (which I duly exaggerated). Whatever impression I made, I was asked to come to a rehearsal in the Anglesea Tennis Club the following Saturday afternoon. This I did, jammed with the band on some of their stuff and sang a couple of Chuck Berry songs which seemed to hit the mark.

I was in.

There followed a year and a half playing two or three nights a week in the various venues springing up around the city, the No. 5 Club, the Carousel, Sound City, the Cavalier Club, Stella Mount Merrion, The Anchor Club and the many tennis and rugby clubs around Dublin. A few times we travelled to Limerick and Cork for a gig.

—————— 22 CLUB ——————

STELLA BALLROOM
MOUNT MERRION

WED. JULY 7th — **SOME PEOPLE**
Plus Supporting Group

WED. JULY 14th — **THE KULT**
Plus Supporting Group

Dancing 8-12 — Admission 4/6

STUDENTS WITH CARDS - 4/-

In the course of that time I played in four different bands: the Inmates, the Kult, Rootzgroop and Rockhouse. We were contemporaneous with the Black Eagles featuring a young Phil Lynott, the Chosen Few, the Creatures, the Gentry, Rory Gallagher's Taste, the Action featuring Colm Wilkinson, the People, which became Eire Apparent featuring Henry McCullough and many more.

Back then, many of the happening international acts like the Animals, Roy Orbison, the Who, Marmalade and the Alex Harvey Band came to town. The band I was in then, Rockhouse, supported the Who in Dublin's National Stadium on 7 May 1966 and on another date at the same venue, Roy Orbison. One of the band members, Ozzie Kilkenny on rhythm guitar, moved on to become one of the best known accountants in the global music business and a dear friend and adviser to me ever since.

And I had a steady girlfriend who I'd met at one of the gigs. Hilary Elliott from Sandymount, nice while it lasted, even though her family hadn't much of an opinion of me: 'A student? A musician?' Her family all worked. Her father had been a captain or a pilot of a tugboat down at the docks. True-blue Dubs, working people.

Of course no lectures were being attended, no study was done. I moved through a bewildering succession of flats and bedsitters, sometimes sharing, sometimes not. On one occasion, flatless, I slept in a hut by the railway lines at Seapoint where guys were making glass-fibre kayaks. The chemical smell nearly killed me. I'd wake up with a headache, stiff all over. I was, in one way, having the time of my life, but in another, avoiding the elephant in the room.

For most of my time in UCD I was in a low-grade depression, a state of denial and a fog of guilt. I didn't want to be in college. Time passed and I *still* wasn't attending lectures or studying. My parents asked every so often how things were going. I'd bluff it out and change the subject. It was generally left at that. Unfamiliar with university life and routines, they were happy to assume I was getting on with it.

My guilt increased with the knowledge that here I was, down from the North with my free UK education and subsistence grant each term of about St£90 (c. St£1,200 in today's money) while the rest of the students from the South had to pay for everything and looked like they appreciated their time in college and wanted to be there.

In spite of the enjoyment I was getting from playing in bands and having a girlfriend who seemed to care for me, my self-esteem was low. I had this dreadful feeling all the time that I was making a mess of it.

This phase ended abruptly in late spring of 1966 approaching the end of my second year in UCD. One of the cool hangs in those days was the café in the basement of Switzers in Grafton Street (later Brown Thomas), stuffed on late afternoons after school with gorgeous young things or teen wannabe modelly types from Dublin 4 or Blackrock. It was a Mecca for cool dudes and since I was now just eighteen and played in a band, I was undoubtedly one of them (yeah?). Then out of the corner of my eye I saw ...

Mollie ... followed by Sean!

... walking through the café, clearly looking for *me*.

Up like a flash to avoid the embarrassment of them actually arriving at our table, I went to meet them and immediately knew it wasn't a social call.

We went outside to where their car was parked. It was revealed that a letter had come to my home in Strabane addressed to me from the Registrar's office in UCD. My mum had opened it 'thinking it might be important'. Basically it said that it had been noticed that for the past year my attendance at lectures was minimal and I had failed to sit my second year exams. I was cordially invited for an interview to explain the situation.

The game was well and truly up. It became clear that for the past couple of years I had been codding everybody, including myself, and that my college career was in deep trouble.

They were horrified.

Ultimatums were delivered. Either I leave the band I was in at the time (Rockhouse) and come home for summer to study for my final year or else ... world war three.

Guilt engulfed me. There was no contest. I shamefacedly told my fellow band members that I was leaving the band. It meant the end of the band, as it happened. Something else to feel guilty about.

11

THE FOLK SCENE

Summer of 1966 saw me hanging round Bundoran in our family's rented summerhouse making half-hearted attempts at studying and codding both myself and my parents that it was effective or significant. They seemed content that I was back in their orbit and, unfamiliar with what I was supposed to be doing, left me to my own devices.

I wasn't working at the Holyrood Hotel this year. It was deemed too distracting. But in reality, I had outgrown the Holyrood show. After a couple of years of playing in four exciting Dublin bands, the thought of chasing round the keyboard after some amateur singing 'By the Banks of My Own Lovely Lee' in three different keys had lost its appeal. I had moved on. Few college textbooks were opened all summer. I went to Dublin in September to have the dreaded meeting with the Registrar. Memory deserts me now as to what exactly was said in the room. A lot of blagging from me undoubtedly and the proffering of a medical cert to cover certain absences sticks in my mind. Whatever, the result was that in October I found myself, incredibly, starting my third year in UCD.

In a symbolic farewell to my beat group days, and needing some money, I sold my much-loved white Fender Mustang guitar to Phil Lynott. Phil and I crossed paths often on the beat club circuit and we got on well. We both loved soul music. A few months previously he'd admired the guitar. He was still living at his mother's house in Crumlin, and I rang and asked was he interested in buying it. We agreed a price of £60. I took the bus out and handed it over. He then said, 'I've only 44 quid on me. Can I owe you the other 16 till next week?'

I laughed and said okay.

I'm still waiting!

I now had a Harmony Sovereign acoustic guitar. I had to study but had no desire to and persisted in a state of denial. Living in 80 Moyne Road, Ranelagh in the upstairs flat shared with a couple of UCD students, still ex-Columb's boys, I became aware of music in the flat below. I'd pass by their door and hear folk songs being sung and played on acoustic guitars and mandolins, seafaring, whaling songs and Irish ballads, the odd jig and reel on a tenor banjo.

Eventually I met up with them. One was a UCD student a year ahead of me, Limerick man Mick Moloney doing politics and economics. Tipperary man, Johnny Morrissey was another resident. Frequent visitors were Kildare Street College of Art student Dónal Lunny from Newbridge and Brian Bolger, the louche, long-haired guy I had noticed around UCD.

Together they were a folk group, a fairly new invention in Ireland, and they called themselves the Emmet Folk after the Irish patriot from the end of the eighteenth century, Robert Emmet.

We began to play poker long into the night and I began to hear more about newly opening folk clubs in the city: the Coffee Kitchen in Molesworth Street; the Oul' Triangle in Mount Street; the Universal in Parnell Square; and the 95 Club in a basement of 95 Harcourt Street.

The 95 Club was formerly a restaurant called the Green Tureen. It was a notorious location. In one of the upstairs flats there had been a recent and, for that time in Ireland, rare murder. An African medical student, Shan Mohangi, had murdered and dismembered his girlfriend and had tried to get rid of the evidence by boiling the body parts in the restaurant kitchen. It was all over the news. The Green Tureen became the butt of several grisly jokes about the contents of its soup. Understandably the owner decided to wind up the restaurant and move in this new folk club direction, though he would still séll soups and sandwiches to unsuspecting late-night folk music fans, already fast growing in numbers.

I was still not a 'folk' fan at this stage, preferring blues and soul music to 'whaling songs' as I disparagingly characterised the folk repertoire, but Mick and Dónal, on one of our poker nights, talked me into coming to a session in the 95 Club and before long I was checking it out.

It seemed to welcome all kinds of stuff: English and Scottish ballads, American old-timey music and acoustic blues, as well as Irish songs in both languages. I started to hang with my new Harmony Sovereign guitar in clubs, hoping for a floor spot. These gradually materialised and I steadily got a reputation and started to do regular spots, mostly playing country blues songs like John Lee Hooker's 'Boom Boom', Tommy Tucker's 'Hi-Heel Sneakers' that I used to sing in the recently departed Rockhouse and even Burl Ives' 'Wayfaring Stranger', still secure in my repertoire from the Holyrood days.

It was only the very early days of the Dublin folk scene and things hadn't yet become commercialised. The clubs were unlicensed for alcohol, and no one was paid for their performance. The pubs in the city, however, seeing how this folk music fad was drawing in big crowds, began to offer their clientele 'folk nights' and the ballad lounge, as it came to be called, appeared on the scene.

Musicians and singers were just getting to know each other and coming from a myriad of different musical styles towards what was becoming a new collective 'folk' consciousness heavily influenced by the US folk scene of a couple of years previously. I remember one afternoon being downstairs in Mick Moloney's flat and seeing the first Bob Dylan album someone had recently bought. Dylan was being talked about as the great new thing though I didn't get it then. His quasi-Woody Guthrie vocal affectations sounded comical to me and faintly ridiculous, though I did pick up on a singular commitment and rare individuality. I had heard nothing like this before. Amazing now to think that it was only getting noticed in Ireland in 1965/66, though it had first come out in the USA in 1962. The cultural ground shifted a lot more slowly in those days.

It was an exciting time in Dublin. There was the feeling that musically we were all on the verge of something new. In the space of a few months, it became a countrywide phenomenon. Dozens of groups started forming and record companies were signing acts and releasing records. Radio began presenting folk shows and playing these records. The press began featuring articles about the comings and goings of the new folk stars.

Gradually Mick Moloney and I were seeing more of each other and one day in early 1967 he told me he had been asked to join the Johnstons, one of the newly successful folk groups (now being called 'ballad groups' with the music being called 'the ballads'). Several other ballad groups were also shooting to national recognition. The Ludlows, with 'The Sea Around Us', singer Johnny Mc-Evoy with 'Mursheen Durkin', the Wolfe Tones, Sweeney's Men and of course the Dubliners. What the Clancy Brothers had started in New York at the beginning of the decade was finally percolating down to Ireland in a commercial way. It took some years but by the mid-1960s the Irish folk boom was well and truly up and running. The scent of money was in the air.

My floor spots at folk clubs were getting noticed too. I'd started appearing at ballad lounges and getting a modest fee ... and a reputation. Through Mick, the Johnstons offered me an opening slot

at their Monday night residency at the Embankment in rural Tallaght, as it then was. I can still recall riding my Lambretta scooter
out there in the winter afternoon, guitar slung over my shoulder,
a couple of newspapers stuck down my front to ward off the cold.
It was there in late 1966, early 1967 that I had my first introduction to real traditional music through the playing of accordianist
James Keane, younger brother of Sean Keane, who later joined the
Chieftains.

James, too, was doing an opening spot at the Johnstons'
residency with a young bodhrán player called Carmel Quinn. I
was doing stuff like Lead Belly's 'Duncan and Brady', a couple of
Hank Williams songs and, still an old favourite that first got me
into open tuning on guitar, Mississippi John Hurt's 'Frankie 'n'
Albert'. After a few nights James asked me would I back them up. I
had never accompanied reels and jigs before and wasn't quite sure
about it, but James' playing was so masterful, musical and exciting
that I saw it as a challenge and decided to have a go. I discovered a
similarity between the way I instinctively felt rhythm and the way
James liked to throw a tune around the place. Within a short time
we were all locking together. It was great to see the smile on James'
and Carmel's faces as the excitement factor of their set grew in this
new direction.

Guitar accompaniment of Irish tunes was still comparatively
rare. I was one of the first to do it. Coming fresh to the music and
having spent the last couple of years playing rock, blues and soul
music, I had a dynamic approach that, when married to James'
brilliance, created an exciting new sound.

I began to pick out the subtle melodic and modal differences
between tunes and gradually discovered a new and rich vein of
music that until now had eluded me. It was always there in the
background, but had I really listened? To say I fell in love with
Irish traditional music in those weeks of playing with James would

not be an exaggeration ... it's a love affair that has never waned no matter where my musical muse has taken me since.

Another convenient result of my support spot with the Johnstons was that the sisters, Adie and Lucy, got to see me in action onstage. They liked what they saw. In addition to opening for them at the Embankment, I was offered support slots at some of their bigger concerts, Liberty Hall for one. My star was in the ascendant.

Bit by bit, James Keane introduced me to other players. Before long, I was doing an opening solo spot at the Old Sheiling in Raheny and on the same night playing with the new generation of trad music heavyweights Matt Molloy, Seán Keane and Tommy Peoples. Matt and Seán would go on to join the Chieftains and

Tommy, the Bothy Band. My rep as a spirited and increasingly knowledgeable accompanist of traditional tunes was growing fast. On my free nights I became a regular in O'Donoghue's on Merrion Row, then the epicentre of the fast-growing Dublin folk scene. Luke Kelly of the Dubliners and increasingly a Folk celebrity in his own right, was always in and out. I'd see him commuting between O'Donoghue's and the Shelbourne Hotel with his *Irish Times* under his oxter. While we weren't bosom buddies, I would get the 'How-are-ye' nod of greeting and the odd smile. Ah, noticed at last!

Ronnie Drew, Barney McKenna and Ciarán Bourke were habitués too. At first they were called the Ronnie Drew Ballad Group but when John Sheahan joined in 1964 they became the Dubliners. Andy Irvine and Johnny Moynihan of Sweeney's Men often dropped in. The back room was where the singers hung out; Ted McKenna on mandolin and Ballyfermot's Liam Weldon on bodhrán singing their hearts out every night.

The front cubby near the door was for the hardcore trad players. I regularly sat in on sessions with fiddler Ted Furey – father of Finbar, Eddie, Paul and George who were soon to enjoy their own fame as the Fureys. Ted was a soft-spoken gentleman, very welcoming and appreciative of my accompaniment. Sometimes I'd play a new mandolin I'd acquired, learning tune after tune, but mostly it was guitar.

Friday nights the older, highly respected players John Kelly and Joe Ryan (musical collaborators who brought the true country-kitchen music from County Clare to the international stage) were in session. I loved their music. That long slow loping Clare style of reels and jigs became my favourite to listen to.

John was already bringing this magic to the international stage as a member of Seán Ó Riada's Ceoltóirí Chualann. In O'Donoghue's front cubby, however, they didn't quite approve of this newly arrived guitar accompaniment by some young long-haired hippy-looking geek who wagged his head round as he played. 'We'll have none of them head waggers in here,' I overheard John muttering one night as I arrived in O'Donoghue's with my guitar.

At the same time, I was making really good progress on the mandolin, playing the tunes rather than just accompanying. I guess it became clear to the older guys that I was capable of some sensitivity and musicality. I was tolerated if not embraced.

Many's the night I just sat, sipped my pint and listened. It was a free crash course in the best music Ireland had to offer. I was like blotting paper soaking up hundreds of tunes that I still remember note for note to this day.

Back in 80 Moyne Road we had a visit from the landlord one morning to say that he was selling the house and that we'd all (that is, the Derry boys and me upstairs and Mick Moloney and his flatmates downstairs) would have to find alternative accommodation. Mick and I decided to share rent on a basement apartment at 61 Palmerston Road in nearby Rathmines.

12

THE JOHNSTONS

The Johnstons – Michael and his two sisters Adrienne (Adie) and Lucy – were a group that sang for years at their family-owned pub in Slane, County Meath. Lucy remembers singing with her older sister on children's radio programmes in Dublin when she was as young as 10 or 11. Later, Adie played piano with the local Darby Céilí Band. Their brother Michael eventually joined on guitar and the Johnstons folk group came into being.

Their repertoire was made up of pop-folk songs of the day like 'If I Had a Hammer', 'Roses Are Red' and Del Shannon's 'The Swiss Maid'. Gradually Irish folk songs were added like 'Johnson's Motor Car', previously recorded by the Clancy Brothers and the Dubliners. Later a slew of recent American folk compositions, like 'Remember the Alamo', recorded by Johnny Cash and Tom Paxton's 'Leaving London' entered the repertoire.

Due to a stroke of luck, helped by their elder sister Margaret's husband Joe Kennedy (then an influential columnist with the *Irish Independent* newspaper), they entered the 1966 Wexford Ballad Contest. They won it. They got a record deal with Pye (Ireland) Records. Their first release, a Ewan McColl song 'The Travelling People', went to No. 1 in the Irish charts in August 1966, catapulting them to fame overnight.

Managed by Tom Costello, one of the most successful Irish showband managers of the time, there followed a year of intense touring within Ireland with lots of concerts, clubs, radio and TV.

The two girls were excellent singers. Adrienne was ambitious and enjoyed the new limelight. Lucy was a natural harmony singer. Michael, the only instrumentalist, played twelve-string acoustic guitar competently if uninspiringly. As their success grew, it was clear the group had musical limitations and needed to develop and expand.

Their brother-in-law Joe Kennedy, in addition to being a columnist with the *Irish Independent*, had his finger on the pulse of the rapidly growing folk scene. He stepped in as their mentor. He wanted them to acquire credibility as authentic folk singers like the Clancy Brothers and the Dubliners, as opposed to being just a pop act. The Seekers from Australia had burst on to the world stage and while they had several huge and melodically strong global hits and were considered by the media to be 'folk', any hardcore folkie, which Joe Kennedy was, considered the Seekers saccharine, politically uncommitted and lightweight.

Every record label wanted their own version of the Seekers. The Johnstons' overnight fame brought them dangerously close to that world of show business. The fact that their current manager, Tom Costello, came from the showband tradition didn't help. Kennedy, however, wanted success for the group, but felt the way to achieve it was to stick to the increasingly popular Irish folk-music scene rather than lose themselves in the superficial world of pop-folk. The Clancy Brothers had done it. Why not the Johnstons?

Mick Moloney, then playing with the politically left-leaning Emmett Folk group, came to the band's attention, having come second to the Johnstons at the 1966 Wexford Ballad Contest. Mick was exactly what the group was looking for: authoritative, charismatic, politically educated, well versed in the rich Irish folk-song canon, a convincing singer and a rapidly improving instrumentalist on guitar, tenor banjo and mandolin. He was approached by the group and joined up in early 1967.

Now that Mick and I were sharing accommodation, I was kept in the loop about his progress in the group. Internal musical tensions were developing. A different dynamic was at work since Moloney joined. Ambitions ratcheted up a notch. The brother, Michael Johnston, now forced to stretch outside his musical comfort zone, was challenged by this new reality.

Discussions were held between Mick and the girls about this. The possibility of me being asked to join was mooted. Adie came to the decision that her brother Michael was holding things back and had to go. It was an awkward situation which Moloney says he kept out of. After all, they were family and Michael had been there from the start. To what extent sibling dynamics played a part I will never know, but Michael got the push and I was asked to replace him.

It came as a shock. From being an unheard of 'floor singer' and opening act I was (just turned twenty) on the verge of being catapulted into a nationally famous group – 'Stars of TV and Radio' as the posters would say. I wanted it, definitely, but I was still in my final year at UCD and as far as my parents were concerned I had forsworn involvement in music to complete my degree. The conflict resurfaced. It could not be avoided.

I went back to Strabane to have high-level discussions about the future. A couple of days of intense bargaining began. I knew I hadn't a chance of getting my degree that year. Nothing but a dismal relay of exam repeats lay ahead. I felt sorry for my parents. They were doing their best to offer me opportunities they never had. The knowledge that I was one of the privileged few at UCD from Northern Ireland, with college fees and living expenses paid for by the UK government, while my classmates from the Republic had to find the money themselves, became harder to bear. Now, throwing it all away, I was creased with guilt and plagued by doubts. But this opportunity to join the Johnstons was the chance I'd been waiting for. I had a clear goal in mind for the first time in my life – I was not about to let it slip away.

Sean, who had never wanted to be a teacher, who in a later generation might have done the same as me, was ambivalent, quietly supportive. Mollie, in spite of her fears, was not immune to the attractions of having a son in a nationally celebrated group. Eventually they gave in. Soon I was on the express bus back to Dublin to get fitted by Dublin's show-biz tailor, Louis Copeland, for the regulation mohair suit. Johnstons' manager Tom Costello's background in the showband world stretched to influencing what we wore on stage. I think Tom was, in a patriotic way, enthralled by the ballad boom, but for him, 'being on stage' meant wearing the mohair suit. It was the first time I'd ever worn one. Suitably besuited, I joined the famous Johnstons officially in July of 1967.

A week after I had committed to join the Johnstons, Andy Irvine, unaware of my decision, asked me to join Sweeney's Men to replace Galway Joe Dolan (so-called to differentiate him from the even more famous showband singer of the same name). It never rains but it pours. A major 'Oh, shit!' moment.

I had stood-in for Joe on a Sweeney's gig in Cruise's Hotel, Limerick a few weeks previously and really enjoyed it. They did too. Sweeney's Men were more my kind of music than the Johnstons. I was a huge fan of the band. They had a current Irish top-ten hit with a trad song 'Old Maid in a Garret' and had almost as high a profile nationally as the Johnstons. I loved their singing, choice of material, Andy's harmonica and mandolin playing and Johnny Moynihan's bouzouki.

Johnny is genuinely credited with introducing the bouzouki into Irish traditional music when he bought an original Greek round-back model from a friend and later had a flat-back version made in London by John Bailey. This was seriously real stuff.

Andy's music reminded me of the New Lost City Ramblers (Mike Seeger, Tom Paley and John Cohen) whose Folkways recordings I'd been listening to for years. The Ramblers recreated songs from the Great Depression of the 1920s and 1930s. I loved the sound they made on a variety of instruments: fiddle, mandolin, banjo, autoharp, harmonica, dobro. Because I knew their music so well it was a breeze to fit in with Sweeney's Men.

The difference between Sweeney's Men and the Johnstons was that the Sweeney's were *all* good instrumentalists. They were totally into the music, less concerned about entertainment value. Besides, I liked their striped shirts and waistcoats. Not a mohair suit to be seen. Ah, how life turns on these small events. Who knows what my future would've been like if I'd gone that way? I would have avoided all the later grief that came down the road in the Johnstons. As it was, it would be eight years before my path and Andy Irvine's would cross professionally again.

Life went into high gear straight away. The Johnstons played all over Ireland for the rest of that summer. We travelled in a chauffered limo. 'The Curragh of Kildare', a song the group introduced to the Irish folk canon worldwide, was recorded and released just before I joined and was getting heavy airplay. Michael Johnston's twelve-string guitar playing on that recording was his last contribution to the group.

Within a few months of my joining, and at my suggestion, the new band line-up recorded an old song 'I Never Will Marry'. Originally recorded in the USA in 1933 by the Carter Family it was also a part of the New Lost City Ramblers' repertoire in the late 1950s. Already striving to make my musical preferences count, this was the first group recording to feature me on lead vocal. The arrangement was a strange hybrid. Opening with a four-part

harmony a cappella verse, and heavily influenced by the style of the emerging English folk band the Watersons, it dovetailed into an old-time country-waltz against a background of six- and twelve-string guitars and mandolins. My high lonesome vocal harmony in the second verse and harmonica in the chorus heralded an eclectic input to come. It was the first time I heard my own voice on any record. The significance of it passed me by at the time. For now, if I couldn't be in Sweeney's Men, I'd bring some of that music with me.

'I Never Will Marry' was an immediate hit in Ireland. The Johnstons were the star attraction at a plethora of showband dances managed by Tom Costello. The showbands generally hated us. They'd be playing from 9 p.m. through to 1.30 a.m. We'd swan in around 10.30 p.m., use their sound system, play for twenty to twenty-five minutes and disappear with a fee twice, three times what the showband earned all night.

Sometimes we did a 'double header', moving on to another dance twenty or thirty miles away and doing the same thing. At best there was a begrudging making way for us with little or no help with the gear. 'No you can't use our echo chamber' or 'You can only use *one* mic.' That kind of thing. We'd find ourselves stuck around one Shure open-head mic on an upright stand to pick up four voices and two acoustic instruments. An odd time there was outright sabotage with mics left screaming in feedback and the host band sniggering as we struggled to sort it out. But I was a quick learner technically and somehow things worked out. We always left the stage to cheers and huge applause. Heady days.

TV and radio beckoned too with live performances and a *Late Late Show* appearance that autumn. Famed and respected US folk singer Tom Paxton with his hits 'Can't Help but Wonder Where I'm Bound', 'Ramblin' Boy' and 'The Last Thing on My Mind' played Dublin's National Stadium that October and asked for the Johnstons to open. It was a big deal to be handed this imprimatur. In the pantheon of successful singer-songwriters in what was now a global folk scene, Paxton was the 'right sort' of artist to be respected by. Both he and Bob Dylan cited Irish folk music as a wellspring to which they frequently returned for inspiration. We were getting noticed in the right quarters and this didn't hurt our reputation at home.

Concerts mushroomed nationwide, often with other acts like Paddy Reilly and Jim McCann supporting us. I enjoyed being a professional musician. I was finally doing what I was supposed to. The relief from not having to pretend I was a student left me on a permanent high.

The fact that I was making good money too, for the first time in my life, didn't go unnoticed back home in Strabane. To see the legendary Gay Byrne, host of the biggest TV show in the country, introduce their son Paul to the nation must have gone some way to ease my parents' doubts about my choice of career.

Mick Moloney and I complemented each other instrumentally,

me on Michael Johnston's Hagstrom twelve-string guitar (which somehow remained a group asset after his departure) and Mick on a Levin six-string guitar, tenor banjo and mandolin. I was improving on mandolin and tin whistle. I even tried my hand at the fiddle, though that didn't last long.

As the round of concert, TV and radio engagements careened on, there began a subtle change in the Johnstons' musical personality, reflecting changes in the folk scene itself in Ireland, the UK and continental Europe.

The golden age of popularity of indigenous music and songs of these islands and our nearby neighbours was upon us. In England, recently formed bands like Pentangle, Fairport Convention and Steeleye Span were drawing huge audiences and attention from mainstream media, even appearing in the UK charts with centuries old folk songs.

Similarly in France, Alain Stivell, the Breton harpist, was breaking through and all over Europe, folk festivals were mushrooming – the Cambridge Folk festival being one of the most respected.

The common feature throughout this movement was the celebration of the music of our own countries and localities. American music, previously dominant in the repertoire of many folk groups of the time was, for the next few years at least, out of favour. We in the Johnstons were quick to scent these winds of change and were already planning to focus more on our own native repertoire. We moved away from US material like Johnny Cash's 'Remember the Alamo' or Tom Paxton's 'Leaving London' or established popular Irish rebel songs like 'Johnston's Motor Car' that now seemed glib, lightweight and crass.

Mick and I were now frequent visitors to the Tradition Club in Slattery's pub on Dublin's Capel Street. The club met weekly on a Wednesday night. Run by Tom Crean of local singing group the Press Gang, singer and bodhrán player Kevin Conneff (later to join the Chieftains), vocalist and folklorist Seán Corcoran, and singer Finbar Boyle, the Tradition Club provided a platform for a host of Ireland's best native traditional singers and musicians, many of whom were being plucked from obscurity and celebrated for the first time. Many future stars in the younger generation of instrumentalists – fiddlers Seán Keane and Donegal native Tommy Peoples, uilleann pipers Liam Óg O'Flynn and Paddy Keenan, flute players Matt Molloy and Cathal McConnell – took flight from the Tradition Club.

We were at the start of a huge growth of interest in singers from all over Ireland, North and South. The cream of Irish-language singers like Darach Ó Catháin, Seán Mac Donnchadha and Nioclás Tóibín were regulars at the Tradition Club. Ulster singers in English: Paddy Tunney, Geordie Hanna and Eddie Butcher, all graced the stage. These Ulster singers and their songs heavily influenced me as I worked at finding my own voice.

It was around this time I realised that for me, melody was the most important and interesting aspect of a song in any form of music. Rhythm and words came second. If the melody had no internal life force, then a song never held my interest for long. What made me fall in love with the big traditional songs, in Irish or English, was that internal life force of tune that could stand alone, with no instrumental accompaniment or arrangement. This love of melody has stayed with me through all my musical reincarnations ever since.

For young musicians and singers like us, going to the Tradition Club provided a feast of material and stylistic education. For the next decade it remained the go-to place in Dublin for anyone wanting to hear the best in Irish traditional music and song. Anytime I was in Dublin and free on a Wednesday night I rarely missed it. For the moment I was heart and soul into the pure drop of Irish traditional music.

13

THE MOVE TO LONDON

In late 1967 the UK folk revival was gearing up. We were hearing records by Martin Carthy, the Watersons and the Young Tradition and were mightily impressed by these new folk albums. From our own tradition, we picked songs that we would later record as our first album together, songs that would move the group away from 'show business' into a space that would become a force to be reckoned with in the international folk scene. This tension between credibility and commercialism, folk and pop was always in the background and would return to bite us later. For now though, we were all of one mind and this period remains one of the most enjoyable of my time with the Johnstons.

While I was settling in, in fact, even before I had joined, the group came to the attention of the UK label Transatlantic Records. Owner Nat Joseph was a pioneer in the British record scene. He started the label in 1961 on graduating from Cambridge University. Where most UK labels were old school and only interested in high turnover pop acts, Nat realised there was a growing market firstly for folk, blues and jazz artists from the US whose records weren't available in Europe, and secondly for local UK, Scottish and Irish artists outside the mainstream who were drawing big audiences in the expanding folk scene.

Nat had already been scouting in Ireland and signed the Dubliners in 1964. Other recent signings were the Humblebums (featuring Billy Connolly and Gerry Rafferty), singer-songwriter Ralph McTell, a cappella folk group the Young Tradition and the folk-rock band Pentangle.

Nat picked up on the Irish success of the Johnstons and wanted to bring us to world attention. He would have seen and been tempted by the commercial pop potential of the Seekers-type groups popping up all over the place, like the UK's Settlers, and the Johnstons' sound was similarly accessible. But he was happy to let his acts choose their own material, even if most of it didn't sound like what was currently in the charts. He understood that with the arrival of Bob Dylan, popular music and songwriting had gone through a fundamental revolution and that it was smarter to see what developed naturally out of this new wave of music rather than prolong the artists and repertoire (A&R) methods of the old guard who told artists what to sing. He foresaw the growth worldwide of the late 1960s and early 1970s folk boom and the resulting successful business model. After all, who could have predicted that the Dubliners, although they were no longer on Transatlantic Records when it happened, would be riding high in the British charts with an Irish folk song, 'Seven Drunken Nights'? As in the US some years previously with groups like the Weavers, and Peter, Paul and Mary, folk had entered the UK mainstream.

We soon got an offer from Nat Joseph and Transatlantic Records. After a Christmas concert in Dublin's Gaiety Theatre, 17 December 1967, we were flown to London for the meeting. The prospect of being introduced to the UK and European market was exciting. A twenty-minute cabaret spot in the middle of the dance in the New Hall, Ennis didn't seem quite the future we wanted any more. Even though we still had that top ten hit 'I Never Will Marry' in Ireland, in January 1968, we were determined to look further afield. It was a strange time. I couldn't help thinking we were walking into an unknown void, turning our backs on an innocent and fun world that we would never see again. How right I was.

We were offered a two-year contract at the royalty rate of 4 per cent of 90 per cent of the net retail price of a record with the option on Transatlantic Records' side to extend the contract for a further two years at the increased rate of 5 per cent – a 1 per cent rise between the four of us. A sweetheart deal (not).

On 12 February 1968 we signed. This is the way it was back then. Obviously, something was worked out between Transatlantic and Pye Records and our Irish manager Tom Costello, but I wasn't aware of the details, nor cared less.

Juggling with an increasing workload in Ireland, the beginning of 1968 saw us spending a lot of time in London. Regular flights on the old Aer Lingus Viscount turbo prop or British Airways Vanguards brought us over for further meetings about future directions, UK management and when to begin recording. The label paid for all the flights, to be deducted from our future 4 per cent, naturally.

From 25–30 March we recorded the album *The Johnstons* (colloquially called the *White Album* because of the sepia group photo on a plain white cover) in Sound Techniques – a trendy new independently owned studio on Old Church Street off Kings Road, Chelsea.

We each got UK £9.00 per three-hour session, around £100 each over the five days, to be deducted from future royalties. That was the last and only money we ever got from that record. Engineered and mixed by John Wood and produced by Nat Joseph, it has remained one of our most popular and well-loved.

On one of our trips, at Nat's suggestion, we met with Jim Lloyd about UK management. We had just performed to some acclaim at a St Patrick's Day concert at the Royal Albert Hall on 15 March with the legendary songwriter Dominic Behan (writer of 'The Patriot

Game' and 'Liverpool Lou'), Margaret Barry & Michael Gorman, and the Grehan Sisters.

Word was out on the Johnstons. Nat was working his contacts. Talk was we were destined for big things. First up as a potential manager was Londoner Jim Lloyd. He was freelance at the time. He hadn't yet become the BBC voice of *Folk on Two*, which would have prevented his relationship with us as a conflict of interest. One clear present advantage, however, was that Jim's partner and future wife Frances Line was a senior producer at BBC Radio 2. She was at the helm of most of the programmes that dealt with folk and country music. This meant that in 1968 we were on *Country Meets Folk* four times and *My Kind of Folk* three times. On one of these programmes, we were the guests of the trailblazing Clancy Brothers and Tommy Makem on one of their rare visits to London.

Radio shows worked well for us. We were recognised as a consummately professional group with an attractive sound and a currently relevant and exciting repertoire. Plus, we were 'a dream to work with' apparently and required a very simple set up technically. What's not to like if you're a BBC producer?

All this time we were hopping back and forth between Dublin and London. On 21 February 1968 we played a famine relief week gig at Trinity College exam hall with Sweeney's Men, Luke Kelly, Jon Ledingham (later called Jonathan Kelly), Anne Briggs, Jim Mc-Cann, the Press Gang and Dubliner Barney McKenna. In June it was the Sligo Smithwick's Ale Festival, a couple of RTÉ TV shows: *Guth Na nÓg* (*Voice of Youth*) and *Summer Scene*.

But it was back to the UK in August for our first big festival gig. The weekend of 9 August 1968 saw the annual open-air National Jazz and Blues Festival in Sunbury, Surrey. We were a late addition to the bill, engineered by folk impresario Roy Guest, then working with the English Folk Dance and Song Society at Cecil Sharp House in London.

KEMPTON PARK
RACECOURSE
Staines Road (A308)

SUNBURY

Previously held at
Richmond & Windsor

8TH NATIONAL
JAZZ·POP·BALLADS &
BLUES FESTIVAL

An NJF/MARQUEE presentation

THIS WEEKEND

FRIDAY, AUGUST 9th, 8-11.30 p.m.   Tickets 15/-
THE HERD   MARMALADE   THE TASTE   TIME BOX
plus only appearance in Great Britain of
JERRY LEE LEWIS

SATURDAY, AUGUST 10th, 2-5.30 p.m.   Tickets 10/-
JON HENDRICKS   RONNIE SCOTT QUINTET
THE DON RENDELL-IAN CARR QUINTET
ALAN HAVEN TRIO   THE MIKE WESTBROOK BIG BAND

SATURDAY, AUGUST 10th, 7-11.30 p.m.   Tickets 15/-
ARTHUR BROWN   THE NICE   JEFF BECK   TEN YEARS AFTER
TYRANNOSAURUS REX   JOE COCKER   DEEP PURPLE   CLOUDS
NITE PEOPLE   plus special guest appearance of **GINGER BAKER**

SUNDAY, AUGUST 11th, 2-5.30 p.m.   Tickets 10/-
INCREDIBLE STRING BAND   AL STEWART
FAIRPORT CONVENTION   ECLECTION   THE JOHNSTONS, etc.

SUNDAY, AUGUST 11th, 7-11.30 p.m   Tickets 15/-
TRAFFIC   SPENCER DAVIS   JOHN MAYALL   CHICKEN SHACK
JOHN PEEL   JETHRO TULL   Tramline, Dynaflow Blues, etc.

Why not make a
weekend of it?
Stay at our
CAMP SITE
For details contact NJF Secretary
Bring your own tent,
etc. We provide
water and toilets

Tickets: In advance from NJF Box Office, Marquee, 90 Wardour Street, W.1. 437 6601
Keith Prowse, 90 New Bond Street, W.1. HYD 6000. or at Box Office on Festival Ground

Roy was a one-off. Born in Izmir, Turkey, he decided he was really a Welshman. (This was 1960s London. Everyone was reinventing themselves.) He became embroiled in the British folk scene where he heard *The Johnstons* (our *White Album*) and liked it.

Roy was flamboyant. Around lunchtime that sunny Saturday we all drove down to Kempton Park Racecourse in his huge Mk10 Jaguar. I was thrilled, nervous and excited. We were innocents in this flower-power world. The air was rife with patchouli oil, incense and marijuana. The sight of Mick Moloney and me in Louis Copeland's mohair suits (the uniform of the newly arriveé Irish showband) and of Adie and Lucy in their Irish dressed-up country girl outfits must have looked weird to the audience, sandwiched as we were between the Eclection and the Incredible String Band with their scarves and head dresses and tie-dyed outfits, bell-bottoms and high-heeled boots. I suppose we looked kinda cool ... if you were tripping, perhaps.

I felt out of place at the festival. The hippy dress code ruled – everyone vying to look more outrageous than the next. But there was more to my discomfort. Here we were, Paddies singing 'The Dublin Jack of All Trades', 'The Travelling People', 'I Never Will Marry' and 'The Curragh of Kildare' and probably Joni Mitchell's 'Both Sides Now', which we had just released as a single.

The inherent musical schizophrenia in the band was plain to see. I was beginning to feel conflicted with what my instinct saw as a long-term unworkable combination of styles. Up to just a year previously I probably had more in common musically with the other acts of that day – Traffic, Jethro Tull, John Mayall and Spencer Davis – than with the material on our *White Album*. But it was the 1960s and anything went. I kept my instincts under wraps for now. I was staying on board this mystery ride no matter where it went.

14

BOTH SIDES NOW

That summer everyone was talking about new kid on the block Joni Mitchell from Canada. Nat Joseph gave us her first album *Song to a Seagull*. I loved the record, loved her voice, loved the songs, but it was her guitar playing, which featured lots of open tunings, that for me was the really interesting part of the package. Adie, too, loved Joni's songs, especially 'Marcie' and 'Michael from Mountains' and before long she was learning them.

As a guitarist, open tunings were a favourite of mine. When the musical relationship between the individual strings is changed from orthodox tuning, it opens up a bunch of entirely new harmonic movements and rhythmic possibilities to the player. These movements are sometimes compared to those used on a keyboard and they can result in music that sounds hauntingly different, that brings the listener to another place. Two years previously, after I bade farewell to my Fender electric and my college band Rockhouse, I started experimenting with different tunings on my Harmony Sovereign acoustic. I was a fan of John Fahey's 1965 US album *The Transfiguration of Blind Joe Death* recently reissued in the UK on Transatlantic Records. Fahey made an art form of the open tuning. Joni Mitchell was taking it in a new direction, almost as an essential part of her songs.

The group had several meetings about our recording future with Nat over those summer months. Already, Transatlantic wanted another record although we had only released the first album that previous March. Folk records didn't cost a lot to produce and were quick to record. To give him his due, Nat was a mover and shaker. He knew the moment was now, knew that the Johnstons could be very successful on the back of the exciting new wave of music rolling in from North America. He suggested making an album of contemporary songs by Joni Mitchell, Leonard Cohen, Jacques Brel and Britain's Ewan McColl.

Alarm bells started ringing for Mick Moloney. He didn't want to make a record without *any* traditional folk songs. He already feared that the group might go in a direction that would see us losing our original Irish fans. It was confusing. We were all a little ambivalent about Nat's idea. We loved the trad Irish side of our music and saw its value both aesthetically and career-wise. It's fair to say, however, that Mick felt more strongly about this than the rest of us. Bar my reservations about the inherent musical schizophrenia of the band (which I was keeping to myself), musically I wasn't afraid of any new direction. I was intrigued, found it an exciting challenge. I looked forward to it. The girls did too. But Mick was still unsure.

As a compromise, Nat suggested a novel concept. Why not record two albums at the same time, a traditional one and a contemporary one and put them out on the same day? Nat even enthused that this would be an unheard-of event in the British record business and therefore very cool and newsworthy. Like I said, a mover and shaker.

All were in agreement. Deal done.

We settled on a bunch of songs by the aforementioned luminaries and then it was back to Dublin to research, learn and rehearse. Friends with local songwriters Shay Healy and Jon Ledingham, we decided to include a couple of theirs. Finally, with songs from Dave Cousins of the Strawbs, the American composer Stuart Scharf and the Australian singer Pat Carroll, we were ready to record.

Nat wasn't finished yet, however. He wanted the contemporary album to be arranged for strings and small orchestra with a rhythm section, bass and drums, keyboards and electric guitar. He knew some arrangers who were interested in the project. Barry Booth (Roy Orbison's UK musical director at the time) and David Palmer (who would go on to join Jethro Tull) were drafted in to arrange different songs.

In an incredibly short period of time, we were back in Sound Techniques Studio from 22–26 September. Even more incredibly,

Royal Festival Hall
(General Manager: John Denison CBE)

Saturday, 28th September at 8 p.m.

festival of contemporary song

Featuring:

AL STEWART **FAIRPORT CONVENTION**

JACKSON C. FRANK **THE JOHNSTONS**

and special guest star from America

JONI MITCHELL

Tickets: 20s. 15s. 12s. 6d. 10s. 7s. 6d.
from ROYAL FESTIVAL HALL (Tel. 01.928.3191) or USUAL AGENTS

Printed by Hastings Printing Co., Drury Lane, St. Leonard-on-Sea, Sussex Telephone Hastings 2434 we completed the recording of two albums, *Give a Damn* and *The Barleycorn* in that time. True to Nat's word, both were released on the same day – 14 January 1969.

It's hard to believe now how busy the band was in 1968. As a separate project, presumably while we were putting together the two albums, we recorded a single of Joni's 'Both Sides Now', the B-side being another Joni song 'Urge for Going' taken from *Give a Damn*. This single was released in Ireland in midsummer and entered the Irish charts at No. 12 for a six-week run from 31 August 1968.

Just two days after we completed the recordings, we found ourselves on the bill of Joni Mitchell's first ever concert in the UK at the Royal Festival Hall. She was a 'special guest star from America'. I wonder what that avowedly Canadian lady thought of that? Appearing in the 'Festival of Contemporary Song' that, in addition to us, included the currently hot Fairport Convention, was American songwriter Jackson C. Frank, whose new album was produced by Paul Simon, and finally London's bedsitter bard, Al Stewart.

We were thrilled to be on the bill. And since our recording of Joni's song 'Both Sides Now' was out in the UK as well as in Ireland, and was getting airplay, we hatched a plan to find out if she'd mind if we sang it in our set.

Our manager Jim Lloyd went backstage to see Joni's manager Elliot Roberts. He explained the situation, 'We've a hit with Joni's song in Ireland, could we sing it in our own set?'

Jim came back all smiles, 'No problem. All cool.' So, we went on stage and finished our set with 'Both Sides Now'.

After the interval we went upstairs to the circle where, surprisingly, there were plenty of free seats. We settled in to hear Joni's set. All went well till we heard her say, 'I'm now gonna sing a song of mine that I'm told is a hit in Ireland for an Irish band ...' (or words to that effect).

Whatever had gone down backstage, she hadn't been made aware we were *on* the same bill as her, or even what our name was and that we had already sung the song too. A mega cringe-worthy moment, so embarrassing it was actually funny. But not at the time. We were raging with Jim Lloyd for ineptly exposing us like that.

Nonetheless, Joni's set was brilliant. It included all her big songs from *Song to a Seagull* including 'Michael from Mountains' and 'Marcie' plus songs from her second album *Clouds* including 'Chelsea Morning' and of course, 'Both Sides Now'. At the end she disappeared. We didn't even get to meet her.

As it happened, a month later *Give a Damn*, including the song 'Both Sides Now', was released in the US. It was on a new label, Tetragrammaton Records, founded by comedian Bill Cosby and A&R executive Artie Mogull who, well named, went on to be just that over the next few decades in the US record business.

'Both Sides Now' was put out as the Johnstons' first single. To our surprise it took off on American radio. We got excited, watched it climb the US Hot 100s, 90s, 80s, 70s, 60s. By the time it got to No. 56 in *Cash Box* magazine's 'Cash Box Top 100', Reprise Records finally woke up to realise that another act of theirs, folk singer Judy Collins, had recorded a version of the same song on her 1967 album *Wildflowers*. They rushed it out as a single, spent some money, and after a battle between our version and Judy's lasting three weeks, Judy's gained traction and gradually airplay of our record slowed and stopped. Judy reached No. 8 in the US top 100.

It's tempting to posit that she owes her career success to the Johnstons. If our single hadn't come out and started happening, it's likely Judy's version would have languished on *Wildflowers*. The battle itself left a strange surreal feeling, as it all happened at such a distance.

Reprise Records, who Joni Mitchell was also signed to, then added Joni's own recorded version of 'Both Sides Now' to her second album *Clouds*. That album was a huge success and established her career globally.

We got over our disappointment. We had to. We were busy. We did our first solo London concert, 26 November 1968, at Hammersmith Town Hall. It sold out. There was a large contingent of Irish there of course, but also lots of British folkies came out for a look.

In between several more live recordings of BBC radio's *Country Meets Folk* and *My Kind of Folk* we still found time to go back home for two concerts in Dublin's Liberty Hall on 11 October and 14 December, and record for RTÉ's *Music Hour* with Irish showband star Dickie Rock on 26 December.

But things were coming to a head. Over the course of that year, we spent most of our time and energy in the UK with less and less focus on our Irish fans. The constant toing and froing took its toll on younger sister Lucy, who had a boyfriend at home and who was finding the pressure more than she felt comfortable with. She didn't share the blind optimism of the rest of us. Since Adie, Mick and I were determined to move to London and go for broke, Lucy decided to leave. We became a three-piece band.

A couple of days after a Farewell Johnstons Last Irish Appearance at Liberty Hall, 4 January 1969, we loaded up Mick Moloney's VW Beetle, tossed two guitars and a tenor banjo on the roof rack, covered it with a canvas tarpaulin held down with an elastic spider and headed down to Dún Laoghaire to catch the ferry to Holyhead and then drive to London.

Adie's man of the time was a Dublin doctor, Stanley Samuels, and as he had recently moved to London, she moved straight in with him to his place in Wembley. Mick and I stayed in a succession of places over the next couple of months from Harrow to Ealing and then closer to the action in Willesden and Hammersmith. We didn't have much time to relax or settle in as *Give a Damn* and *The Barleycorn* were both due for release on 14 January. We were on call.

The year 1969 was a time of building and consolidation. We spent much of the year travelling the length and breadth of UK doing concerts, folk clubs and festivals and BBC radio and TV shows. The North of England, Yorkshire and Lancashire were always happy hunting grounds. Apart from Manchester and Liverpool, towns like Barnsley, Accrington, Oldham and Sheffield saw us on regular visits a couple of times a year.

One day, on our travels, we came across a young Christy Moore at large in a high-rise flat in Halifax where he was living at the time. He had been to see us play in Barnsley Civic Hall the night before, loved the show and in the throes of post-gig largesse invited us to call in on him the next day on our way north. We took him up on it and spent a raucous afternoon catching up.

Mick and I had first come across Christy in Dublin a couple of years previously when he was working as a teller in a bank and doing folk gigs as a solo performer on a semi-professional basis. Now and again our paths crossed at sessions and parties. Then, on the back of a prolonged and acrimonious national bank strike in the summer of 1966, Christy took off to England to try and make some money, working in various odd jobs and doing 'floor spots' in folk clubs in the evenings. Bit by bit this began to take off for him. He released an album, *Paddy on the Road*, produced by Dominic Behan and containing some of Behan's songs. After a year or two and making a good living now, he decided, to the folk world's eternal benefit, to quit the bank and turn pro. Apart from a few short gigging trips home over the next couple of years, he didn't return to Ireland until 1971 when he came back to record the *Prosperous* album in County Kildare with Andy Irvine, Dónal Lunny and Liam O'Flynn. Out of that association came the legendary band Planxty. It never crossed my mind that day in Halifax that five long and turbulent years later, in a strange twist of fate, I too would join that band.

My Kind of Folk radio programmes followed in February, April and May with Peggy Seeger and Al Stewart, Gordon Lightfoot and a new arrival on the scene from the US, signed to the Beatles' Apple label, James Taylor, with his new single 'Carolina on My Mind'.

Several more *Country Meets Folk* radio shows came along with Sweeney's Men as guests on one of them. It was good to meet up with the lads again, that other band I *almost* joined. BBC producer Frances Line's relationship with our manager Jim Lloyd was indeed bearing fruit.

On 7 February we did a variety show at the Bradford Alhambra in the presence of HRH the Duke of Edinburgh. We headlined folk package concerts at Fairfield Hall Croydon, Newcastle City Hall and London's Queen Elizabeth Hall and topped the bill at the Royal Festival Hall in March supported by Hedy West from the US plus stalwarts of the English folk scene, Shirley Collins, Bob Davenport and the duo Dave & Toni Arthur. We were fast becoming the band to book.

A highlight that year was our invitation to appear at the Singers' Club at the Union Tavern in London's Kings Cross, 20 June. This was a rarely extended honour, an imprimatur of sorts for a folk group that could be accused of having commercial leanings.

The Singers' Club was a weekly gathering of like-minded left-wing politically active singers collectively known as the Critics Group, hosted by Ewan McColl and Peggy Seeger. That title in itself was enough to make me pause for thought. It was rigidly exclusive in that anything that smacked of mainstream entertainment, pop or show business was considered suspect, lightweight and to be avoided. The worst crime was to be politically uncommitted.

We had already recorded a couple of Ewan's songs, 'The Tunnel Tigers' on our 1967 *The Johnstons* album and 'Sweet Thames Flow Softly' on *Give a Damn*, so there was that connection and I liked both songs. It was a scary experience, nonetheless.

We arrived on a damp Friday evening. The room was already full. There was a kind of mini-theatre layout. There were chairs on two levels, it seemed, around three sides of the room and, as my possibly over-imaginative memory tells me, two large throne-like chairs, with their backs to the fourth wall where McColl and Seeger sat. I found the atmosphere totally intimidating. Adie was equally nervous. Mick, who was already more politically committed and outspoken than I ever could be, was terrified too. Everything was so serious. Songs were sung with an overtone that was almost religious. The hand-on-the-ear affectation that most of the acolytes present adopted in mimic of Ewan's well-known style was, to me, comically pretentious.

Coming from Ireland, where the singing of folk songs, even those politically based, was naturally joyous and uninhibited and much more of a social activity, the occasion seemed stilted and artificial, and I couldn't wait to start singing and get out of there. That said, we were warmly welcomed and afforded the stage to do our stuff.

We sang Ewan's 'The Tunnel Tigers' (though he gently reprimanded Mick afterwards for getting a word wrong), his London anthem 'Sweet Thames Flow Softly' and then Mick and I played the instrumental 'O'Carolan's Concerto' on guitars, after which Ewan chided his own gang for not being proficient enough instrumentalists.

The reception was spontaneous and genuinely effusive, so my initial fears were perhaps unfounded. Ewan and Peggy loved us, it seemed, phew. Still, for all my ifs and buts about Ewan McColl and his high priestliness, I'm a huge fan of his songs. I also loved his singing voice, which was warm, tuneful and real. He was indeed a genius who lived a full and productive life, leaving behind a legacy of some of the greatest songs of the last century.

From the lofty heights of the Singers' Club, we played the

Cambridge Folk Festival with the Dubliners, Ralph McTell, the Young Tradition and American singer-songwriter Patrick Sky. Sky (whose real name was Lynch), a southerner from Georgia, of Irish and Cree Indian heritage, was one of the early 1960s Greenwich Village folk heroes. A contemporary of Dylan, Dave Van Ronk and Eric Andersen, he was a skilled folk/blues guitarist with a biting wit who wrote satirical, anti-establishment songs. He went on to further explore the Irish side of his makeup, founding Innisfree records with Lisa Null in 1973, which became the successful Green Linnet label. Later, Sky was a great support to me in difficult times.

From there we progressed to BBC One's *Monster Music Mash* in November where we shared the stage with ex-Animals organist Alan Price (now an artist in his own right), Bob Kerr's Whoopee

FIFTH CAMBRIDGE
FOLK FESTIVAL

CHERRY HINTON HALL
1·2·3 AUGUST

The DUBLINERS ★ PATRICK SKY
ALEX CAMPBELL ★ The YOUNG TRADITION
DAVE & TONY ARTHUR ★ JOE LOCKER
NOEL MURPHY and SHAGGIS
The JOHNSTONS ★ MAGNA CARTA

Plus! Plus! Plus! ●Licensed Bar ●Buffet ●Camping

Tickets 17/6 day, 30/- weekend, from:
MILLERS, Sidney Street, Cambridge 54450

Band and Slade. We made short trips back home to do some radio and TV and a one-off concert in Gweedore, in the Donegal Gaeltacht. This was at the newly opened Amharclann Ghaoth Dobhair (Gweedore Theatre) which resulted in the release on the Gael Linn label of a single in the Irish-language 'Gleanntáin Ghlas' Ghaoth Dobhair' ('The Green Glens of Gweedore'), written by local schoolteacher Prionnsias Ó Maonaigh (Francey Mooney), father of Máiréad Mooney of later Altan fame.

All this time we were preparing a new record. *Bitter Green*, an album with the now familiar Johnstons mix of traditional folk and contemporary songs, was released on 1 December 1969. It had two Gordon Lightfoot songs: the title track and 'The Gypsy', a Leonard Cohen song 'The Story of Isaac', a Joni Mitchell song 'Marcie' and Ewan McColl's 'Jesus Was a Carpenter'. Also included was 'Fiddler's Green' an English folk song that has become a staple in the repertoire of many a folk band ever since. We learned it from Tim Hart and Maddy Prior's album of the previous year, *Folk Songs of Olde England Vol. 2*, though it wasn't really a folk song of Olde England but a contemporary composition by a Lincolnshire man, John Connolly. Tim and Maddy shortly went on to found the soon-to-be-huge folk-rock band Steeleye Span. My first recording of 'Lord Thomas and Fair Ellender', a song I first heard sung on an old Folkways album by Mike Seeger also went on the album. I fell in love with it so much that I re-recorded it on my 2017 *Unfinished Business* album. 'The Spanish Lady', a Dublin street song, became one of the group's most popular recordings. A traditional song 'The Penny Wager' and a few selections of jigs and reels rounded the record off. I still think it was one of our best records.

15

RUNNING ON THE SPOT

On 12 March 1970 we played at the Royal Albert Hall on a strange bill. Promoted as a charity concert in aid of the National Society for Mentally Handicapped Children, it was headlined by legendary Irish tenor Joseph Locke, by then in the autumn of his career. The Johnstons and the Ken Mackintosh Band were in support, further down the bill. In fact, the opening act was an up-and-coming singer-songwriter called David Bowie.

Heralded by a muffled, barely audible introduction from offstage, he came out alone, long shaggy blonde hair practically covering his face, in a blue tie-dyed button up T-shirt and salmon pink bellbottoms. No band, just a twelve-string acoustic guitar. He played for about fifteen minutes, finishing with a strange song 'Space Oddity' about some guy called Major Tom that was greeted with muted, disinterested applause. This was not a music crowd; the audience was mostly there to support the charity. I liked the song. Enigmatic and visual, it immediately took me somewhere else, somewhere I hadn't been.

Afterwards we chatted a bit backstage. I was playing an acoustic twelve-string too, the sunburst Hagstrom. He said he had one exactly the same which he loved, though that night it was a Gibson B45 he played. We compared string gauges. He said he liked Irish folk

music but didn't expand. He was quite nervous really but sweet and accessible. How he came to be on the bill I never found out. Often charity gigs had a disparate mix of acts, with exposure to a ready-made crowd the main attraction for the artist. A few months later 'Space Oddity' was all over the radio. The rest is history.

We recorded Ralph McTell's great song 'Streets of London' around about then. It was arranged by David Palmer, who had worked on *Give a Damn*, and produced by American producer Richie Gottehrer. Already a co-founder of the legendary Sire

Records (later home for a time to the Ramones, the Undertones and Talking Heads), Gottehrer started as a songwriter in New York's Brill Building in the company of Carole King and Gerry Goffin, Bacharach and David, Leiber and Stoller and Neil Diamond. 'Hang on Sloopy' by the McCoys was one of his first hits. He went on to produce Blondie's eponymous first album and the Go-Go's 'Beauty and the Beat'.

It was quite a coup to have Gottehrer behind the desk on our behalf in Sound Techniques, though I wasn't fully aware of his pedigree at the time. I think he and Nat Joseph were friends. He was easy to work with, complimentary of our efforts and good fun. It was a really good recording featuring a harpsichord and a beautiful piccolo trumpet solo in the middle. Adie sang a storm on it and it got a lot of attention and airplay, definitely more than any other recording of ours in the UK, but we still got no significant chart action.

All this took place against the backdrop of renewed violence in Northern Ireland. Following the split in the IRA (into the Officials and Provisionals) the summer of 1970 saw rioting and gun battles in Derry and Belfast. Though it would be a few years before the violence spread to Britain, as an Irishman I was increasingly feeling uncomfortable in London. The old British prejudices about the Irish resurfaced and the gutter press were sharpening their claws. While it didn't immediately impact on the success of the Johnstons, the innocence, laissez-faireism and open atmosphere of the late 1960s was slipping away. It was hard to believe that just a year earlier, a song from our 1968 *Barleycorn* album, 'The Fenians from Cahirciveen' about an 1867 West Kerry attack by 'the boys' on the dastardly occupying Redcoats, was a 'good time' concert-closer and one of our most popular songs in the British folk-club circuit. Things were changing fast.

We were still doing loads of radio and gigging like mad, but no one was talking about the elephant in the room. Northern Ireland was exploding. It started to feel surreal. Who or what were the Johnstons? Were we the group that recently got the blessing of the hardcore left at Ewan McColl's Singers' Club? Or were we the group that on UK nationwide TV welcomed in the New Year/ Hogmanay from Aviemore Ski resort in Scotland to a drunken audience who threw snowballs at us? Or were we the group that did endless recorded sessions for the cosy Jimmy Young BBC radio shows singing songs by Leonard Cohen, Ralph McTell, Gordon Lightfoot, Joni Mitchell and Ewan McColl with the odd Irish folk song thrown in like 'The Dublin Jack of all Trades' or 'The Spanish Lady' to get the foot tapping?

And what *was* the British folk scene in 1970? A genuine movement of people who learned to love and enjoy listening to traditional songs and music from the past? Or just a middle-class, flavour of the era, acoustic knees-up that took place once a week in 300 or so rooms above pubs throughout the UK?

It became a musically fragmented world, the traditional folk element to the fore but increasingly with contemporary songwriters and even comedians sharing the same stages. Gerry Rafferty, still in the Humblebums with Billy Connolly, had started writing songs like 'Her Father Didn't Like Me Anyway' and 'Mary of the Mountains'. Nick Drake too had just released his first album which was an exciting development to me. But you could just as easily have been at what was billed a 'folk' concert where, rather than a brilliant singer and guitarist like Martin Carthy or Nic Jones headlining, it might be a political commentator with a few funny songs, a dodgy voice and three chords on the guitar.

Pre internet and mobile phones, the need for social cohesion that gave the folk scene one of its main *raisons d'être* also offered a platform to a host of entertainers whose communication skills often enabled them to present themselves as leading lights in the folk movement. Nothing wrong with them tasting success. It was often great entertainment. But did it have much to do with music? Not a lot, really. I began to need something else. I began asking myself: what was this folk scene anymore and what was I doing in a 'folk' group anyway?

In the mid 1970s Nat Joseph introduced us to an American songwriter, Chris McCloud. McCloud had come to the UK after hearing a Johnstons record and wanted to work with us. Nat predictably was trying to encourage us to keep moving in a commercial direction so whatever spiel Chris McCloud gave him obviously convinced him that he was going to be useful. Little did I know at the time just how pivotal, destructive and devastating, both career-wise and personally, this was to prove.

Chris' arrival coincided with my own restlessness. I was itching to write songs but didn't know how to start. I was bursting with music but lyrics were my problem. What to write about? A very unformed twenty-three-year old, I lived day-to-day in a psychic daze. Chris was a prolific lyricist and while I didn't instinctively relate to his subject matter or style – in fact found some of it overblown and sentimental – I hoped that by getting involved with him I might learn something and get a breakthrough in my own writing.

In the beginning things went well. I wrote some music to lyrics of his. Songs appeared. He was spending a lot of time with us and was enthusiastic and positive about our mutual association. It looked like he saw the group as his vehicle to express himself as a writer and indeed, a businessman.

Everything was possible: a new album, a release in the US, tours there and in Europe. Massive success all within our grasp. So long as we followed his advice and suggested direction, we would all benefit from our relationship.

Adie in particular was impressed with Chris and not just on a professional level as it turned out. I don't really know what Mick's first impressions of him were, but he seemed happy to go along with things to see what developed. An album would be recorded. Chris would produce. Nat Joseph and Transatlantic Records approved of the plan.

After many binned attempts at songwriting over the previous months, I had finally written 'Brightness, She Came', which would be the first of my own songs to appear on a record. I quite liked it. The tune was catchy enough and I had fun playing the guitars on the recording, the lyrics perhaps a little mawkish in hindsight, but it was a credible start. I wrote two others with Chris, 'I'll Be Gone in the Morning' and 'Colours of the Dawn', which eventually became the album title.

Over the next couple of months Chris and Adie started going out together and became romantically involved. This changed the dynamic in the professional arena. Working methods that involved taste, criticism, opinions on individuals' creative offerings were more difficult to negotiate in that atmosphere. If, for instance, one of us thought an input from Chris lacked something or didn't work, it was harder to achieve consensus within the group itself. Chris was sensitive about his lyrics and didn't easily accept negative comments. He picked up on the sense that Mick was more interested in political songs than love songs and saw that as a way to engage him and ensure his support.

A cause célèbre of the time was the case of the American black woman Angela Davis. She was implicated in a drama where a black man, Jonathan Jackson, initiated the armed kidnapping of superior court judge Harold Haley, prosecutor Gary Thomas and three jurors from a courtroom in Marin County, California. Fleeing with the hostages, Jackson demanded the release from prison of the Soledad Brothers. Black activists for prisoner rights and for civil rights, the three Soledad Brothers (none of whom were in the courtroom that day) included Jackson's elder brother George Jackson. In the ensuing shootout, Jackson and Judge Haley were among four people killed, the others being two inmates who, already in the courtroom, had promptly aided Jackson. The prosecutor, Gary Thomas, was paralysed and a juror was seriously injured. Since the guns that Jackson used were registered to political activist Angela Davis, who had formed a committee supporting the Soledad Brothers, Davis was implicated and stood trial for alleged involvement in the kidnapping. After some time on the run, she was eventually arrested and brought to trial. She was acquitted.

It became one of the most widely publicised trials of the era. John Lennon and Yoko Ono had already recorded a song 'Angela' on the album *Some Time in New York City*. Bob Dylan had entered the fray with his song 'George Jackson'. The Rolling Stones song 'Sweet Black Angel' on their album *Exile on Main Street* was dedicated to Davis. Chris McCloud had written his own song 'Angela Davis' and suggested to Adie that she sing it on the record.

Mick liked the song and enjoyed working on it. Not being a huge fan of the 'protest song' genre which always tends to favour the message over the musical content, I wasn't crazy about it but concede it was a popular song in our live act, playing to the predominantly left-leaning gallery of the era, who supported the cause.

With further songs by Leonard Cohen, Peggy Seeger, Gordon Lightfoot and British folk-scene stalwart Ian Campbell, the album *Colours of the Dawn* was completed in early 1971 and released on the Vanguard label in the US and Transatlantic Records in the rest of the world.

In London, in March 1971, the BBC radio programme *Folk on Two* (produced by … you've guessed it, our manager Jim Lloyd's partner Frances Line) gave a preview of songs from the album. We played Belfast's Ulster Hall on 12 May supported by the Chieftains, who had recently turned professional and begun to tour. A month-long hugely enjoyable tour of Scandinavia followed in June.

While we were in Sweden, Chris and Adie got married. Things were moving fast. After one more appearance on a BBC radio programme in early August with the ineffably twee title *Sing Hi, Sing Lo*, shared with Alan Price, Georgie Fame and the BBC Scottish Radio Orchestra, we headed to the US for a tour to promote the Vanguard records release of *Colours of the Dawn*.

We didn't realise it at the time, but this would turn out to be the last Johnstons record to involve Mick Moloney.

16

SO NOW, AMERICA

We started off by supporting Joan Baez on a huge open-air concert on Boston Common, finishing off at the Philadelphia Folk Festival on the last weekend of August. This was a successful, effective trip. Following a well-received performance at Philadelphia which set the PR drums beating, came a week-long booking in September at the famous Greenwich Village club, Gerde's Folk City, that had given a start to so many successful US folk artists including Bob Dylan and the Clancy Brothers. We got a great write up in *The New York Times* by music critic John S. Wilson:

Without losing the vital spark that fires their singing, they have achieved a performing polish and a kind of relaxed but cogently directed showmanship that lifts them into that special area that Duke Ellington has described as 'beyond category' ... the group is so stirringly and beautifully musical, so full of shadow and spirit, that the listener is swept up in the drama or the humor or the poignance of their songs ... they have presence, a warmly communicative performing personality ... they are much more than the essentially instinctive performers that folk singing suggests.

While we were in Philadelphia in August, we met up with Dr Kenneth (Kenny) Goldstein. He was professor of Folklore and Folklife at Penn State University but was also a record producer of long-standing in the folk and blues world.

Goldstein's records of Ewan McColl and A.L. Lloyd were among the first English and Scottish folk albums ever recorded in the US and they opened up a vast new market that transformed the folk scene. Jean Ritchie, Reverend Gary Davis, the Clancy Brothers and Tommy Makem were others he recorded. Some of these were definitive moments, not only in the histories of these artists but in the music of the era. The albums from Reverend Gary Davis, Lightnin' Hopkins, Sonny Terry, Brownie McGhee and Lead Belly had a similarly profound effect on American blues and rock 'n' roll.

He also was a big fan of the Johnstons. He and his charming wife Rochelle offered us hospitality and support while we were in town. Mick had an immediate rapport with Kenny. His academic and historical interest in folk music appealed to the professor. They were of similar minds.

We made a return to Philadelphia in September the week after Folk City to do a four-night stint at the Main Point club supporting Jerry Jeff Walker – a leading figure in the Outlaw Country Music Movement. This further developed the relationship with the Goldsteins.

Things were very cordial, indeed open-armed and welcoming, but my emotional memory has me feeling increasingly ill at ease. While I still had no clear idea of who I was, no defined artistic identity yet, I had a growing feeling of what I was not … and that was 'part of a movement'.

There was a cosy collegiality in this US folk scene that I couldn't quite feel at home in. In terms of how I saw my musical sensibilities tying in with anything that was going on around me, I had a hundred standpoints and none. How the group was spoken about, written about or even introduced onstage had me feeling ... that's not what this is, that's not what I am. This was probably my first conscious awareness of a trait that I would later describe as being 'terminally non-aligned'.

I admired and liked Kenny and valued his perspective on music, but there was something about the academic and historical view that made me uncomfortable. I was a fledgling songwriter. I loved folk music but was increasingly more interested in what *might be* as opposed to what *was*. I was finding the US folk world – the folk world in general – confining and dogmatic. I saw the pitfalls in the commercial pop/rock world but ... was it a more appropriate place for me to find my feet?

I wandered in and out of this state of mind for years. Ultimately, I'd be grateful that I could traverse the folk/traditional and pop/contemporary musical arenas with ease, but the old feeling of 'not fitting in' that dogged me all my young life began to reverberate inside me again.

I can't speak for how Chris McCloud and Adie felt around this time but knowing the man as he was already turning out to be, he would not have wanted to dance to anyone's tune but his own. I was already under his spell, throwing my eggs into his basket. I didn't know it at the time (I feel shocked by it still) but I was moving along a road that would lead me into the darkest period of my life.

Tensions increased in the autumn of 1971, musical, personal, directional, leaving the current status quo on a knife-edge. I didn't want to spend all this time in America just to transfer from the British folk scene to the US one. I wanted to become a songwriter in a more contemporary style while, to me, Mick seemed right at home in Kenny Goldstein's academic world.

I finally admitted to myself that I was no longer musically stimulated working with him. I didn't want to continue with the schizophrenic 'Are we a trad band or a contemporary band?' conundrum. I'd had it with being in a folk group and dealing with all the spoken and unspoken rules as to what was legitimate folk or not.

I didn't care.

I wanted to move into areas that challenged me – areas that Mick had no desire to visit.

Things were good at this time with Adie and Chris McCloud. I was writing more songs myself and with him. Mick would surely have been unhappy with what he probably rightly saw as him being bypassed in the band with Chris, Adie and me wanting to move away from traditional music. In the past he was used to being considered the band spokesperson, if not leader. He was probably reacting against what he saw as Chris starting to dominate and control things. There was a lot of manipulation going on that I wasn't directly involved in, though I admit it suited me to acquiesce. This kind of pattern is endemic in groups as they develop and individuals' musical preferences and personalities change. The upshot of it was that Mick left the group in late 1971 and decided to go his own way. It was inevitable and in the long run for the best. Mick has certainly made a significant and well-deserved mark on the world of Irish music since. I have heard him described, not unjustly in my opinion, as 'Mr Irish Music America'. I am only sorry that our association ended messily after all the good times we'd had, though we now are on cordial terms again. But there were lots more messes to come.

In the autumn of 1971 Adie, Chris and I went back to London, the Johnstons now a duo for the moment. We immediately went into the studio to record what became the 1972 album *If I Sang My Song* produced by Chris. There were a bunch of songs already in the pipeline. Two I'd written myself: 'Continental Trailways Bus' and 'December Windows'. Both were newborn expressions of my current inner feelings. The songs 'If I Sang My Song', 'Won't You Come with Me', 'You Ought to Know', 'The Wind in My Hands' and 'Border Child' I wrote with Chris. Though I was still struggling to get a clear sense of who I was, it was exciting to finally be a songwriter.

My lyrics were still callow and self-absorbed, but I was beginning to flex my muscles as a singer, guitarist and piano player and to play with a string section was a thrill. 'Bread and Wine' and 'The Morning of Our Love' Chris wrote with Adie and one, 'I Get to Thinking', he wrote on his own.

We put a rhythm section together for the record that included Steeleye Span's Rick Kemp on bass and Phil Chesterton on drums – a definite departure from the acoustic folk sound of the previous record. Steeleye's Tim Hart and the Young Tradition's Royston Wood joined us on backing vocals and Barry Dransfield on fiddle. There was a string section on some of the arrangements. The rest of the instrumentation, guitars, piano, keyboards, harmonium and tin whistle I played. My confidence as a singer and instrumentalist was growing apace.

We needed to find a replacement for Mick for live gigs. Now that we were heading in a more contemporary direction it didn't have to be someone who was into Irish or folk music. It didn't even have to be an Irish person. We put the feelers out and word reached producer Sandy Roberton.

Sandy was one of the best-known record producers, movers and shakers of the London folk-rock scene having produced Steeleye Span, Decameron, Keith Christmas, Ian Matthews and Shirley Collins among many others. He had a new group he was working on at the time and mentioned to one of the members, twenty-year-old Gavin Spencer – that we were looking to expand.

Gavin liked the sound of our situation and auditioned with us. Adie and I jammed with him for a few hours and liked him. He played bass, acoustic and electric guitar, and sang. We asked him to join. One of the first things was to bring him into studio towards the end of the recording of the album to play bass and sing on 'The Morning of Our Love'.

If I Sang My Song came out on Transatlantic in spring of 1972 and got positive reviews. It was released in the US on the Mercury label. Now a three-piece again, we gigged through the spring of 1972. The highlight was a concert in the Queen Elizabeth Hall, London on my twenty-fifth birthday, supported by the Woods Band (Terry and wife Gay Woods, Terry originally of Sweeny's Men and later with his wife Gay Woods in the first iteration of Steeleye Span). We had the album string section backing us, which was a blast.

On the cusp of being cool, we did a couple of sessions for the high priest of cool, John Peel, for the *Sounds of the Seventies* BBC Radio 1 programme with other happening acts like Kevin Ayers, the Strawbs and Mick Softly. This was a hard club to access in the London of the early 1970s. Gavin settled in well and was enjoying himself.

In July we headed back to the States with Chris to gig at New York's Gerde's Folk City and Club Passim in Boston. These were promotional gigs for the Mercury album in the US and there was no money in it. This was soon to be the story of the next year and a half, and from here on in things for the Johnstons began to stall. The gigs were fun for a while. The new Johnstons were making a great sound, but the record was not a success in America.

The record business itself was in deep crisis due to the spiralling costs of vinyl caused by an acute worldwide oil shortage. Chris, who had taken over management of the band, was upset at the lack of promotion for *If I Sang My Song*. The current strategy of the group had become 'break America at all costs' and put the UK and Ireland on the back-burner in the meantime.

Overnight, the group's five-year relationship with UK's Trans-atlantic Records came to an end. Chris was now talking for the group to anyone we had dealings with. His temperament began to undergo a change. For the first time I was seeing him in a different light. He started to become dogmatic, confrontational and secretive. Could he have had a row in some discussion over the lack of promotion for the album both in the UK and US? Could he have fallen out with Transatlantic's boss, Nat Joseph? I was never told, but suddenly it seemed we were looking for a new record deal in the US at the worst possible time.

Not only were labels not signing new acts due to the economic crisis but they were actually dropping acts they already had on their rosters. I remember being shocked that a well-known New York folk artist of the time, Eric Andersen, had been dropped by Vanguard Records. What chance had we?

The rest of the autumn of 1972 was taken up with Chris going to meetings with various record companies in the city to try and get a deal. Labels like Brut (owned by the rich son of the Fabergé global cosmetics), Bell Records, RSO records (Robert Stigwood's label), United Artists, Elektra, Epic; all were apparently positive to the group and wanting to sign.

By now we had moved out of prohibitively expensive New York city to a rented house in Shorefront Park, Norwalk CT – about forty minutes on the train from Grand Central Station.

We did showcases for A&R people, taking the train from Norwalk, carrying our instruments with us, returning in the evening with the nine-to-five commuters. We shuffled into the office of the already legendary Clive Davis of Columbia Records to play for him. He was charming. He really liked us. He 'just needed some time to think'. We had arrived. It was all going to happen! We managed to afford to put a pretty good demo tape together of a couple of songs. The drummer on the session was a young Rick Marotta.

Stu Woods played bass. Both would go on to play on some of the greatest records of the 1970s with Bob Dylan, Paul Simon, Steely Dan, John Lennon, Roy Orbison, Crosby, Stills & Nash ... the list is endless.

We started doing non-paying support spots in places like Kenny's Castaways, a now legendary but defunct music club on New York's Upper East Side. Pat Kenny was a music fan who had emigrated from Ireland some years prior. Kenny's Castaways was a refuge for up-and-coming wannabe stars. Acts like the as yet unknown Bruce Springsteen or Bob Marley's Wailers were regular patrons. Pat took a fancy to us as we were Irish and he was very supportive. Only problem was our showcases were early in the evening where the main act might be a glam rock band. When we went onstage there were few in the audience except some glammed-up fans of the headliner and whatever record-company types came to see us. It wasn't the best environment for us to shine in. Mostly we didn't.

There was a lot of waiting to hear back from people – 'So-and-so's gone to the coast and won't be back till next week. He'll listen to the tape then ...' kinda thing. It went on and on. We were running out of money. I had nothing but a credit card on a bank account in London with minor funds in it. Chris had a chequebook in use all the time, but there never was any cash. So we were now dependent on Chris' choice for everything: food, travel, accommodation, entertainment. I was expected to donate whatever was left of my financial resources to the kitty for the greater cause of the band. So I did.

As 1972 drew to a close, there was still no deal in sight. The constant stress and lack of control in my life was beginning to have a dreadful effect on me. The mythical record deal and the band meant less and less to me. I felt like I was in prison. I was homesick too and decided to go back to Ireland for Christmas ... at my own expense. I had just about enough money left in my London bank to pay for the trip. I was pretty nervous about the flight as I had outstayed my three-month visitor's visa and was worried I mightn't get back in.

I spent Christmas at home in Strabane with my parents. This was a difficult enough visit. The violence in the North was still in full spate. The day before I arrived, five civilians had been killed in a suspected UDA gun attack in the Top of the Hill Bar on Derry's Old Strabane Road. After so long away, the muted atmosphere on the streets, with few signs of Christmas celebration, was surreal and depressing. The errant son, whose career to date just about deserved his parents' blessing, had run aground. They hadn't a clue what was going on with the Johnstons in America and I was at pains to avoid telling them.

In mid-January I had a yearning to go back to Dublin and see some old friends. It was difficult to face. I was a member of the famous Johnstons and though our profile had lessened in Ireland since we moved to London, the group's activities were still of considerable interest to the musical fraternity and to some extent the media.

But I was reluctant to be dragged into inevitable discussions as to what was going on. I was ashamed and embarrassed to admit that in fact nothing was going on, that we were stuck in America on an endless losing ticket and that I had no idea where things were going. Out for a pint with close friends, they sensed after a few queries I wasn't happy to talk and didn't push me. That pressure apart, I was delighted to be home again.

17

TRUE LOVE WAYS

I was in Dublin when news broke of the death of Willie Clancy, the great piper from Miltown Malbay in County Clare. This was a huge occurrence in the Irish traditional music world. Willie was one of the most respected musicians in the country. I had been privileged to meet him several times in 1967 and 1968 in my travels round Ireland before the Johnstons moved to London.

I remember a quiet afternoon session in the back room of Friel's pub in Miltown with Willie and that other great piper and singer Séamus Ennis. Séamus I already knew from the odd afternoon session in O'Donohue's pub in Dublin and from a TV show that the Johnstons and he had both appeared on. We had played together before. I had my guitar in the back of my car and Willie and Séamus had encouraged me to retrieve it and join in with them.

I will never forget it. I felt like I'd died and gone to heaven to be sitting and playing with the two of them and no one else around but us. They were both very open and encouraging to me, which of course spurred me on to play some reels and jigs on the guitar, something no one was doing at the time. They evidently enjoyed what they heard. It was an exciting experience for a then twenty-year-old boy from Strabane and I always had a fondness for both men after that. So, this news of the death was a big shock.

Friends and musicians in Dublin made plans to go to the funeral. Tom Crean from the Press Gang was going to Miltown Malbay the night before and offered a lift to me and Kevin Conneff of the Chieftains.

We arrived at 9 p.m. Miltown was full of funeral goers and the Central Hotel, where we stayed, was alive with music till the wee, wee hours. It couldn't have been further away from the Johnstons' New York showcasing for record companies.

The funeral on 26 January 1973 was a big and solemn affair with music at the graveside and everyone went back to the town to celebrate Willie's life and legacy in the only way musicians can. Later that evening Tom, Kevin and I were soon ensconced in our favourite pub, Friel's, having a quiet pint and singing a few songs, when in the door came two girls who had also just arrived from Dublin. One I recognised as a regular at the Tradition Club in Capel Street, so I knew they were there for the funeral ... but I was immediately struck by her friend and I couldn't take my eyes off her for the rest of the night. We got to talking after a while and I rather gauchely offered her my seat, much to her embarrassment. Seats in a session were sacrosanct and not to be given up to non-musicians no matter the gender. She was aware of that (like it wasn't glaringly obvious what was on my mind?). We all saw the funny side of it. No harm was done, and we were getting on well. She, Mary Elliott, had just that morning handed in her thesis as culmination of a master's degree course in Trinity College and was well ready to relax.

The night progressed. Mary's co-traveller friend Ann Cox had a cottage a mile outside the town at Spanish Point by the sea and that's where the two girls were staying. When the pubs closed, we repaired to the cottage and chatted by the fire for another hour or two. I was seriously smitten, losing myself in her jade green eyes and velvet voice. Emotions engulfed me. I suddenly knew that whatever was going on here, I did not want to go back to my life in America. It made no sense anymore.

Next day we all went back to Dublin. I blagged a lift with Ann and Mary. We were getting on well and I didn't want it to end. She seemed equally eager to keep it going. Over the next week there were various musical parties on the go at a large communal house in Palmerstown in the west of Dublin where some of our friends lived and we spent some time there. Mary was living with Ann and another girl Kathy in Fitzwilliam Square in the centre of Dublin. Each had her own room and for some time afterwards I stayed there. As February progressed Mary and I became more closely involved and I, for one, was falling in love. But back in the real world I knew I couldn't just pretend the Johnstons didn't exist. I'd have to return to America.

After a blissful month in Dublin, at the beginning of March 1973 I headed to the airport for the journey back to Norwalk. Would I get back into the country? Did I care? I was deeply conflicted. Part of me hoped I'd be refused entry. Though I was slightly panicky at immigration, I breezed through.

Things were strained on my return to the fold. Adie was vague and uncharacteristically withdrawn. Chris was eager to know all about my trip and whatever implications it might have for the stability of things in the group. Who had I met? Other musicians? Had I talked about the Johnstons?

I told them I had met Mary, that we had got on very well and that before I left Dublin, we had agreed she would come over and visit me in May. This was greeted with what felt like token enthusiasm.

Things had got a lot worse now financially. Nothing had happened while I was away in terms of a new deal. I became very dispirited with the constant, 'Oh, so and so loves the band and it'll all be agreed and sorted out in a few days and then we'll get a cheque.' Not only was I missing Mary, but I was back in the same old quicksand as before.

I ask myself now why I stuck it out so long, but it was complex. Chris was convincing with all his stories. Having not been present at these 'meetings' with record companies – 'It's too expensive for us all to take the train into the city so I'll go alone' – I couldn't figure out whether it was all genuine or whether he believed his own spiel or indeed was hiding some larger truth from us. He had also become quite manipulative: 'We all have to stick together. Don't ask questions. Don't complain. Trust me.' Loyalty was expected. A four-day series of gigs came up in June in Passim's, the well-known Boston folk club. That was the focus now.

Things were surreal. The house we were in was right on the water's edge on Long Island Sound. It was comfortable and picturesque. Idyllic even. But I didn't have a cent in my pocket. If I wrote a letter to Mary – something I now did every couple of days – I'd have to ask Chris for money for stamps. I learnt that if I wrote four pages on a certain notepaper the postal cost was 21c but if it went to five pages it was 42c. It was that bad.

I began to feel unwell. I stopped sleeping regular hours. I'd lie awake all night, sleep all day. I got pains in my neck, back and shoulders. I became withdrawn. This was noticed by Chris and was deemed disloyal. 'Don't bring Adie down!' was the mantra. Adie had to be protected at all costs.

Mary arrived in May. I was thrilled to be with her again. To have this warm and open girl from a totally different world to share my thoughts, fears and desires with was liberating and inspiring. I felt I had an ally, someone in my camp.

There was an outward show of welcome from Chris and Adie, but before long her presence posed a threat to Chris' control. Tensions arose, though never boiling to the surface. I think she was a

little shocked to see the state of things and the general air of un-
reality in the house. It was great to have an outsider's take. Mary
wasn't prone to taking everything Chris said to heart and after
many late-night talks between the two of us, it was clear to me just
how big a mess I was in. Mind you, knowing it and getting out of
it were two very different things.

After a couple of weeks, Mary went back home with a plan to
return in October if I was still there. I was not going to let this fall
apart. I had changed inside and would bide my time.

Things ground on. We did the Passim's gigs in Boston in June,
the fee just about covering our expenses. Gavin met a girl there,
Susan Sky, whom I knew well. She was the ex-wife of singer-
songwriter Patrick Sky. She and Gavin hit it off and he moved out
of the Norwalk house and in with her.

Though I had first met Patrick Sky at the Cambridge Folk festival back in 1969, I only got to know him at the Philadelphia Folk
festival in 1971 where both he and the Johnstons played. Through
us, at the same festival, he had met up with piper Liam Óg O'Flynn,
a meeting that for Patrick started a life-long love affair with Irish
traditional music and uilleann piping in particular. In the years
ahead he not only learned how to play the pipes but started making them. As things developed (notwithstanding the fact that one of
our band members was seeing his ex-wife) I would see a lot more
of Pat in the next few months.

Chris had started to borrow money from, well, whoever he
could borrow it from. Though he never discussed the financial situation in detail, one case I knew of was a loan from Robert Adels, a
writer from the music magazine, *Cash Box*.

Bob, as he was known, was a big fan of the group since our
brush with fame in the US charts with 'Both Sides Now' in 1969.
In particular, he loved Adie's voice and perhaps was a little smitten.
In any case, Chris asked him to help us out 'till our record deal

advance came through' and he generously did. He gave us a couple of months' rent money. I doubt he was ever paid back.

That was only one instance of several friends and colleagues being hit up with no repayment. Now, however, money had run out again. Most of the time I never knew precisely what was going on, but I was aware the owners of the house had been complaining about delays or even lack of rent. They had even visited one weekend to check up on things but were mollified in that instance by Chris' silver tongue. Before long, however, came all kinds of tense phone calls behind closed doors. Finally, the talking ended, and we were forced to leave the Norwalk house in the summer.

On the day of the flit, we borrowed a car from Gavin's girl Susan and drove into the city with all our belongings in suitcases. We checked into a downtown hotel using my London credit card as security. It was an incredibly tense time. I was in a kind of daze and felt 'this is not really happening'. I knew it was all crazy and would end in tears, but I couldn't imagine a way out of it without upping and leaving the band and being the cause of its collapse after all this time. Out of a desperate sense of loyalty I hung on in there.

Early in the morning of the third day the hotel bedroom phone rang. It was reception saying 'Good morning Mr Brady. There seems to be some problem with your credit card. Would you please come down and see us?'

I was in a state of shock. I called Chris and Adie, told them the news and in a couple of minutes of frantic conversation we decided to do a runner. The alternative seemed catastrophic with police and immigration coming into the picture and the whole thing crashing down, not to mention a jail sentence.

The hotel had a number of permanent residents who from time to time brought their laundry and dry cleaning through the lobby in plastic bags on their way to an outside operator. We were afraid that if we walked through the lobby with suitcases we would be seen and stopped so we decided to abandon our suitcases in the rooms and transfer all our belongings into plastic bags as if we were just going to the cleaners.

Down we went in the lift separately and walked through the lobby looking straight ahead and out the front door. It was terrifying. No one stopped us. We met outside on the pavement a block away and gathered ourselves.

The mad thing about it was we had nowhere else to go. Chris was in discussions with another rental place on Long Island, but it hadn't yet come through. God knows how we were to pay for that. Right now, we were on the streets. We got in a cab and went uptown to another hotel on 57th.

Chris knew of an apparent norm whereby any hotel transaction up to $200 (over $1k in today's money) on a credit card would automatically go through. Anything above that had to be verified by phone. We checked in, this time Gavin and Susan with us, again using my card as security. The precise cost of a night's stay was worked out. All were warned not to put any extras on the room. The plan was to leave next morning and use the same device in different places till the Long Island rental came through. We'd worry about paying the credit card back 'when the record deal came through'.

Check out the next morning saw me at the front desk nervously asking for the bill. $215! My heart sank. How could this have happened?

'Sorry to keep you Mr Brady,' the clerk said, 'but rules say I gotta make a call to verify your card – it's over $200.'

I was caught between rage and terror. He went into the back room and through a window, I could see him in line waiting his turn to get on the phone. Two minutes passed, three, four. The queue wasn't moving. He turned to me, shrugged his shoulders apologetically, then suddenly quit the line and came back out.

'It's okay, Mr Brady, as you can see, we're busy, it's only $15, Fuhgeddaboudit. Have a nice day!'

Those were the best words I'd heard in a long while.

We met up outside. I was shaking. I told them what had happened. Had anyone run up room charges? Ordered room service? Turned out that Gavin or Susan had made a phone call from their room at the then exorbitant hotel prices and that's what made the difference. I was incandescent. There were apologies. I didn't hear them.

All this was before credit cards were computerised. Even if a card was invalid in one establishment you could still use it else-where for a considerable time before it got on a defaulter list. That's how we got away with it. My nerves were shot. I wasn't built for this stuff. I binned the card and never used it again.

A couple of days later, we moved into a house in New Hyde Park, Long Island, just off the Jericho Turnpike about half an hour out of New York city. How Chris had pulled this deal off I hadn't a clue, but it was with 'borrowed' money. I was at my wits end. I didn't have a cent in my pocket. I was keeping myself to myself. My friendship with Adie came to a standstill. I couldn't discuss my doubts about the Johnstons situation with her as I knew it would get back to Chris.

I wandered the area and came across an Irish bar, the Dublin Pub, advertising live music. One evening I walked past it and heard a succession of standard Irish ballads blaring out in the summer air. My emotions welled up. To hear music from home, played just for fun and with no stressful game plan for global acceptance, made me feel giddy.

I took a look inside the pub. The clientele was mostly young blue-collar American twenty-somethings with a smattering of older people who looked Irish. Onstage was a tall dark-haired Irishman with a Kerry accent playing acoustic guitar and singing in a typical ballad lounge style with lots of 'hups' and 'how-are-yis' and exhortations to 'have the craic'. This was the kind of 'Oirishness' I would run a mile from at home, but here in the middle of Long Island in the awful state I was in, I was overcome with loneliness and homesickness and this old familiar sound was a comfort. With hindsight I now see this torrent of emotion as the first real turning point in the nightmare I was living in. Along with the pain came a rush of primal survival instinct. I felt the urge to burst into something different, whatever the outcome, and leave this disempowering chaos behind.

I walked up to the bar. Behind it was an American guy in his twenties who had a proprietary air to him. I heard myself asking:

'Any work going?'

'What kind of work?' he said.

'Any kind, bartending, cleaning, *anything*.'

I had never worked in a bar in my life.

'Where d'you live?' he asked.

'Just round the corner.'

He thought for a while, pulled a pint and said, 'Come in tomorrow afternoon. We'll talk.'

Next day I arrived in. The two guys were there. The singer was a Kerry man, Timmy Moloney, and the guy I'd asked the previous evening about work was an American, Billy Dennis. Both were partners in the pub.

I decided not to say anything specific about my situation, that I was a singer, musician, none of that. I just said I was in a difficult position and needed to make some money. I was straight up with them and said I knew little about bartending. They laughed. We chatted on. Whatever chemistry came about they decided to give me a start and before long I was behind the bar being shown how to make a Bloody Mary and a Margarita.

'Come in this evening,' Billy said, 'let's see how you get on.'

I told Chris and Adie I'd got a job. I was starting work that evening. They were surprised, curious, hesitant, but positive. I went in that night and things were fine. I didn't disgrace myself and the rest of the staff were helpful. After a couple of days, they handed me $30. I felt like a millionaire. It had been months since I had felt a dollar note in my hand.

18

BUSTED LOOSE

I was working in the Dublin Pub about a week when I was overheard singing along behind the bar to some song or other coming from the stage. One of the girls jokingly said 'Hey Paulie, you should be up there with Timmy.'

I shrugged and laughed, a little too loudly. A slew of panicky thoughts: *Am I going to jump into this pool? Or will I just play dumb?*

Timmy came up next afternoon and said, 'I hear you're a bit of a singer, laddie. Fancy having a go up there?'

I prevaricated, bleating, 'I don't have my guitar.'

'Ah sure, no problem, laddie, you can borrow mine!'

The shoulder strap was too long, the strings too light, the pick he gave me, too soft, but I sang something, I don't remember what. Probably a Hank Williams song. Nods of approval.

'Come up tonight and sing us a couple of songs,' he said.

I did, opening with 'Paddy's Green Shamrock Shore' which seemed to hit the spot with the crowd, then my Hank Williams staple, 'You Win Again' and one other 'The Lark in the Morning' (I think). The earth didn't move, but neither did the sky fall. This was the pattern for a week or so, working behind the bar and getting up for a song or two. I started to earn more, which was great. I was also kind of enjoying this alter ego, incognito game.

One afternoon, as I was slicing lemons, Timmy and Billy approached me. Billy was carrying the Johnstons' *White Album*. Timmy pointed to me on the sleeve and said, 'Is that you?'

My heart thumped. There was nothing to say except yes.

There was a river of well-well-wells! What's all this about? Why are you here? WTFs?

While the Johnstons weren't a household name in the US like the Clancy Brothers, anyone who was in the Irish folk and ballad scene anywhere in the world at that time knew 'The Travelling People', and 'The Curragh of Kildare', as did Timmy and Billy. I told them a very shortened version of the situation.

'We felt we had achieved all we could in Ireland and UK and were having a go in the States. But the record business was in deep shit, closing shop and it was, uh ... bad timing. So ...'

They sat open-mouthed for a while but acknowledged that these things happen and that I was the same guy they'd known, worked with and sung with over the past few weeks.

I owe Timmy and Billy a debt. They saved my soul at the time. Their company and support were the catalyst that set me on the path of deliverance.

I went home to the rental house every night, handed over my earnings to the kitty, but something was different. I had lost my commitment to the Johnstons. Chris, Adie and I related distantly now. Instinct said if I told them I'd been 'discovered' as a Johnstons band member while bartending in the Dublin Pub, they'd not be happy. But now I decided my life outside the Johnstons was none of the band's business – none of *Chris'* business.

Soon I met new people, others, friends and colleagues of Timmy and Bill. The Johnstons story got about and for a while was a subject of interest in the New York Irish music scene, not that Chris and Adie picked up on it, isolated as they were.

At the Dublin Pub one night I met with another Kerry man,

Sean Fleming, who had his own burgeoning career as a singer and guitarist of some stature in the Tri-state area. He offered some gigs to me, playing with him. I would play bass and sing a bit. I earned more with Sean than I did in the Dublin Pub. I owe him a huge debt too. He was very generous to me. I couldn't have survived at that time without his help. Sean remains at the top of his game in the Irish music scene on the US East Coast.

The empowerment that came from earning money of my own and experiencing a life outside the Johnstons' fishbowl slowly bore fruit. I'd no idea where to go or what to do next, but I put that to the back of my mind, decided to go with the flow. I needed some fallow time to let things take their course.

Late summer, I called up Patrick Sky, the folk singer I'd met and become friendly with back in 1971 at the Philly Folk Festival, and he invited me up to stay with him in his place in Rhode Island. Since we'd last met, he was now firmly into Irish traditional instrumental music. We'd a lot in common through that. He picked me up where I was staying in his big Dodge.

He thought I was mad to be sticking with the Johnstons' situation and wasn't shy of saying it. The folk boom was over. We were never going to get a record deal in this climate and Chris McCloud was a con man and a nutcase and why couldn't I see that? You could have lit a bonfire with the electricity that flew between Chris and him when they squared up to each other the day Pat called for me. Here was yet another threat to Chris' carefully controlled self-image.

Rhode Island was a breath of fresh air. Where Pat lived was in the country in a tiny old wooden house dating from the late 1700s on the Old Post Road in Perryville near Wakefield. The surrounding area reminded me of Ireland, with small fields and hand-built stone walls everywhere along the roadsides. Pat introduced me to some of his friends including a writers' agent Chuck Neighbors – another visitor from New York. I would see a lot more of Chuck in the city over the next few months. We hung out, played music, listened to records. For the duration of my stay, it was easy to forget the situation I was in and imagine other possibilities.

Pat was a good guitar player, singer and songwriter. Looking back, he was one of the 'nearly made it' acts of the early 1960s New York folk scene that gave the world Dylan and Simon & Garfunkel. He had already had a couple of successful albums and a decent career as a live touring act, but by the time we met he was disillusioned with all of that and was ready to jump into something entirely different: enter … the Irish piping tradition, stage left.

Pat was obsessed with the playing of the greats, Séamus Ennis, the recently deceased Willy Clancy and the younger Liam Óg O'Flynn who I knew well from many sessions in Ireland in the late 1960s. Before too long Liam would become a founder member of the now legendary Irish band Planxty.

The Rhode Island house was full of interesting books and records. I spent hours browsing through Pat's collection. One book I came across was called *A Heritage of Songs: The Songs of Carrie Grover*. I was taken by it. Carrie Grover (1879–1959) was a Nova Scotia-born woman of Irish, Scottish and Welsh ancestry, who had settled in Maine. She had a huge repertoire of folk songs from Britain and Ireland that Alan Lomax recorded in the early 1940s, and this collection was recently published with single-line musical notation.

Many of the songs were familiar to me in other versions but the tunes Carrie had were frequently different and often more attractive. I came across the song 'Arthur McBride', which I'd first heard recorded as 'Arthur McBride and the Sergeant' by England's Martin Carthy on his 1969 album *Prince Heathen*. I always loved the story and set about deciphering Carrie's version from the musical notation.

The melody was strong and captivating. She sang it over fifteen four-line verses with the melody resolving at the end of each verse. I felt by doing that the story was fragmented and harder to engage with. What if I joined up each section of two verses and made them into one with no final musical resolution till the eighth line? That way it would give me more time to build the dramatic tension in the story. There were a few confusing words and repeated lines which I changed to suit me. The word 'burgoo' I'd never come across. I now know it to be a word in use in America from before the Civil War meaning a rough stew or porridge. I thought 'thin gruel' rhymed, kind of meant the same and would be more understandable to Irish people.

There was also a six-line verse in the middle which was musically superfluous and which I dropped. So,

The soldier he always is decent and clean
While other poor fellows go dirty and mean
While other poor fellows go dirty and mean
And sup on burgoo in the morning

became

For a soldier he always is decent and clean
In the finest of clothing he's constantly seen
While other poor fellows go dirty and mean
And sup on thin gruel in the morning

I had been enjoying experimenting with different open tunings on the guitar and found myself tuned to open G that day. I started trying to sing and play it and it gradually came together in a way that excited me. I wasn't to know then that the arrangement and performance I cobbled together in Pat Sky's house that winter of 1973 would become one of my most successful and celebrated musical creations, loved by musicians and singers the world over. Right now, however, I was still broke and in a rudderless drift.

Years later when I listened to Bob Dylan's recording of 'Arthur McBride' on his 1993 *Good as I Been to You* album, I knew he had learned it from my recording on *Andy Irvine and Paul Brady* as he also followed my eight-line verse arrangement and sang the lyrics I had changed.

More recently I heard from Happy Traum – a friend of Bob's since the 1960s Greenwich Village days – that Bob regularly called in on him if he was passing by, asking what he was listening to these days. One of those times in the late 1970s, Happy played him the *Andy & Paul* album. Bob loved it and took it with him. It's worth saying here that, stuck in America, I wasn't familiar with Andy Irvine's different version of the same song on the first Planxty album. Neither did I then have the remotest notion that in the not-too-distant future I would actually *be* in the band Planxty and singing my version on stage with them.

My visit to Pat came to an end and he dropped me back to New Hyde Park one day on his way into the city. Things were in crisis again. There was still a 'new deal just around the corner' but the game was up in the rental house. Another midnight flit was called for.

Chris had found a small two-bedroom house just off Elmhurst Broadway in Queens and somehow managed to put a month's rental down. This meant the end of any work in the Dublin Pub, it being way out of reach.

All this time I was writing every second day to Mary in Ireland. For some weeks we used the address of Pat's friend, Chuck Neighbors, on Waverly Place in the Village as the only reliable point of postal contact in a rapidly changing situation. I never knew how long we would be in any accommodation anymore. A couple of nights I slept on Chuck's floor.

One of those times, totally broke and at my wits' end, I decided to go into the city next morning and busk on Wall Street. The financial centre of the Western world ought to be good for a few dollars. I had gotten pretty good on the tin whistle and thought that was the instrument that would work best. I took the subway downtown. I still remember the cost: 35 cents, one way. All I had. I'd at least make that to get me back to Waverly.

I set up on a corner with my baseball cap on the ground and began to play reels, jigs and hornpipes. It was mid-morning. Loads of people were passing by but nobody, not one person, put their hand in the pocket and gave me a red cent. This went on for two hours. I was getting disillusioned when this old down-and-out denizen of the streets walked past me a few times, laughing to himself. He finally came to a standstill before me. I stopped playing.

'Say Buddy,' he said, 'you've lost your snake!' Off he went, cackling hysterically at this Irish snake charmer.

I called a halt to my busking and faced off into walking uptown. I didn't even have enough for a subway token. A low point in the career, perhaps.

Mary came over again in October. As she said years later, it was to finally see if the thing between us was real and worth sticking with. I still think she must've been mad. It's not like I was a great catch. I was a basket case all the time she was with me and 'prospects had I none' as the song goes. But she chose to believe in us.

We stayed in the house in Queens. Things were fluid with me time-wise. Though the job in the Dublin Pub was gone, I was still doing the odd gig with Sean Fleming to pick up cash wherever I could. Pat Sky had just introduced me to an Irish music session in a pub on Lexington called the Monk's Park. I began to play there. The clientele was a motley crew of folk music enthusiasts from many ethnic and stylistic backgrounds. There was an uilleann piper with the unlikely name of Bill Ochs who would go on to become one of the foremost US authorities on Irish wind instruments. There was a singer of sea shanties, Dan Milner, who remains one of the leading lights of the New York folk scene. Many other performers, and at least two people, singer and musician Jeff Davis and Renée Lawless, became lifelong friends. It was there I performed my version of 'Arthur McBride' for the first time in public.

The enthusiastic reaction did wonders for my confidence. I had mostly taken a back seat in the Johnstons while Adie and Mick were the main singers. Up to this point I had no experience as a solo performer. I had to learn fast.

Pat Sky was a constant friend through difficult times. I went back up to Rhode Island with him as winter arrived, this time with Mary. We stayed for a few weeks. He suggested I put some songs together, get a gig on my own. There was a club called Salt in Newport nearby and he knew the booker. He secured a forty-minute support spot for me ten days ahead.

It would be my first ever solo gig. It was a challenge. I had the few songs I'd written for the Johnstons albums, 'Brightness, She Came' and 'Continental Trailways Bus', but what else? 'Arthur McBride' was an obvious choice. I'd no idea what sort of an audience, if any, to expect but felt they'd be more into a singer-songwriter thing rather than a trad-Irish set. Hank Williams' 'You Win Again' was always a guaranteed crowd-pleaser as was Lead Belly's 'Duncan and Brady' – they went on the list. I always loved Van Morrison's 'Into the Mystic' so added that. The final two were strange choices. 'The Blacksmith' and the Beatles' 'I Should Have Known Better'.

I rehearsed my set daily the week before the gig. Pat, a seasoned solo performer with a great onstage patter, gave me tips on how to present myself, what to say ... or not to say.

The night arrived and it was bitterly cold with heavy snowfalls. The roads were treacherous. We crawled the twenty miles to Newport in an old VW Beetle belonging to a friend of Pat's. The

Down the Line
Jacobites
Shamrock Shore.
Reels on guitar
(The Wild side of life
(I should've known better
Into the Mystic
Bonny Bunch of Roses.
Continental Trailways
Blacksmith
30 ft Trailer
Reels whistle
Rocky Road
Border Child
Frankie & Albert.

club was at the water's edge and there were fewer than twenty people there yet to see the headline act.

No one knew who I was ... including myself. I did my set, played well, I thought, to a decent swell of applause. I had got through it. The ice was broken. It could only get better, surely.

I wanted less and less to stay in the Queens rental place. Mary and I moved around a lot. We spent time with our new friend Renée Lawless, originally from County Wicklow, who had an apartment in Manhattan. We stayed with Chuck and Dorothy Neighbors in

Waverly Place. Christmas came and went with no developments on the record deal front. I had given up on that. Mary and I had thoughts of bailing out, going home to Ireland even though for me there was nothing to go home *to* except the prospect of starting again – bottom of the ladder.

Also, there was the matter of a plane ticket: I didn't have one. The return date on my ticket from the previous March had expired.

In early 1974 we moved back into the house in Queens for a few days. Things were on an exponential downward spiral. Adie was spending most of the day in bed. We rarely saw her. Chris brought food and drink into their bedroom saying Adie 'wasn't feeling well' or that she 'had a bit of a bug'. Was she in a serious depression, I wondered, having some sort of mental breakdown?

I walked for hours all round the area to get away from the atmosphere in the house. Chris McCloud was still disappearing into town to meet someone about a record deal or another about a showcase gig at Kenny's Castaways. By now I guessed these meeting were probably to talk someone into loaning money to pay for next month's rent.

There was a bar called the Last Post we went to at the time. The big record at the time was Paul McCartney and Wings' 'Band on the Run' and it seemed to be played in high rotation on the bar jukebox all night. I never felt so lost, so much of a failure in my entire life and seriously wondered what on earth Mary was doing with me.

One light in the gloom was that we got in touch with Alan Pepper and Stanley Snadowski. We had met them running Gerde's Folk City on West 4th Street when the Johnstons had played there to acclaim before Mick left the group. We had all got along well. It turned out that Al and Stan were opening a new club close by called The Bottom Line. They actually took us round to see the venue while it was still being fitted out. At this time they offered us a support spot on the second show after it opened. The headliner was folkie Eric Andersen on 23 and 24 February 1974. We did well that first time and were immediately offered a week of gigs from 26–30 March supporting the Strawbs, then Ricky Nelson.

But something was wrong. Adie was in trouble by the March shows. Whether it was her medication or the effects of a break-down, she lost confidence. Gone was the gutsy frontwoman of old. She was nervous, withdrawn and really unable to perform. It was a nightmare on the stage. She forgot arrangements, where she was in a song, mixed up words of songs she had sung for years. At one time she seemed about to collapse but righted herself. It was one of the most uncomfortable times ever on a stage. It didn't go unno-ticed – we weren't booked again. I spoke to Chris about it the next day. He was in denial: 'She's just tired, she's run down.'

One April morning, shortly after that gig, I came out of the bedroom to see a letter with an Irish stamp on the hall floor. It was addressed to me. Who was it from and how were my where-abouts known? I took it back into the bedroom where Mary was still asleep. I nervously opened it, instinctively expecting bad news. It was from my old friend the piper Liam Óg O'Flynn – he must have got my address from Pat Sky as they were regularly in touch. It was a one-pager. He was now with the successful Irish band Planxty. Singer and founder Planxty member Christy Moore was leaving the band. Would I come back to Ireland and take his place?

I still remember the shock and fierce excitement that hit me on reading this. It was like a miracle. Here I was at the lowest point in my working life, twenty-six years old, broke, marooned in the States with nothing on the horizon that offered any kind of relief and, bang! Out of the blue, this lifeline appeared.

I woke Mary up in my excitement and told her the news. There was no doubt in my mind that this was my 'get out of jail' card and I immediately decided that my time with the Johnstons, the band

I'd been with since mid-1967, was finally at an end. I decided to say nothing about this to Chris McCloud yet. I still had to find the money to get home.

I contacted Liam and said I'd do it but I'd need some time to sort myself out. He suggested a starting point might be Planxty's appearance at the UK Cambridge Folk Festival that coming July. That gave me enough time.

I told Pat Sky about the development. He was delighted. It did not escape my notice that after a couple of years of trying to extricate myself from the folk scene I was heading back into it in a big way. The difference here was that there was no confusion as to what kind of music the band was playing. There would be time enough later to go back and explore the songwriter side of me.

Mary and I moved out of the Elmhurst house and stayed with Renée Lawless. Through my friends at Monks Park, Jeff Davis and Jean Stewart, I got some work teaching 'Irish guitar' at the Guitar Workshop in the town of Old Roslyn, Long Island. After a couple of weeks I had earned enough for a ticket home.

I told Gavin about my decision first. He understood. He was mentally moving in other directions too and wasn't entirely surprised. Next was to tell Chris and Adie. It was a predictably nasty scene. I was a traitor, letting the band down after all this time, blood sweat and tears. All the guilt-making buttons were pressed, the exact ones that to date had messed with my head and kept me from seeing reality. My own lack of self-confidence and fear of stepping out into the unknown played its part too. But all that was at an end. Like a man released from jail, all I felt was excitement about the future. A few weeks later Mary and I were back in Dublin. A new life stretched out before us.

Chris and Adie, incredibly, kept on going. They came to Ireland not long after us. Chris made another attempt to talk me into staying on. It ended in a screaming match on the phone as he played the same old games. That was the last time we spoke. I never saw them again.

Adie got a local deal and made an album for RCA Ireland in 1975 which included some of my co-writes with Chris. After months hanging around Dublin, tales of friends and acquaintances being burned by loaning money to them emerged, and they went back to the US. In fact, they disappeared from sight and never returned.

The Johnston family were distressed at not being able to know where Adie was. When her parents both died in that period no one could reach her. She wasn't at either of their funerals. It was clear to me that Chris McCloud was singularly intent on controlling Adie, isolating her from her past life.

Remembering her fragility in the final days in New York I can only imagine how her emotional and mental state would have continued to deteriorate. In 1981, after many attempts by her old mentor and brother-in law Joe Kennedy to use his journalistic contacts for information about her, it was learned that Adie died in the US in 1980. The official cause was 'death as a result of injuries sustained in a fall'. The coroner expressed doubts about whether this was the reason for her death but there was no proof of foul play and the verdict stuck.

Chris McCloud (whose real name it turns out wasn't McCloud at all, but Miethe), after at least one recorded period in prison later for an unspecified offence, died in 1989. A troubling mystery till the end.

The Johnstons was a big part of my life. Seven years. It was my introduction to the professional music world, live performances, radio and TV appearances, studio recordings. It was fun. I made a good living in the beginning. But I had no sense of who I was. I drifted as if my *real* life's purpose had yet to be. This feeling of 'waiting' persisted long after I split from the band; it dogged my footsteps, caused me grief.

I regret how my friendship with Adie ended. She was spirited and talented. We had a great time in our heyday. Gavin and I drifted apart. He married and settled down in New York where he developed a successful career in music, but we got back in touch in later years. Equally with Mick Moloney whom I see every so often.

As for my relationship with Chris McCloud? When I look back, I recognise it as an abusive relationship. I'm uneasy about who I was and how I reacted to events back then. Like many abuse victims, I blame myself for what happened to me. The final two years in the band darken my recollections of the Johnstons. Apart from one (for me) uncomfortable reunion in 2011, with Mick Moloney, original members Lucy and Michael Johnston and singer Niamh Parsons in Adie's role, painful memories have me shying away from any well-meaning attempts to honour their legacy.

19

PLANXTY

Mary and I arrived back in Dublin early June 1974. Our friends rallied round to get us accommodation and we gradually found the beginnings of our way. I met with the Planxty boys, all of whom I knew from before: Andy Irvine and Johnny Moynihan from Sweeney's Men; Christy Moore from when we crossed paths in the North of England in my Johnstons days; and the piper Liam Óg O'Flynn whose letter led to my being here.

But this was different. To my initial surprise I discovered that Christy was still in the band and would continue to be for another six months. No one said anything by way of explanation as to why he had decided to leave or indeed why, if I was supposed to replace him, he was still there.

By this stage original Planxty founder member Dónal Lunny had moved on to a band called Bugle with musician and composer Shaun Davey. No one was particularly forthcoming about this either; as the new guy I wasn't inclined to ask questions. To be honest, after the two-and-a-half-year nightmare I'd just woken up from, I was just happy to be playing music again and making a living. All else could wait.

The first time we were together in public was in Buncrana, County Donegal. It was a Planxty gig. I didn't join them onstage, but was brought along to hear the band, familiarise myself with the repertoire and imagine how I might fit in. At some stage we found ourselves in a pub and as the soon-to-be new member I was pressed upon to sing a song. The only one I felt comfortable with was 'Arthur McBride', which of course was already known to the public via Andy's recording on the first Planxty album; a wonderful version that I really loved.

It was a strange occasion. My performance was received very well with lots of whoops and hollers. I can only imagine how Andy felt at the time. As it turned out, he would never again sing the song in Planxty, at least in that incarnation of the band.

In 2018, in the course of writing this, I decided to call up Christy and finally satisfy myself as to why things were the way they were then. He was very accommodating and forthcoming. I asked him why he decided to leave the band in 1974. He said that after Dónal left, late the previous year, he didn't feel musically comfortable any more. He relied a lot on Dónal's musicianship as they went back many years, even before Planxty, and with his absence he found it hard to find his place. New entrant Johnny Moynihan who replaced

Planxty as a five piece at the Ice Rink in Edinburgh during the run of 'The Fantastical Feats of Finn MacCool' at the Edinburgh Festival, 1974. *Left to right*: Johnny Moynihan, Andy Irvine, me, Liam O'Flynn and Christy Moore.

Dónal had a singularly individual approach to instrumentation and performance that didn't suit Christy; after a while in this line-up he wasn't having fun anymore.

When I asked him why he remained on after I joined he said he felt an obligation to the band to stay on until I had settled in rather than leave them exposed. That came as a surprise. I was further surprised to hear him say that it was he who had first suggested me as his replacement. Up to that point I was under the impression it had come from Liam and perhaps Andy.

It was a strange time for me. Christy was, even then, a larger-than-life figure with many fans and followers. The news of his departure left many aghast. While pretty well-known from the Johnstons, I had been 'off the scene' for some time; the mantra going round was that Paul Brady could never replace Christy Moore, that I might possibly be a 'better musician' but that I could never be a 'front man' like Christy, or words to that effect.

I felt that pressure and it was an unpleasant feeling. It left me determined, however, to stand my ground and show my worth. I threw myself wholeheartedly into the band with a 'feck the begrudgers' attitude.

Reading between the lines of my conversation with Christy, there were possibly other troubling issues bubbling under the surface that helped him come to his decision to leave. He said something (that I too believe) that Planxty were never as 'big' then as people now think; their international legend grew up after they had ceased to be. Granted the first couple of albums were groundbreaking and became the sound of early-1970s' Ireland, but by the end of the first year things were not so rosy.

According to Christy, Dónal's reason for leaving in late 1973 was that musically things were at a standstill and that he wanted to develop in other directions. There were many tensions within the band as to how to exploit their sudden newfound success. Fiscally, as I eventually found out much to my great cost, the band was a total mess.

One interesting development that may have encouraged Christy to stay on awhile was an invitation to the band to create the music for a major play in the upcoming famed Edinburgh International Festival. Irish playwright, Kerryman Sean McCarthy had written a play *The Fantastical Feats of Finn McCool* which was to open at Edinburgh's Haymarket Ice Rink from 19 August–7 September 1974.

The band was commissioned not only to compose the incidental music (there was a lot) in support of several scenes, but to perform it live with the cast every night. This found us perched on a raised podium at the back of the theatre from which we overlooked what was indeed a fantastical event.

Musically it was an ideal situation for me. None of us knew what we were going to come up with, which took the individual pressure off me and spread it equally. It suited me. I was good at this kind of thing. Over the month of July I enjoyed contributing to this project.

We arrived in Edinburgh a week before the opening and were thrown into rehearsals with the cast of the Young Lyceum Company. We made many friends in those few weeks, young actors who went on to greater things: Patrick Malahide, Billy Paterson, Alex Norton, Tony Haygarth, Johnny Bett, Jeananne Crowley and of course singer Hamish Imlach who played a musical role. By the end of this event I felt like a bona fide member of the band.

At this time there was no talk of further recording. Firstly, since Christy was leaving, things were up in the air; and secondly there was some dispute going on between the band and their record company Polydor UK. Irish songwriter Phil Coulter was somewhere in the mix too as producer of their last album *Cold Blow and the Rainy Night*, though precisely what part he played,

Tomorrow Night **CARLTON**

Thurs. 5th Dec. 11.15 p.m.

PLANXTY

Seats : £1.20, £1.00, 80p

Special Guest

DICK GAUGHAN

Booking 2-7 p.m.

or side he took in this dispute, was unclear to me and was never explained.

At any rate, recording was not on the agenda in late 1974. We did a lot of live performances, however, and some television work. Gigs in London's King's College and Battersea Town Hall in November followed. BBC TV's *Old Grey Whistle Test* showed us playing 'The Blacksmith' (recorded at the Cambridge Folk Festival earlier in the year) and a BBC TV Northern Ireland programme helped keep the band in the public eye.

Christy's last gig with the band, in Dublin's Carlton Cinema, 5 December 1974, was coincidentally the occasion of the first enthusiastic public response to my version of 'Arthur McBride'. Though I felt secure in my position as a Planxty member over the summer gigs in England and Scotland, that was the first time I felt really accepted in the band in Ireland. It was a good feeling.

The year 1975 saw the consolidation of the band's reputation in the UK and continental Europe, particularly France. We began a relationship with a Paris promoter/agent Lionel Rocheman and with our first engagement sold out a concert headlining in the famed Paris Olympia in February.

More French shows arrived with gigs in Brittany and, in November, a full French package tour with two French 'folk' bands: Malicorne and the Occitan singer Joan Pau Verdier. That took us to back to Paris then Lyon, Marseille, Montpellier, Aix, Nancy, Strasbourg, Lille, Rouen, Caen, Rennes, Nantes, Tours, Bordeaux, Toulouse, Poitiers and Brussels.

This was the golden age of the European folk music revival, which only lasted a few more years. Alain Stivell, the Breton singer and harper, was one of the biggest acts at the time; selling out large venues throughout Europe, the UK and Ireland. Fairport Convention and Steeleye Span ruled the roost in Britain.

Earlier that year, 15 March to be precise, Mary Elliott and I were married by my uncle Joseph McElholm in the University Church in Dublin's St Stephen's Green. Including the bride and groom, there were twelve people at the wedding: my parents Sean and Mollie; Mary's father Willie; my sister Anne and her husband Maurice; my brother Barry; Mary's elder brother Harry with his wife Eadaoin; her younger brother Des; and her good friend Anne Cox. My mother, God rest her, was dismayed that there was no one there from the press! If her son had eschewed academic security in favour of show business then where were the attendant paparazzi? What a let down.

We all headed down for the wedding celebration to the Clarence Hotel on the quays. Years before it was bought by U2 in the 1990s and 'coolified', the hotel was a long-established favourite of country folk and clergy on a visit to the big city. It was old-fashioned and traditional in its fare.

Shown into a small private room, we had champagne and a choice of sirloin steak or salmon. It was a convivial gathering. Speeches were made and all wished us well. The entire affair cost the staggering sum of IR£42.18.

We were set to honeymoon in County Clare. We both had a strong connection with West Clare as that was where we had first met two years previously at Willie Clancy's funeral. It was pleasant to anticipate returning in these very different circumstances. We headed off around 4:30 p.m. and stayed overnight in the bridal suite in Hayden's Hotel, Ballinasloe. From there, next morning, to Kilshanny to stay with my old friend from my Johnstons' days in London, Mike O'Connor and his then partner Jackie. I had lived across the road from them in Bolingbroke Road in Shepherd's Bush. Mike was an accomplished artist even then, with lino-cutting among his many talents.

We were soon back in Dublin and had by then moved into a mews apartment in Lad Lane off Baggot Street. Mary had started working in a government body, the Institute of Public Administration. Planxty were at their zenith, reputation-wise, at this time. A typical set list would include lots of instrumental music; jigs, reels and airs, with songs from Andy: 'The Blacksmith', 'Baneasa's Green Glade', 'The West Coast of Clare', 'Farewell to Old Ireland' and a harbinger of the later album Andy and I would make, 'Bonny Wood Hall'. Johnny's contribution might include 'P Stands for Paddy' from Planxty's most recent *Cold Blow and the Rainy Night* album, and 'Love Will You Marry Me'; while I would sing 'Arthur McBride' and 'Mary and the Soldier'.

Within the band, though, things were stalling. While we all got along personally, there was an absence of any management with vision, indeed management at all. While Planxty's first three albums: *Planxty*, *The Well Below the Valley* and *Cold Blow and the Rainy Night* (released just before I joined the band) were produced by Phil Coulter and licensed by the Coulter/Martin production company to Polydor Records UK, there was no talk about future recording.

The band's original Irish manager, Des Kelly late of the Capitol Showband, seemed to have disappeared off the scene. There was a secretary, Carmel, who apparently took care of financial and general administration, and there was an accountant somewhere supposedly looking after tax. There were many issues record deal-wise, accounting-wise and tax-wise in hiatus; nobody was talking to me about any of this. It was clear; no one in the band wanted to hold the reins in the day-to-day running of business. It's scarcely credible now when I think back on it, but we didn't even have a tour manager.

Whether by accident, default or because of my newly acquired need to be in control of my life and reasonably well organised, bit by bit I found a lot of management work landing in my lap. On the marathon French package tour I became a quasi-tour manager, dealing with the ups and downs with concert promoters, hotels and venues; soon I was collecting the gig fees due directly to the band as opposed to those that came through Lionel Rocheman. Our touring situation was fairly primitive. We all travelled – the band, Johnny Divilly the driver (a butcher by trade), and Nicky Ryan the sound engineer – in a basic Ford Transit van. It was really cold in France that November and the Transit's heater was about as effective as a panting poodle. We froze on the journeys between gigs. Johnny Moynihan, a talented visual artist, recorded the traumatic and memorable episodes of our journey in a series of cartoons accompanied by *Rupert-Bear*-type explanatory rhymes. He called it *The Humours of Planxty*. It wasn't very funny at the time!

As with any group of young men thrown together at an age before the real exigencies of adult life forced them to grow up and learn the art of compromise, personality differences and conflicts often came to the fore. There was a lot of moodiness with individuals withdrawing into themselves during the long daytime journeys.

Considerable alcohol consumption, before and after shows, probably didn't help things. All kinds of head-wrecking Belgian 9 per cent alcohol beers were the regular tipple. Wine was barely considered to be alcohol. Great to be young!

I started to lose my enjoyment of it. The gigs were 'OK' and we were getting great receptions everywhere, but something was missing. Apart from when Andy and I engaged and I felt musically challenged, my heart wasn't really in it. I didn't feel as a band we had a shared sense of purpose.

Undoubtedly a lot of this came from the fact that there was no management, no strategy or long-term plan. We were just drifting along. There was even an unspoken vibe that having some concrete goal in mind was actually somewhat crass, like it was all about the music, man! I envied the English bands Steeleye and Fairport who had professional management and a sense of direction.

It seems petty now but onstage I'd find myself getting frustrated at the length of time Johnny, in particular, took to tune his bouzouki between songs. It could last several minutes for each song. This, of course, was in the days before electronic tuners – folk audiences were used to a certain amount of tuning, but Johnny took it to extremes. Granted he was a consummate and witty racconteur and this accompanied the tuning, often prolonging it, but while that might have been an asset in English-speaking territories it was unnecessarily indulgent and ineffectual in France where most of his in-joke repartee passed over their heads, indeed some of it over mine.

I bit my tongue during those episodes. Johnny was not going to tune any faster. There was no alternative to 'sucking it up'. Andy on the other hand, though he had many more strings to worry about over his countless multi-stringed mandolas, mandolins and the dreaded hurdy-gurdy, managed to handle it all much more easily. I found myself enjoying playing with him and wishing we could expand that.

One of the more explosive outbursts came between me and sound engineer Nicky Ryan. Nicky had been with Planxty from the start. He was autocratic and used to getting his own way as far as the band's sound was concerned. The others were terrified of him and never argued; but he wasn't always right and his demands made it difficult for us onstage.

I began to challenge him. One day in Brussels it came to a head in the lobby of our hotel a few hours before our gig in the Bourse that evening. Both of us refused to back down which resulted in Nicky 'taking the hump' and heading straight for the airport to fly home. That was a bit of a shock. No sound operator for the gig. Silence for five minutes. Then driver Johnny Divilly chirped up in his Galway accent, 'Sure, I'll do it. I've stood beside him every night and I know exactly what he's doing.'

We were sceptical, but it was the only option. We had to trust him.

The soundcheck went surprisingly well with all of us managing to hear what we wanted to hear. Johnny Divilly professed himself happy with the out-front sound in the hall. The gig was a success with no complaints from the audience and the tour was completed with Johnny at the sound desk.

It was probably twenty years before I spoke to Nicky Ryan again. His next port of call was as sound director for the band Clannad. From there he graduated to being the manager and producer of Enya. I guess he didn't need to dwell too much on his Planxty days.

As we neared the end of this tour word came back from Carmel in the office that the band's accountant had been on to her talking about tax liabilities. Apparently, since the band's inception no accounts had been submitted to the Irish Revenue and there was now a serious arrears situation and a large bill demanding immediate attention.

The amount pretty much equated to the entire takings from our French tour. I was shocked and upset. By this stage I was the band's on-the-road treasurer, carrying a large amount of cash in French francs. The thought that this would all have to be handed over on our return and that we had all worked our asses off for a month for nothing was devastating. More galling was that this liability accumulated when I wasn't even in the band!

I remember arriving at the passport area as we were leaving France to see a notice to the effect that it was illegal to take more than 10,000 French francs out of the country. I was carrying more than three times that amount in a shoulder bag. I was terrified. What if we lost it all and still had a huge bill to pay on our return?

Thankfully, no one asked me any questions and we got through unscathed. But something happened to me. I wanted out of this mess. I had been in the band for eighteen months and I'd had enough.

After a final late 1975 gig in Egremont – a small out-of-the-way town on the west coast of Cumbria, UK – all of us seemed to arrive at the same decision at the same time. At a meeting in Kiely's pub, Donnybrook, we mutually dissolved the band.

20

ANDY IRVINE AND PAUL BRADY

Andy and I took up together almost immediately after the Planxty demise. We decided to play as a duo. We made plans to tour together and record an album. We asked old friend and original Planxty member Dónal Lunny to produce the record and approached the Bothy Band fiddler Kevin Burke to see if he'd play. They both agreed. I was excited. I was itching to make a record.

But first I had something else to do. In the summer of 1975, in a gap in the Planxty schedule, I was approached by Richard Nevins and Dan Collins of the recently formed Shanachie Records to make a record of fiddle and guitar music with one of the great Irish fiddle players of the era, Tommy Peoples. I had played live with Tommy many times in the Tradition Club in Slattery's of Capel Street; he really enjoyed the way I drove his music along. I agreed to do it and we recorded an entire album in one crazy day, 28 August, in Peter Hunt's studio on St Stephen's Green in Dublin.

Tommy was nervous. A total perfectionist, he had set the bar so high for himself that it stood in front of him like an insurmountable barrier. After a lot of false starts, eventually Richard Nevins suggested perhaps a drink to loosen up. He went out to the nearest pub and came back with two pints of Smithwick's. Things improved dramatically and the red light went on. Magic started happening; within an hour or so we had six or seven tracks cut. More drink was called for. Rather than keeping coming back with solitary pints, Nevins went out to Woolworths and bought a ten-litre plastic bucket. We kept on going and by around 5 p.m. we had finished.

Things were understandably a bit hazy by this time so, as I recall, we said our goodbyes and went our separate ways. The record, *The High Part of the Road*, came out a couple of months later and was an instant success.

A month or so later, Shanachie came back and asked me if I'd come to New York and make more records with some of the great older Irish fiddlers living there. They also asked if Andy Irvine and I were interested in recording for them as our reputation as a duo was growing fast. However, a new Irish label, Mulligan Records had just been formed by Seamus O'Neill (a former employee of the Irish-language label Gael Linn), Dónal Lunny and singer/guitarist Micheál Ó Domhnaill. Andy and I thought we'd be better off in that direction, particularly as Dónal was going to produce.

The New York fiddle records project interested me, however, and I agreed to do it. I flew back to the US in January 1976. It was my first trip back since Mary and I left in 1974. I was nervous about re-entry and about how I would feel coming back to the scene of the nightmare. But I settled in quickly enough and over a couple of weeks, I recorded three albums: a solo album with Andy McGann, *It's a Hard Road to Travel*; a duet album with Andy McGann and Paddy Reynolds; and a record with Sligo fiddler John Vesey, *The First Month of Spring*.

The music was among the best the Irish tradition had given birth to in the twentieth century. It included some of the oldest tunes side by side with great ones from the previous few decades – some of which would have been composed in New York by recent emigrants. Andy McGann was a living legend, revered both in the States and back home in Ireland. All these guys were famous within the tight world of Irish music; the more I played with them, the more I appreciated my involvement and the one-off historical nature of what we were doing.

I remember spending a Saturday afternoon in Paddy Reynolds' house in Brooklyn rehearsing with him and Andy. They were so easy with each other having played together for years in various situations and there was a lot of humorous banter flying around the room. I was stretched in all directions as an accompanist. While I knew a lot of the tunes and had played them often in sessions, it was one thing playing in a session but another making a permanent record. For every set of tunes I had to write out a chart. I knew that when we got into studio, time and energy were of the essence and that in most cases all we would get was a run-through of the changes between tunes before the red light went on. No pressure, Paul!

The recording went at a breakneck speed. To me, a slightly bizarre aspect of it was that producers Nevins and Collins were insisting on complete acoustic separation between me and the other players. The purported reason was that they wanted a stereo mix that would allow the listener to hear less guitar if desired! Just turn your balance dial to the left and the guitar would be less audible. It was clear that guitar accompaniment was revolutionary in terms of recording Irish music in the States and not everyone of the old school would be into it. I thought it was narrow-minded and demeaning but said nothing and got on with it.

The records were done, mixed and released. Throughout the Irish music fraternity worldwide the response was extremely favourable and to this day I am regaled by younger players, especially accompanists, who say the albums were a huge influence on their own development.

Job done, I headed home to begin touring and rehearsing with Andy. One of the first things we set up was a weekly residency in the Baggot Inn in Dublin, the popular music venue then for both folk and rock acts. This took off in a big way and by the second show we had crowds queuing round the block. We were putting together new material that included 'The Jolly Soldier', 'Bonny Woodhall', 'Lough Erne Shore', 'The Plains of Kildare' and the rest of the songs that would eventually make up our album. We further drifted into American folk where Andy's and my interest in Hank Williams and Woodie Guthrie crossed. Andy's harmonica playing in those old styles is still as good as I've heard anywhere.

We spent the first half 1976 alternating between duo gigs and our own solo ones; I was gaining in confidence as a solo performer all the time. We had a shared common purpose but could each be our own boss, which was great, and it was only now that the Planxty thing was over that I realised how confining and lacking in direction as a unit it was and how free and exciting the future appeared.

Meanwhile back on the domestic front, Mary and I made the big move and bought a house. We had been living in a tiny one-bed apartment in Dublin's Lad Lane for the previous year and we wanted more space. We were beginning to think about a family.

We found a new three-bedroom house on Dublin's Northside opposite Glasnevin Cemetery in a small, terraced development called The Willows and paid the princely sum of IR£9,400 for it. It was tiny. Downstairs there was one large, combined living–dining area including a modest kitchen. Upstairs two small bedrooms, a bathroom and a child's room that might just about hold a cot. Still, it was brand new, everything worked, and it was ours. I bought a cheap Chinese upright piano and put it in the corner of the living space. I loved it. Mary continued to work, now as a researcher for the Poverty Committee. Andy and I started working in earnest.

First off, as well as a round of Irish gigs, we went on a tour of Brittany in June with piper Liam Óg O'Flynn, allowing us to revisit

some of the Planxty material. That was fun. Next was to record the album.

We signed with Mulligan Records and in August 1976 were booked in to Rockfield Studios in rural Wales – well-named as it turned out since things got off to a rocky start. The plan was for Andy, Dónal Lunny and me to fly from Dublin to Bristol on Monday 23 August and drive to Rockfield in Monmouthshire. But the previous weekend, Andy was playing with Dónal at a boutique festival on Sherkin Island, a ten-minute sea trip from the village of Baltimore in West Cork. Transport to and from the island was primitive and achieved solely via a small, open boat that held around twenty people and their baggage. How anyone thought of running a festival with this limited access was beyond me but that's how things happened in the 1970s. As it turned out, three or four hundred people were there and by the standards of the era it was a success. Next day, however, there was chaos on the quay as people tried to get off the island. As evening approached, and after many trips back and forth, the two lads were still waiting to get off.

In the confusion they managed to get their instruments on board the open boat, but before they themselves could board the boat took off! It was the last trip of the evening as darkness had set in. To cut a long story short, Andy and Dónal arrived at Rockfield a day after me and Kevin Burke (who had travelled by train up from London). Not a great start!

Summer of 1976 in the UK was the second hottest summer since records began. We were staying on top of a hill across the main road from the studio in a house that was reputed to be haunted and was mentioned in a publication *The Haunted Houses of Britain* as such. There was indeed a strange atmosphere in the place though I personally didn't witness anything supernatural. However, later visitors, Matt Molloy and Paddy Keenan of the Bothy Band, said they definitely had unwelcome nocturnal experiences including visions of people at the foot of beds and the like.

The main problem we had was a plague of houseflies due to the heat. Otherwise, things were good. The catering was first class and the studio facilities top notch. All in all, the recording took about two weeks.

Engineer Ted Sharp had probably been more used to recording rock bands as many famous ones like Black Sabbath, Dr Feelgood, Dave Edmunds, Ace and Hawkwind had passed through there in the previous few months. But he did a great job of 'going acoustic'.

We invented the arrangements on the spot. I still remember my satisfaction on the completion (and acceptance) of the 'Plains of Kildare' take, also my enjoyment at hearing Andy's harmonica lock-in with my mandolin on 'The Jolly Soldier'.

I recorded 'Arthur McBride' for the first time. On the first take I had almost got to the end of the seven-minute piece when I made a mistake in the words. I think I stumbled and said 'froud' of your clothes instead of 'proud'. This of course was in the days when you couldn't 'drop in' to a multi-track recording, particularly if it was a solo performance with no rhythm.

I had to do it all over again.

To this day I'll swear that the original take of the song was much better than the one that eventually became the much-loved classic. I recently heard from Andy on our fortieth Anniversary Album Tour that the multi-track tapes are still in storage in the studio all these years later. Perhaps one day I'll get to hear the original take, fix 'froud' and even release it?

Then again, maybe not ...

Back we came to Ireland in September, feeling good about the recording. We decided, in a fever of inspiration, on an album title: *Andy Irvine and Paul Brady*. We knew we had made something different to the usual folk album but never for a moment imagined that it would become so popular or that forty years later we would embark on a celebratory anniversary tour.

21

BEGINNINGS OF METAMORPHOSIS

Later that year, both Andy and I made separate programmes as part of an RTÉ TV series *Live at the Embankment*. We were that famous now. Our own TV shows! Even now in late 1976, I was beginning to imagine playing other kinds of music than Irish folk, maybe even writing songs in earnest.

The Embankment was the celebrated music venue situated in what was then rural Tallaght outside Dublin where I had started my own career back in late 1966 as opening act for the Johnstons. Andy and I both contributed to each other's shows. I also invited Dónal Lunny as a guest; and as a foretaste of the direction I would go in a few years later, Arty McGlynn.

Arty was new to the folk scene having spent the previous decade playing electric and pedal-steel guitar in Irish showbands, mostly in the country style. A few years older than me, I first knew of him in my teenage years when I was working in the hotel band in the summers of 1963 and 1964 in Bundoran. I regularly saw him play with the Plattermen Showband in the local Astoria Ballroom and was in awe of his ability. He was fluent in all kinds of music: jazz; blues; rock and pop; as well as country. I too was attracted to all those forms – I had stood spellbound on so many occasions as a seventeen-year-old watching him play his beautiful cherry-red Gibson 335. Arty always remembered this young red-haired geek with glasses at the foot of the stage gawking up at him and drinking in every note.

Several years later I had started seeing his sister Anne which led to my meeting Arty for real. In the early 1970s when I would be back home on a break from the Johnstons in London, we began to hang out and play together in Omagh where both he and Anne were from. A great bond, both musical and personal, grew between us at that time and stayed firm until his death in December 2019.

We would talk for hours and spend ages duelling on guitars playing Irish dance tunes, each of us vying to come up with a strange one the other hadn't heard. Though he wasn't playing Irish traditional music professionally then, it was very much a part of his background. His father had played the accordion and in fact that was Arty's first instrument as a youngster. At that time, he was playing with a local band, Brian Coll and the Buckaroos. For several reasons he was getting fed up with the dance-band life which often saw him playing in far north Donegal one night and Kerry, the other end of the country, the next. It was a brutal existence with little sleep, too many stimulants and a lot of boredom. He became interested in the kind of life I had, playing different kinds of music, living in London, touring in Europe, and making records, all of which seemed more attractive and exciting. At the time I guess it was.

He quit the showbands and started working with Tommy Makem and Liam Clancy, who were all that was left of the famous early-1960s' band Clancy Brothers & Tommy Makem. That brought him firmly into the folk scene where he put down deep roots and over time acquired the major reputation his work now enjoys. Of course, for most of the 1980s he became the MD in Van Morrison's band; a whole other story. No end to his talents. In any case, after several more years where we didn't see much of each other, we hooked up again in Dublin in late 1974 after my return from the Johnstons' break-up in the US.

Now two years later, as I was beginning to get the glimmer of a songwriting instinct in a more rock-pop style and since Arty was a master of all that, it seemed natural to invite him to play on my upcoming TV show. Though it was very early days in my song-writing odyssey, one of the songs I did on the show was an early version of 'Crazy Dreams'; at the time it was called 'Another Day Without Her'. Arty played guitar on that plus pedal-steel guitar on my version of the Hank Williams classic 'You Win Again' that also featured Andy on harmonica. The shows were well-received and enjoyable to work on. Still, it would be another couple of years before Arty and I worked together again.

Andy Irvine and I were 'hot' in Ireland in late 1976 with pres-tigious bookings, full houses everywhere and a tour in the UK with the recently formed Bothy Band. Belfast beckoned in January 1977; we were offered a second TV series, this time with BBC Northern Ireland, called *The Gig in the Round*. Directed by Tony McCauley, it was one of the first 'folk' shows on TV in Northern Ireland.

Over the fortnight's filming we had as our guests: the Bothy Band; Christy Moore; Liam Óg O'Flynn and Tommy Peoples; Shannon, Stewart & Baillie; Red Peters and the Floating Dublin Blues Band; and Ballymena songwriter David McWilliams. Filmed on a circular indoor set in the Balmoral Showgrounds in front of a live audience, the series was an instant success; decades later it is still spoken of fondly.

But by early 1977 the work dynamic between Andy and me was changing. We were in demand all over Europe as a live act, but our individual responses to these offers exposed a differing attitude to lengthy touring. Was there also a part of me tiring of the need for consensus in everything we did? Musically, I increasingly felt the urge to be free to find whatever was still dormant inside of me ... music I knew that Andy would not relate to, music that would not reveal itself as long as our partnership was the focal point. Though we were still playing as a duo and celebrating the success of our album, we were already doing our own solo gigs. I had gone to the UK myself for a two-week tour in February just after the Belfast TV series. Next, at the end of February, I recorded an album in Dublin with Matt Molloy and Tommy Peoples for the Mulligan label. Andy and I had a three-week US tour booked in March, the highlight being a concert in Town Hall New York put together by our friend Renée Lawless.

It was while I was in America that Mary told me she was pregnant. I was shocked, terrified and excited in equal measure, the fathering instinct gratified only until the fear of the coming changes raised its voice. I arrived home from the States for some solo Irish gigs in April and a concert with Andy in Dublin's National Stadium in May supported by Clannad. With a calendar full of one-off Irish gigs, and more trips abroad stretching out through the year, I began to feel pressure building up.

On 3 July 1977 I made a trip to Gormanstown beach north of Dublin for the filming of the *Arthur McBride* short movie directed by Tiernan McBride, the son of Seán MacBride, Nobel Peace Prize winner and assistant Secretary General of the United Nations. Tiernan owned a very successful ad agency in Dublin. He had seen my performance of 'Arthur McBride' on television and was so taken with the story and performance that he approached me about making a film of it. It was shot on 35mm film and starred Paul Brennan as Arthur, Paul Wilson as his cousin, Godfrey Quigley as Sergeant Napper, Don Foley as Corporal Vamp and Paddy O'Neill as the wee drummer boy.

My diary at the time reads like an endurance test:

Outside our house in Church Street, Strabane with my first guitar, 1958.

Sean and Mollie on the town in Bundoran.

Me and Cormac McCready, the resident singer, at the Holyrood Hotel, Bundoran in 1963.

With my new Fender Mustang in the Holyrood in 1965.

My first photo session with The Johnstons in the summer of 1967, having just turned pro at the age of twenty. © Roy Esmonde

My bandmates (left to right) are Lucy, Mick and Adrienne. © Roy Esmonde

In studio in London with Lucy Johnston on the recording of *Give A Damn* and *The Barleycorn*, 1968. © Roy Esmonde

Celebrated photographer Eva Rubinstein took this shot on a visit to mutual friends in Rhode Island in early 1973.

Me with a Schaefer beer and a cigarette, in New York City for the fiddle recording project pictured below.
© Wren Di Antonio

In New York with (left to right) Andy McGann, Paddy Reynolds and John Vesey on a fiddle records project in 1976.

Planxty on BBC NI in 1975. From left to right: Johnny Moynihan, Andy Irvine, me and Liam O'Flynn.

Me and Andy Irvine on the set of BBC NI gig *In The Round*, 1977.

Me and Andy in New York City, 1977, prior to our concert in Town Hall.
© Wren Di Antonio

Me and Phil Lynott
at a photo session
for the cover of *Hot
Press*, 1982.
© Colm Henry

On stage with Phil and Rory Gallagher at Punchestown, 1982. © Colm Henry

With Bob Dylan ahead of his headlining performance at Slane Castle in 1984, the day after his 'Lakes of Ponchartrain' tutorial in Wembley. © BP Fallon

With Eric Clapton at Slane Castle in 1985, a couple of years after touring with him throughout Europe.

On stage with Tina Turner for her performance of my song 'Paradise Is Here' at the RDS in May 1987.
© Paul Bell

With Carole King, Stephen Tyler, Mark Hudson and Gary Burr in New York in 2001, recording our song 'Monday Without You' on Carole's album *Love Makes The World*.

With my family at Mary's fiftieth birthday celebration, Colm to the left and Sarah to the right.

In New York as maître d' of the Chrysler Building's 'Cloud Club' in Matthew Barney's 2002 film *Cremaster 3*. Photograph by Chris Winget © Matthew Barney, 2022.

At Marlay House on the set of the TV series *The Paul Brady Songbook* with (left to right) Steve Fletcher, Liam Genockey and Jennifer Maidman. © Kieran Slyne

With Harry and
Pamela Belafonte
after my New York
City Winery gig,
2018.

With Lee Pardini,
Louis Cato, Theo
Katzman and Joe
Dart at the Ulster
Hall, Belfast, 2019.

With Bonnie
Raitt and David
Crosby in LA.

- Solo tour Holland
- Solo tour France
- Solo Dublin Folk Festival, mid-July
- Late July, a week in the UK with Andy culminating at the Cambridge Folk Festival
- August, again with Andy, at the first Ballisodare Folk Festival, County Sligo
- September, producing an album in Dublin for a new Irish folk group Oisín

It was all getting crazy. So much of what was happening was increasingly hard to hold on to. One thing I do remember was coming home from a big Folk Music festival in Leiden, Holland in early September where I had been performing solo. There were loads of Irish acts on the bill including the Wolfe Tones, renowned for their Irish Republican and anti-British outlook. Born in Northern Ireland, at the time I was travelling on a UK passport I had got for a trip to the USA while I was living in London with the Johnstons in the late 1960s. I found myself in the queue at passport control in Dublin airport sandwiched between two members of the Tones. I was mortified they might see my UK passport. Oooh! The shame of it!

There was a ton of life in the Irish folk scene in 1977 with the advent of the summer outdoor weekend folk festivals. The first of those was the Ballisodare Folk Festival in August of that year. Started by local brothers Philip and Kevin Flynn as a laudable but by no means certain gamble, it was nonetheless an immediate success.

Headlined that first year by Andy and me and the Donegal group Clannad, with a stellar cast including Christy Moore and Midnight Well, many of the country's greatest traditional instrumentalists like Tommy Peoples, Seamus Tansey, Fred Finn and Peter Horan rounded off the bill.

The event captured the mood of people in their twenties and thirties in Ireland who flocked to it from all over the country joined, surprisingly, by many visitors from continental Europe. The previously rare sight of Volkswagen camper vans with German, French and Dutch registration plates full of young music fans all heading for Sligo soon became the norm across the country as more festivals, like the Lisdoonvarna Folk Festival, began appearing. Equally it wasn't long before Irish folk artists began getting invites to the many new folk events coming on stream in continental Europe.

In contrast, one of the guaranteed occurrences that would greet any traveller who strayed into Northern Ireland in those days was the Ulster Defence Regiment (UDR) roadblock. The Provisional IRA and Loyalist violence was still in full spate and the British Army would set up lightning random checkpoints all over the North.

Once I was stopped between Omagh and Ballygawley on my way back to Dublin from visiting my parents in Strabane. It was the usual stuff: the soldier in the road waving me down, two or three others lying flat by the roadside pointing their rifles at my car with a jeep or armoured vehicle in the background; I rolled down my window.

'Licence please, Sir.'

I handed it over. Immediately there was silence for a moment, then, 'Paul Brady? A pleasure to meet you! I love that record you and Andy just put out. I'll be up to see you in Belfast in a couple of weeks!'

Well, you could have knocked me down with a feather!

His name was Weir, a good old Protestant name.

But it shouldn't really have been that much of a surprise. The interesting thing about that record was that it appealed across the board, across the religious divide. Normally the loyalist Protestant community would see Irish folk songs as the music of the *other* side. Indeed, what a lot of Irish folk groups and artists were singing in those days was just that – songs of rebellion against England and by extension against those who favoured British rule in Ireland. On the *Andy & Paul* record, however, a lot of the songs would have originally landed in Ireland via the ancestors of the Protestant community: Scottish planters' families and soldiers with their music; great songs like 'Mary and the Soldier', 'Bonny Wood Hall' and 'Martinmas Time'.

These were originally all from Britain's wars in Europe in the previous couple of centuries in which many ordinary Irish people of both religious persuasions fought and died. They were, in many cases, collected from the Protestant community in the North. I never lost sight of that. I was very aware, not just then but lasting into the future, that my own music appealed to all sides. I was always reluctant to be drawn into overtly partisan events. My own wife's ancestry was from the Protestant community, although a couple of generations back, and that made me less inclined to exclusively identify with only one side. Having said that, I did not (and do not) agree with 'British' rule in Ireland. They don't care about us. Ireland for the Irish, of all persuasions!

One other thing that stands out in my memory at this time for a variety of reasons – some good, some bad – was the folk-song festival in Drogheda, Féile na Bóinne (The Boyne Festival) on the last weekend of September 1977. Organised by the local Drogheda Folk Club, singer Seán Corcoran and Dubliner Tommy Munnelly, the festival came at the peak of the period of rediscovery and celebration of the older singers from all over the country who had kept the song tradition alive through the previous decades. Guest singer Eddie Butcher from Magilligan in North County Derry, from whose repertoire I would glean the song 'Don't Come Again' that would later appear on my solo album the following year, was eagerly anticipated. Eddie's friends, singers Joe Holmes and Len Graham were with him too, as was Davey Hammond from Belfast. Legends Sarah Anne O'Neill, Paddy Tunney, Micho Russell, Mary-Ann Carolan, and of course the great singer and collector Frank Harte, who became the source of many a young folk singer's repertoire over the next decade and who had written the liner notes to Andy's and my album released a few months previously.

On one of the afternoons there was a mighty session in nearby seaside village Clogherhead in an old hostelry. Most of the above singers were in situ together singing their hearts out. Never before had all those incredible talents been in the same room and it never happened again.

Now for the bad bit; at the main concert on the Saturday night in the Whitworth Hall, there was a series of singers on the bill. Mary-Ann Carolan – Mrs Carolan as we called her – was onstage singing quietly to an enraptured audience when in came three young men at the back of the hall, talking loudly. Word was (later) they were part of a Northern Ireland film crew down to record the festival. It was apparent that they didn't have any respect for their subject material. They even seemed drunk. Several people started 'Shusshhhing' to no effect.

I was standing with my back to them at the end of the hall. I turned and asked them to please be quiet. They laughed at me. I saw red. For the first and only time since I was involved in fisticuffs with Bobby Burns when we were forced to face off against each other as 11-year-olds in boarding school, I got physical. I drove my fist into the spot from where I estimated the ringleader's future descendants would originate. Within seconds he had smashed his full pint into my face. The glass broke and blood mixed with beer streamed down my face from a three-inch gash.

I'm rushed by friends to the local hospital A&E and find myself attended to by a young male doctor. I'm lying on this gurney and he's going, 'Paul Brady? So pleased to meet you. I'm a huge fan, your biggest! Love "Arthur McBride" especially ...'

On and on he goes. I'm holding a cloth to my face pointing at the wound and silently going, 'For God's sake, will you shut the feck up and fix me face!'

Eventually he doctors the wound (that thankfully isn't deep) and I ask, 'Does it need stitches?'

'No way!' he says.

'Will there be a scar?'

'Oh, not at all! Jeez, Paul Brady. Amazing. Last person I expected to meet tonight. You've made my night!'

More than forty years later the scar, while faded, is still visible. I've never cast a blow in anger since.

By mid-1977 there were so many gig offers coming in I needed a booking agent in Ireland. Dubliner, Gerry Harford, who had been working at our record label (Mulligan) took on the role in a firm arrangement that lasted for the next three years. Gerry was a big music fan with a broad and eclectic taste, very knowledgeable about the Irish market. He'd a good sense of humour and was honest – we had a lot of fun together.

As the decade wore on the folk scene exploded throughout Europe. There were festivals popping up everywhere. I don't think it would be overly partisan to say that Irish instrumental music and songs were far and away the most popular genre of the period. The Guinness Irish Music tour of Germany, for example, became an established annual event that would feature a touring party of around half a dozen well-known Irish acts playing a three-hour concert in all the major cities. Many careers were founded and sustained by that touring model. It eventually spread to Australia.

For my own reasons I kept away from it. Already I was beginning to feel constrained by the unspoken confines of this new folk world. Stylistically it was all getting too exclusive and the increasingly accepted definition of 'Irish music' was narrowing. Bit by bit I was starting to look outside the folk world, wondering how I might find a new me.

When I look back, I'm surprised at how slow my metamorphosis was. Yes, I had introduced three songs that were stylistically outside the Irish tradition as early as the RTÉ TV show in 1976, but a cursory recap shows it wasn't until 1979 that I seriously tried to write my own music and think about a career outside the Irish folk scene. What took me so long?

I guess it's easy to forget the almost total lack of infrastructure in the Irish music business to provide a springboard for artists hoping to broaden their market outside the country. The few Irish acts that 'made it' outside Ireland – the Bachelors, Van Morrison, Rory Gallagher, Thin Lizzy, Gilbert O'Sullivan – did it from a UK base.

For me that opportunity didn't arrive till a couple of years later. In the meantime, while I was dreaming of other horizons, I was still very much involved with the folk world. It was my bread and butter for a start, and I was still in love with the music.

All of this took a back seat for the immediate future when our first child, Sarah Eavan Brady, arrived 2 November 1976. It was a long labour and a difficult birth in Dublin's Coombe hospital. But all was well with Mary and our beautiful child.

On discharge we moved back to our house in Glasnevin and began the process of adjustment. A few more gigs were left to do: a UCD Dublin concert I couldn't get out of the day after Sarah was born; a Belfast gig in Queen's University a week later; and a quick trip to London for an early December show with Andy in the National Ballroom, Kilburn saw the year out. I was exhausted but buzzing.

PART TWO

22

GETTING REAL

Early 1978, I was 30 years old, married, with a baby and a mortgage. I had sleepwalked through my twenties with no plan other than to follow wherever musical instinct led me. I had little knowledge of who I really was. There had been ups and downs, lucky breaks at times and unfortunate liaisons at others. Now I had the feeling it was time to get real.

Home life was getting stressful. Sarah, dear child, was a colicky baby and cried for long periods for no apparent reason. We worried she was unwell, that we were doing something wrong. In the evenings we'd put her in her carrycot in the car and drive around the city till she fell asleep only to have her wake up the minute we brought her into the house, and it would start all over again.

Sleep was at a premium. No one who has a first baby has to be told how all-consuming, even terrifying it is, even if there is an enthusiastic support structure in place. We had nothing of the kind.

As parents we were left to our own devices and had little contact with the outside world. Remember, no such thing as a mobile phone in 1978, no landline either. Incredible to think now, but there was a three-year waiting list for a phoneline in any new housing development in Dublin at the time. Our only contact with the outside world was a public phone box at the entrance to the estate.

We had no parents around to seek advice from, to come and relieve us for an hour or two so we could grab a bit of a rest. County Tyrone and Strabane were three hours away and Mary's dad (her mother had passed on) was in Virginia, County Cavan, in the midlands. Our Dublin friends had work and many hadn't children yet, so they didn't really know what the score was.

Neither of us seemed to have much of an instinct for how to handle the endless everyday problems and questions that presented themselves, but what instincts we had seemed at opposite ends of the pole. Mine was that as long as there was nothing *really* wrong with the child then let her cry herself to sleep 'as children were let do forever' – tough love, they'd call it. Mary's was the exact opposite; to always pick Sarah up and try and comfort her which, to me, prolonged the situation. This, given how stressed and sleep-deprived we were, led to escalating tension. The responsibility for this tiny human being was overwhelming. Indeed, life *was* getting real.

I now regret the way I handled things. In my panic and exhaustion, I had little more to offer other than a succession of learned platitudes and empty clichés. It was hard to accept that life had changed, that I had to 'go back to school' and find a new way to be. But at the start of a new solo career that had no blueprint, no rule book, no map, I was consumed with thoughts of what to do and where to go next. Though it didn't fully materialise till almost a year later, I was at the beginning of a total artistic metamorphosis. The added ingredient – that I was in the middle of a personal metamorphosis too, as a supposed-to-be father – made it a double whammy. I didn't know how to do either. I didn't realise it then, but this conflict between parenthood and the demands of a career in music would constitute the painful backdrop to not only my life but that of my wife and family for the next twenty or so years. Time and time again my career plans clashed with domesticity, putting pressure on our relationship. I am still amazed we got through it and stayed together. When I look at my son as the doting father of three that he now is, I feel ashamed. Duh! So that's how it's done?

At the time we had only one car, a Renault 4, so when I was off gigging, Mary was dependent on public transport. In time we got a second Renault 4 which eased the pressure somewhat. We had a good friend, singer Phil Callery, who had a day job working as a mechanic with Renault. He was helpful in sorting out our mobility. But even with the second car, Mary was left for days on end with a fractious baby, no one to talk to or to get help from. It was a difficult time for her. I am full of respect and admiration for how she pulled it all together. I have lasting guilt that I wasn't much help. But now, as Mary had quit her job to be a mother, I was the sole breadwinner. I had to go out and work; given my chosen profession that unfortunately meant being away from home a lot.

I had already planned to record a solo album and had booked studio time in March 1978. The album *Welcome Here Kind Stranger* was recorded in the first couple of weeks of that month. Long hours in studio meant I was getting home wrecked every night. Mary did her best to ensure I got rest, but it was impossible to totally avoid the frequent minor crises that come with a four-month-old baby. We soldiered on, adapting to broken sleep. The show had to go on!

For the recording, which was produced by Dónal Lunny and me, I was joined by Andy Irvine, Tommy Peoples and Noel Hill in what would turn out to be a popular record at the time and a folk classic ever since. It was chosen as folk album of 1978 by the prestigious UK music paper *Melody Maker* and was noticed, and favourably reviewed, by folk music publications worldwide.

I was thrilled by the reception of *Welcome Here Kind Stranger*. Its success led to many gigs throughout Ireland, UK and Europe. Content-wise, I was much influenced by Ulster songs, as sung by Eddie Butcher, Geordie Hanna and Packie Manus Byrne (all

Northerners). Davey Hammond – a fine singer and song collector from Belfast plus BBC TV producer and film-maker by profession – was also a big influence and ultimately became a good friend.

The Northern Irish song tradition in the English language, fleshed out as it was with many imports from Scotland and England over the previous centuries, was quite different to the main thrust of Irish song as it was generally viewed in the south at the time. The repertoire of most of the successful Irish folk groups of the period would have focused on Dublin or Cork urban material, rural songs from the Famine, and the subsequent mass emigration 'rebel' songs from the many uprisings – songs in the Irish language. Ulster songs were a refreshingly 'new' ingredient in the Irish folk song canon.

Happy with how the record turned out, I could synthesise my by now confident inner folk voice with my dormant blues and rock rhythmic sensibility. My use of normal pop production techniques like double tracking, as on the guitars on 'The Lakes of Pontchartrain' and the mandolins on 'Jackson and Jane', and the cross-fading between the sonic landscapes of 'The Creel' and 'Out the Door and Over the Wall' gave a modern feel to what was a 'folk' record.

The inspired input of Tommy Peoples and Noel Hill on fiddle and concertina and of Andy Irvine on harmonica and hurdy-gurdy gave a heft and colour to the musical arrangements that I loved. I still get a thrill listening to the mandolin and fiddle duet with Tommy on 'The Boy on the Hilltop/Johnny Going to Céilidh'. I don't think I've ever played the mandolin that well since. And of course, 'The Lakes of Pontchartrain' and 'Paddy's Green Shamrock Shore' soon became, and remain, two of my most popular songs in concert.

I gigged a lot from March onwards, mostly solo, but in early April Andy and I did a tour of Holland which saw us in Utrecht,

Heerenveen, Almelo and finally Dordrecht for a concert supported by Clannad for which we were never paid – the sometime joys of the folk scene. Next, I went to London for an Irish Music Festival in the Royal Albert Hall on 7 July which also featured the Bothy Band, Christy Moore, De Danaan and Liam Óg O'Flynn.

I was hardly back home when I headed for County Clare to play at the inaugural Lisdoonvarna Folk Festival the following weekend. This was the second in line of the big Irish festivals that spawned over the next four or five years with great success, the first being Ballisodare the previous year. I shared the bill with Christy Moore, De Danaan, The Furey Brothers & Davy Arthur, and Andy Irvine playing with Mick Hanley and a special guest from the UK – the great, and even then, legendary singer and guitarist, Nic Jones.

It was a rough enough affair organisationally. The site was only accessible via a couple of narrow country roads that at some spots barely had room for two normal-size cars to pass. Before long, there developed an almighty traffic jam with dozens of German, Dutch and French camper vans and Irish musicians' touring wagons stuck in ditches unable to make any progress. I was there in my teeny Renault 4 and miraculously found myself just about able to reach the backstage area a quarter hour late for my own gig even though I had started out from my hotel over an hour earlier on a journey that should normally have taken ten minutes. Nobody got onstage on time all weekend. In spite of that, the festival was a huge success. Nothing like this had happened in Ireland before. Ethnic folk music was the zeitgeist of the time and had become the sonic backdrop to the lives of a whole generation of young Irish, British and Europeans who flocked to see their heroes live onstage. Forty years later, as Andy Irvine and I celebrated the anniversary of our 1977 album with a bunch of concerts, a big percentage of our audience would have seen us for the first time at one or other of the great, late-1970s Irish festivals.

The second Ballisodare Folk Festival followed in August and felt like a homecoming. It too featured the best Irish music of the time: the Boys of the Lough; Clannad; the Bothy Band; De Danann; Christy Moore; the Press Gang; the great Junior Crehan and P.J. Crotty; Martin Carthy from the UK; and Tom Paxton from USA. I exulted in being part of this new energy. I felt at ease in Ballisodare having spent most of my childhood summers down the road in Bundoran and Mullaghmore. Plus, I knew the organisers, brothers Philip and Kevin Flynn, having earlier in the year played at Philip's new folk club, Drowsy Maggie's, in Sligo town.

The gigs piled up and the journeys on my own were long.

On those long journeys I found myself listening to a lot of Neil Young, Little Feat, Weather Report, Randy Newman, Bonnie Raitt, Dire Straits, Gerry Rafferty, Ry Cooder, the Band and Steely Dan. More and more, I was itching to write songs myself. Now married with one child and, as we had just discovered, another on the way, the notion of singing about the Napoleonic Wars and the antics of soldiers and women hundreds of years ago, however beautiful these songs were, began to feel unreal and irrelevant to my own life. It snuck up on me, the realisation that I wasn't listening to Irish traditional music on this trip. This was a big turning point. Just like the songwriters I was listening to, I too needed to write and sing about what I was feeling inside. The difference now – from the time I penned my fledgling attempts at songs with the Johnstons back in 1971 – was that I was beginning to believe I could do it.

In Brussels, late October, I sketched out a song that became 'Dancer in the Fire'. Next, I revisited a song I had first approached back in 1971 in the US while still with the Johnstons; originally a rant against the then record company called 'Hey, Mr Promotion Man', it was now beginning to morph into a totally different song called 'Another Day Without Her', the forerunner to *Crazy Dreams*.

'Trouble Round the Bend' came next. Lyrically ominous and prophetic, it was a harbinger of the difficult times ahead as I would walk away from the comfortable and familiar world of the Irish folk scene into a wholly different place.

Felt this hunger deep inside me and I knew I had to go
Left my friends and my companions, everyone I ever knew
Put the old ways far behind me, lost their meaning long ago
But I smell trouble, trouble up ahead

When I got back to Ireland, I felt like there was a different person alive inside me. I was excited to discover where this new person wanted to go. Though I didn't realise it at the time, it was the emergence of an instinct that eventually would become a defining one artistically; once I had learned how to do something and felt it was good, something I was proud of, I didn't want to do it anymore and wanted to move on. This voice became my inner guiding light from then on. I look back today and am amazed at how quickly in my mind I left *Welcome Here Kind Stranger* behind. Been there, done that, bought the T-shirt.

But back in what was still the real world, the immediate future meant more acoustic 'trad' gigs. The Mulligan Roadshow, a promotional tour to publicise Mulligan Records who put out our albums, featured the Bothy Band, singer-songwriter Mick Hanley, and me. We toured the UK in November ending up with a spot on the John Peel show – the biggest BBC music radio show of the time. My previous appearance on his show with The Johnstons, though it was only six years earlier, now seemed from another lifetime.

23

EXPERIMENTATION AND DIVERSIFICATION

The year 1979 dawned with a splash of rural Irish folk club solo gigs, leading into the recording in February of an album called *The Gathering* in Windmill 2 Studio, St Stephen's Green. The brainchild of American folk fan and entrepreneur Diane Meek, *The Gathering* was literally a gathering of several of her favourite Irish folk artists including flute player Matt Molloy, piper Peter Browne, fiddler Tommy Potts, plus Dónal Lunny, Andy Irvine and myself.

I sang two songs: 'Heather on the Moor', accompanied by Andy and Dónal, and a song about an Irishman's experience in the American Civil War called 'Paddy's Lamentation' for which I wrote a quasi-Baroque style piano accompaniment and played the whistle. The record has since become a rarity and something of a collector's item.

After the recording Andy and I made a lightning visit to Cologne in Germany for a live radio show in mid-February. I was home as much as I could be to prepare for the arrival of our second child. Colm Marcus Brady arrived on the planet on 14 March 1979.

Colm was a big baby at almost 11 lbs. It was a long twelve-hour labour and a difficult birth. I had missed being present for Sarah's arrival as it hadn't yet become the norm for dads to be in the delivery room then, but this time I was granted access. Complications as the labour progressed led to the decision to do a Caesarean. I was asked to wait outside while Mary was whisked off to theatre. I felt bereft and frustrated. I had so looked forward to seeing my child being born, watching him take his first breath, cutting the umbilical cord. In any case, apart from the risks of major surgery, all went well. Within twenty-four hours, however, Colm became distressed, had a temperature and after some tests it was diagnosed that he had sepsis, a blood infection that we feel to this day he got in the hospital; he was rushed to intensive care and suffered the indignity of an intravenous needle in his scalp for ten days till he recovered.

The career/parenthood conflict raised its head again while Mary and Colm were still in hospital. Back in the early summer of 1978 (before we knew Mary was pregnant) I was approached by Sean Murphy, an Englishman of Irish descent, with a project to record an album of songs from the plays and writings of the renowned Irish playwright, Sean O'Casey. Murphy had been discussing such a production with O'Casey's wife Eileen for some time and, having put together a shortlist of material, was now ready to move ahead. My proposed involvement was not as singer but as musical director, arranger and in some instances composer where music didn't exist. Murphy was director and producer of the project. He already had an eclectic background, with experience in theatre and, for a few years in the early 1970s, as manager and executive producer of the Soft Machine, an influential British progressive rock band of the era.

O'Casey's plays were full of songs from the early twentieth century – the period that was covered by much of his work. I was always fond of that era where Music Hall and Irish folk songs dovetailed and I agreed to take it on, seeing it as an opportunity to do something new.

O'Casey had adapted and altered many of the songs with his own words to suit the context of his plays. Songs like 'Since Maggy Went Away' to an old tune 'The Auld House' and 'Nora' to a mid-nineteenth century tune by J.A. Butterfield and a traditional song 'All Round Me Hat'. These were melodies that were already familiar to the general Irish and British public in their original forms as they would have been popular parlour songs, music-hall hits. In addition, there were several soliloquies and poems that were in need of music, which I wrote. After many meetings and a lot of research over the next few months we established a list of songs, engaged the well-known Irish actor and singer John Kavanagh as principal vocalist and began approaching musicians.

The problem was that projects like these, where there are a lot of conflicting schedules involved, take on a life of their own. To suit the majority of contributors the newly opened Windmill Lane Studios in Dublin ended up being booked for the middle of April – only a few weeks after the arrival of Colm.

The unforeseen ten days that Mary and Colm were kept in hospital as a result of the infection coincided with rehearsals and I found myself under pressure to keep all the plates spinning. There were days I couldn't be free to look after Sarah so friends stepped in. She became ill with a dramatic, seemingly stress-related digestion flare-up that looked on the surface like a coeliac outbreak. It was very scary. I cancelled a couple of days' work and collected her.

Eventually things quietened down, the coeliac scare never developed and Mary and Colm came home. But the damage was done. Things were at an all-time low between us. I felt awful and it was in these circumstances that on 20 April, five weeks after Colm's arrival, I went into studio to record the O'Casey album.

It was a big challenge. Apart from just producing a folk album for the band Oisín the previous year – where they had brought all the music to the party – I had never before been responsible for someone else's project as musical director/producer, nor had I any experience of arranging for orchestral instruments. Despite having studied music to UK GCE O-level I always found reading and writing music very difficult and much preferred to work by ear. As some of the songs were set in the music hall, light opera tradition they needed instruments like piano, violin, cello, trumpet, trombone, French horn and double bass. I had scant clue how to write for these instruments.

As talks about the project increased, I wondered why I had been approached in the first place. I know I was sort of 'hot' at the time after *Welcome Here Kind Stranger*, not just as a singer but as a kind of all-round Irish instrumentalist and studio-comfortable guy, but I still I felt Eileen and Sean had got the wrong guy.

Not wanting the whole thing to defeat me, I approached the talented Irish composer and orchestrator Shaun Davey and asked for his help. Dónal Lunny and he had formed the band Bugle after Dónal left Planxty so we knew each other a little. Though his first big orchestral suite, *The Brendan Voyage*, featuring the pipes of my former band mate Liam Óg O'Flynn, didn't appear till the following year, he too was getting 'hot' in Dublin musical circles. Shaun, in my view, was probably a much better candidate for the O'Casey thing than me, but I wasn't going to let on that I thought that. In any case he had his own projects to deal with and mightn't have been interested.

He generously talked me through things, arranged one of the songs and before long I was getting a basic handle on stuff and was able to put down on paper what I heard in my head in a rudimentary but effective way. His input was invaluable. I really appreciated it. When we actually got into studio with a bunch of great musicians, a lot of whom were from the RTÉ orchestra and suggested by Shaun, they were well able and happy to interpret my 'scores' even though they lacked any sense of orthodoxy.

I put a huge amount into this album and learned so many things about myself in the process; to trust my first instinct and not to keep second-guessing myself being one of them.

So many of my favourite musical genres that had proliferated up to the middle of the twentieth century found an airing. I had always admired the sound of Seán Ó Riada and Ceoltóirí Chualann where the harpsichord married up with traditional Irish instruments so well. I noticed one in the corner of studio and on the first track, 'Down Where the Bees Are Humming', I started playing around on it. Never in my life had I played a real harpsichord, let alone written for one and recorded the result. New horizons beckoned.

I wrote the melody and piano arrangement for 'My Bodice Neat and Modest', strings perfectly and authentically arranged by Shaun Davey. I was chuffed when people assumed the tune was a 'standard from the era'. No. It hadn't existed until now.

'As I Wait in the Boreen for Maggy' saw me using the experience from my previous decade in folk music where the mandolin, tin whistle and Paddy Glackin's fiddle, underpinned by Ciarán Ó Braonáin's string bass could have graced a Johnstons' album.

'White Legg'd Mary' was a strange one. I still can't quite tell where it came from. I composed the music, arranged it for tenor sax and cello and played piano and six- and twelve-string guitars. Musical Theatre?

'Since Maggy Went Away' written by O'Casey to an old Scottish tune 'The Auld House' set me off on a romantic journey on the piano. In a hint of where I would go in the future, I added a Fender Rhodes electric piano giving the arrangement its unique sound. That kind of 'Edwardian parlour melody' was familiar to me having sat in on countless sing-songs in Donegal hotels in my youth where Scottish tourists from the older generation would get up and do their party pieces.

'A Sour Soul'd Cleric' saw me having fun recreating a quasi-Fairport Convention/Steeleye Span 1960s folk-rock groove. I introduced a new acquisition of mine, an ARP Odyssey synthesiser. My God, what next?

'I Tucked up My Sleeves' from the play *Red Roses for Me*, had a tune that was an artfully slowed down version of a popular Irish jig 'Donnybrook Fair'. I took it back into the Edwardian parlour, played piano and featured Pat Murphy on old-fashioned harmonica, leader of the orchestra Audrey Park on violin and Aisling Drury Byrne on cello. A heartbreaker.

A really satisfying element to the recording was the inclusion of the legendary uilleann piper Séamus Ennis. I had written an Irish 'slow air' to be the background to a poem by O'Casey called 'Lament for Thomas Ashe', the Irish revolutionary who died from being force-fed on hunger strike in 1917, and I asked Séamus would he play it. I knew Séamus for many years, regularly hanging out with him in the afternoons in O'Donoghue's in the late 1960s, me on the 'lam' from college, he sipping his vodka and milk. We'd often play together, guitar and uilleann pipes. He loved the air I wrote and said yes. I had set it in a sort of classical harmony structure which was perhaps a little grandiose – it was a 'big' tune.

When the great man arrived in studio to play, he had transposed the entire melody, which he still faithfully reproduced in all its detail, into a stark modal setting devoid of any sweetness, chordal changes or harmonies – simply the drone. It was a stroke of genius. Buoyed up by this, I asked him would he stick around to play on another tune. He was having a good time and again he said yes. I played him the recording of 'All Round Me Hat', the last song on the record. Paddy Glackin had already played fiddle. Séamus stuck on the headphones and mucked in as part of the band. It was amazing. This surely must have been one of the last recording sessions he was involved in as he died after a long decline less than two years later.

All these years after, I still feel hugely privileged to have been accepted and respected by a man who was a Leviathan in the world of Irish music and of whom I was in awe for so many years. To hear him play a tune of mine and lovingly make it his own still thrills me.

The album *The Green Crow Caws* was completed and released later in the year. To say it didn't set the world alight would be a fair comment. Sean Murphy had done a deal with EMI records in the UK. Their marketing department, insofar as they devoted any time to it at all, seemed unsure as to what it was – a musical item, theatrical item, ethnic Irish? Consequently, it slipped through all the cracks and after six months was 'catalogue', except when a CD of it sneaked out in the 1990s with little or no traction.

When I say the original album is now so obscure it's a collector's item, I mean that recently in 2018, when Shivaun O'Casey tried to source it online, she found only one copy valued at £400!

Finally, in 2021 it was rereleased which is gratifying to me since I firmly believe it includes a lot of diverse expressions of what it was and is to be Irish. In terms of experience, producing the album turned out to be a perfect bridge between my previous mainly 'acoustic stringed instrument' history and the future 'rock' direction I would travel in my songwriting and recording.

After *The Green Crow Caws* I found myself concentrating more and more on songwriting. It was a strange feeling. I had made my way to the top of the Irish music world, made a record I was very happy with (which had sold well) and been fêted in Ireland and the UK. I was in constant demand as a solo performer. Yet I kept getting this feeling that I hadn't begun my real work yet, that I'd been biding time all these years indulging in something that, however successful, wasn't really me or mine.

But how was I going to put flesh on the bones of this feeling? I hadn't a clue beyond knowing I needed to walk away from the folk world, go down the mine and see what I could find there.

In the corner of one of our bedrooms in The Willows I had set up a little recording area. Whenever I had some home time, and temporary relief from active fatherhood, I was working on new songs. 'Busted Loose', 'Cold Cold Night' and 'Nothing but the Same Old Story' began appearing there. I laid down rudimentary demos on a primitive quarter track AKAI 400db reel-to-reel machine that allowed for a couple of overdubs. But working at home meant constant interruptions and minor parental crises. I found it impossible to maintain the concentration necessary to write.

Eventually, I rented space in an apartment with a piano in Mountjoy Square and I started spending afternoons there. Gradually 'Road to the Promised Land' and 'Dancer in the Fire' began to take serious shape. At the same time, I was harbouring thoughts of taking the songs a step further and making some proper demos with other musicians.

I was still with Mulligan Records at this time and began talking to director Seamus O'Neill about making a record of my own songs. Seamus said that if I could put together a bunch of players and work up a half-dozen songs, Mulligan would fund it. This became a priority. I started thinking about who to ask to play.

As I thought more about it, and as the 'feel' of a song was paramount to me, I decided to incorporate just a rhythm section of bass and drums at first. It had been thirteen years since I had worked in a 'rock' band line-up while at UCD and back then it was the drummer who set the tempos and general rhythmic dynamic and we all followed along. We were of course only singing R 'n' B covers and standards and everyone *kind of* knew what was what. But in the years since, where I mostly set my own rhythms and tempos with acoustic instruments, free from an outside structure, I had realised how important it was for the singer to control this. As I moved away from traditional forms into writing my own songs it became even more crucial. The problem was that, once they learned their part in the song, not many 'rock' drummers were used to actually listening to what was going on onstage.

This was never going to suit me. A typical 'rock' drum kit is a very crude instrument. For a start, the noise level dominates everything else on stage and tends to dictate the overall 'feel' of a song. In the hands of an insensitive player it can ruin things. The experience of performing songs solo, either traditional or now my own compositions, showed me how important it was for a good performance to let a song breathe, to vary the tempo and dynamic according to what the lyric suggested. To find a drummer in Dublin sensitive and sympathetic to this, to sublimate their needs and follow someone else's rhythm, was not going to be easy. I asked around but I was an outsider to the Dublin rock scene.

The trad and rock camps never crossed paths those days except for in the iconic band Horslips who skilfully married both. I was unsure of myself too, never having tried to do this. But gradually a few options appeared. On my nights-off, regularly spent in the music pub the Meeting Place in Dorset Street, I had seen drummer Paul McAteer and bassist Garvan Gallagher and thought they were really good, sensitive players. We talked, threw ideas around and they agreed to get involved. Over the next few months, I began getting song arrangements together and sending them tapes to listen to.

Meanwhile in the gig arena I continued building on my profile in Ireland with a host of solo shows in bigger venues round the country and appearances at all the now well-established summer festivals. The second Lisdoonvarna festival came round in mid-July in the company of Loudon Wainwright III, Ralph McTell, the Chieftains, Richard and Linda Thompson and Martin Carthy. The Irish festivals had come of age and were now attracting the cream of international folk artists.

It was at this festival I first met Loudon and his booking agent Paul Charles. Paul, originally from Magherafelt in County Derry, was the co-owner of Asgard, one of the most successful London booking agencies, even then handling some of the biggest rock and folk acts from the UK and the US.

After my set he approached me and asked would I be interested in being represented by Asgard outside Ireland. I was excited and over the weekend we started talking about his ideas for my future. This was the first glimmer of recognition from abroad. I instinctively knew that I would need the backing of someone like Asgard if I was ever to break out of Ireland and before we parted I had agreed to come on board, beginning a long and successful business relationship and friendship that lasted for the next thirty years.

As I felt all these major changes in the offing, my imagination ran riot.

Later that summer I played at the inaugural and (as it turned out) only Causeway Coast Folk Festival in Portrush in the company of Loudon Wainwright III, John Martyn, the Strawbs, the Boys

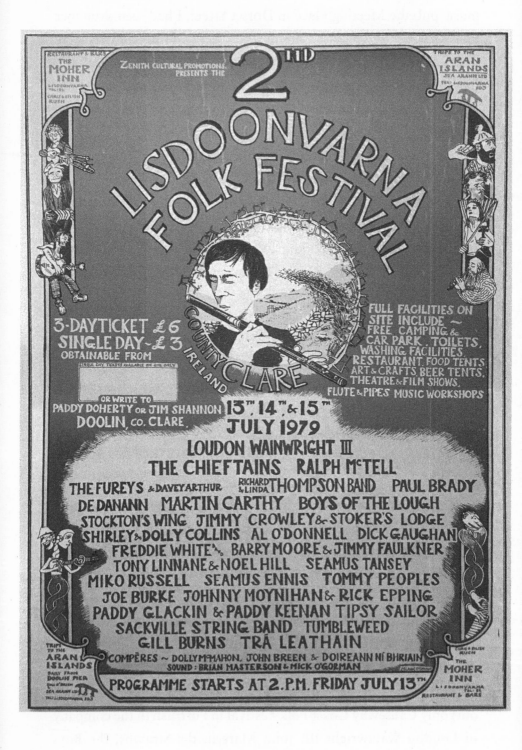

of the Lough and Christy Moore. I remember walking along a deserted beach with recent new friend Loudon who was in a somewhat fallow period commercially after his initial big success of a few years back in the USA. The subject of radio came up. He was lamenting how hard it was for his material to get daytime airplay at the time. I naively suggested that he perhaps write some more pop-style songs with a more commercial sound to which he replied, 'You mean non-Loudon Wainwright songs?'

Duh!

I never forgot that – especially as I was nearly always in the same position myself in the years that followed.

Another memory is from the after-show party in the snooker room of the hotel where we were all staying. I was singing something when in came John Martyn and immediately started badgering me to sing 'Paddy's Green Shamrock Shore'. I didn't really know John at the time, and you'd think I might have been flattered to have registered with him at all. But no! I kept on singing and eventually got stroppy with him in a 'fuck off' kind of way. It was Robin Morton of the Boys of the Lough who whispered in my ear, this was *the* John Martyn who a couple of weeks previously had thrown Sid Vicious through a plate-glass window in the Portobello Hotel in London's Notting Hill. We eventually bonded and I did indeed sing 'Paddy's Green Shamrock Shore'.

The meeting with Paul Charles, and the now ongoing relationship with Asgard, started to dominate my consciousness. I had a load of folk gigs spreading out over the rest of the year in Ireland and a three-week French tour in November that took me from Jersey to Paris through the north of the country to Brittany. But these all seemed distractions now, impeding my progress in this new direction.

The only exception was an October solo concert in the Library at Dublin's RDS showgrounds. It was just after Pope John Paul II's visit to Ireland, which had been the biggest thing all year. I arrived onstage and, with my arms outstretched in a papal embrace, I echoed the Pope's recent words of welcome at Phoenix Park by declaiming in a mock Polish accent 'Young people of Ireland, I love you!' much to the amusement of the audience. The fact that I was raving with a flu at the time made for an out-of-body performance which was, by my wife's account – and she didn't normally go over the top – one of my best to date.

24

NOW OR NEVER

It was 19 December 1979 and time to go into studio to begin recording my new material. I had booked Keystone Studio for a couple of days, which was in a basement in Harcourt Street at the time. With a state-of-the-art eight-track reel-to-reel recorder anything was possible. Andrew Boland, the owner, was engineer. Paul McAteer and Garvan Gallagher were set up and ready to go. We had rehearsed a few times in the preceding week, and we all felt reasonably sure of ourselves. As an extra insurance I had asked old friend and colleague Arty McGlynn to join us on day two. The tea and coffee maker (all self-respecting studios had a tea boy, or in this case, girl) was a seventeen-year-old Norwegian girl, whose family had moved to Ireland, called Mariella Frostrup. Mariella went on to enjoy a plethora of greater things in the years to come ... as a journalist contributing to *The Guardian*, *Observer*, *The Telegraph*, as a TV and radio presenter with Channel 4, Sky Arts and BBC Radio 2 and in 2005 voted the sexiest voice on UK television.

The songs I picked to record were: 'Crazy Dreams', 'Dancer in the Fire', 'The Road to the Promised Land', 'Trouble Round the Bend', Hank Williams' 'You Win Again' and an old Lead Belly song I had loved singing for years called 'Duncan & Brady'. I started with 'Crazy Dreams' on acoustic guitar.

You're tired of dreaming someone else's dreams
When they really don't include you any longer
Miles from home, you're sliding down with each day
And you need a woman's love to make you stronger
And lately you've been getting doubts
A voice inside keeps calling out
That someone else's dreams don't get you nowhere.

If ever a song was written to express the realisation that you were destined to find and follow your own muse and no one else's, it was 'Crazy Dreams'. I sang it in one take. The track felt and sounded good, and the recording went without a hitch. Everyone relaxed and we started to enjoy ourselves.

I moved on to the piano for 'Dancer in the Fire'. This was a different ball game. I lacked confidence on piano. It was fine if I was playing live; I was good at improvising – somehow the tightrope experience increased the excitement factor. I followed the adage 'if you make a mistake, repeat it'. That way it's a choice not a mistake. But when the red light went on in studio, particularly back in those days when, unlike today, the technical possibilities of fixing stuff hardly existed, it had to be right first time, or you had to do it all over again.

It was complicated too by this tendency I had, and still have, to write music that I find really difficult to play. Consequentially, 'Dancer in the Fire' with a piano arrangement that was complicated stood before me like a mountain. Andrew Boland, a talented piano player himself, was encouraging. After a few takes I had a credible version on tape where I sang and played simultaneously. As if to celebrate the achievement, Andrew, a much better player than me, sat down and, on the tail end of the song, overdubbed a fabulously rising flourish that was the icing on the cake.

I stayed on piano for 'Promised Land' which back then had a

totally different 6/8 Gospel feel to the later 4/4 Caribbean-influenced version on the *Hard Station* album.

I hadn't really played electric guitar (and never onstage) since Rootzgroup in 1966, but I'd played my old Gibson SG Standard on the basic demos I'd sent around to the band. Now that I was in studio I wanted to play more. Andrew had a gorgeous matt-gold Gibson Les Paul and he said to try it out. We had just cut 'You Win Again' and I started messing around on it with some country licks. It started to sound good, so we recorded a take. I must've got inspired because after trying it a few more times we went back to the first take and kept it. (I included this recording later on my 2012 *Anthology* album.) Things were on the up.

We moved on to 'Trouble Round the Bend'. I was a J.J. Cale fan at the time. I loved his minimalist blues guitar style. It suited me as I was no virtuoso myself. 'Trouble' sent me in that direction, dark and moody. Again, the initial tracking was just drums, bass and me. This time I sang live too. I overdubbed the electric guitar and that was it. Real simple. I still love that recording.

Next day Arty McGlynn came in and we tackled 'Duncan & Brady'. The basic track was me on acoustic twelve-string with bass and drums. Arty overdubbed a pedal steel part that lifted the song into another place. I finished it, adding piano and electric guitar. I went back to 'Crazy Dreams' again and added the solo on electric. We were all feeling a bit of magic in the room and there were smiles all round. The mix was easy. Everything was so simple, the songs kind of mixed themselves. I felt relief and a sense of achievement when it was all done. Upwards and onwards! Though these were just demos and there was a lot to do yet, I relaxed with the family that Christmas and forgot about music for a while.

In February the next year, Paul Charles had set up a gig for me at the Venue, a happening rock club in London's Victoria. I decided to bring my demo musicians, Paul McAteer on drums and Garvan Gallagher on bass with me.

My big new direction took off slowly. Arriving in London on a cold February day and entering a large stand-up room in Victoria knowing that, if I was lucky, it was at best going to be half-filled with an audience that evening was a sobering experience. I was nervous. I had never done a live gig with Paul and Garvan before. Singing and playing acoustic guitar with just drums and bass suddenly seemed woefully inadequate. There was a piano in the Venue that they let me use. I remember singing 'Dancer in the Fire' and 'Road to the Promised Land' on it. 'You Win Again' sticks out in my mind for some reason, and of course 'Crazy Dreams'. The Venue staff ignored me. Nobody had a clue or cared who I was. I was Thursday night's act. That was about it. We got through the gig but I don't remember the crowd reaction or anything else other than that I was glad to get offstage.

I came back to Dublin, not exactly with my tail between my legs but with the definite realisation that this new direction was not going to be easy. Nothing was going to fall into my lap. The feeling of a rapid descent from the top of one ladder to the bottom of another overtook me and I struggled but I was also beginning to plan how and when to record an album of these new songs.

Over the previous few months, a bunch of new songs had materialised. I felt they were good. With the coolness of my recent reception in London dragging me back mentally and emotionally to when I lived there in the early 1970s, 'Nothing but the Same Old Story' appeared. I quickly recorded a home demo of it. Back then, my time living in London had coincided with a period when the violence in Northern Ireland got worse and worse. Internment without trial had been introduced in late 1971 followed, a few months later, by the massacre in Derry of thirteen unarmed and innocent civilians by the British Army on Bloody Sunday. That day, more than anything, convinced me that for all the British government claims that Northern Ireland was part of the United Kingdom and no different to anywhere else, there was a different attitude to the people there. Irish lives did not matter in the same way as English, Scottish and Welsh lives did. All Irish people in Britain were viewed with suspicion as either being or sympathising with 'terrorists'. My opinion on that hasn't changed nearly fifty years later. Britain (whatever that is) doesn't give a damn about Northern Ireland and never will.

'Night Hunting Time' was a throwback to my days in rock bands in the 1960s.

> *Sweat streaming down my cheekbones*
> *Smoke stinging my eyes*
> *Walls dripping like the jungle*
> *But this ain't no paradise*

Even so, I still loved being there.

'Cold Cold Night' was an attempt to acknowledge the difficult time Mary was going through, rearing two children with long absences from me.

> *The price that you have paid for loving me*
> *And there is nothing I won't do to try to set you free*

'Hard Station' followed, the complex intros and outros heavily influenced by 'Baker Street' and the subject matter directly mirroring
the economic deprivation so many were experiencing in Dublin at
the time. I felt I had something new here.

As I thought about an album and acknowledged an ambition
that it would get noticed outside Ireland, I began to have doubts
about the ability of my current label, Mulligan Records, to give
it the support it would need in the international arena. The label
was still focused on Irish traditional music. It had (at the time)
no effective distribution outside Ireland. There was also grumbling
discontent developing between us about money issues.

UK agent, Paul Charles advised that I find a more established
international outlet for my next record. I valued his opinion. I
started asking around. At the time WEA Records, Ireland (Warners,
Electra, Atlantic) was run by an Englishman, Clive Hudson. I went
to see Clive, talked about my new direction, the UK agency, and my
hopes for the future. I dropped off a cassette of the demos. Before
long he got back to me; he was interested in doing a deal. He also
talked about a UK release on WEA. I was excited. Paul Charles
had several contacts in the London branch too which helped oil the
wheels. I decided to throw in my lot with WEA.

In spite of these new developments, I was still in the dark as
to how to approach the new album or who to get to produce it.
I knew no one in that big world out there with a track record. I
had enough sense to realise I shouldn't try and produce it myself.
An approach to Richard Thompson who I knew vaguely from the
Johnstons' days was a dead end. Then I met with Van Morrison
at a house he had in the country outside London, again set up by
Paul Charles. It was a strange meeting. I played him my demo
tape, song by agonising song. He listened quietly but said nothing
throughout. When it was over, he said, 'I don't know what I can
bring to this.'

I was disappointed. Was he saying that I didn't need any musical input from him, that it was complete already? Was it a compliment?

In truth, I guess I was hoping he would become involved as a mentor or producer, that the association would bring some much-needed attention to me in my new direction. Van was never going to do that!

In April, Gerry Rafferty was coming to Dublin. Being such a huge fan of Gerry's writing and the production on the *City to City* album, I was aware of his producer Hugh Murphy. Was there a remote chance Hugh might be interested in producing me? I managed, again through Paul Charles whose assistance in those days was invaluable, to find out that Hugh would be at the gig and would be happy to meet me for a brief introduction after the show. I arrived with cassette in pocket.

The show was great. The band was phenomenal. Keyboard player Betsy Cook and drummer Liam Genockey stood out. With my Access All Areas (AAA) pass I got backstage, introduced myself to Hugh and left the tape with him.

After a nail-biting, dream-chasing week I heard back. He liked the songs and was interested in going further. Did I have a record deal, a budget, management, all that?

I told him I had a 'single' deal with WEA, that we were talking about extending into an album but that we were still working details out. I was encouraged; if nothing else, it showed me that my songs were good and that as an artist I was worth taking seriously.

By the middle of 1980, Paul Charles had suggested that, in addition to being booking agent, he would become my overall manager. His interest had increased. I said I'd think about it. I talked to a few people including my long-term friend Ozzie Kilkenny, whom I had played with in the band Rockhouse in the mid-1960s and who was now becoming the pre-eminent music-business accountant in Ireland. Ozzie wasn't so sure. He felt that, to avoid possible conflicts of interest, it was best to keep agency and concert promotion (as Asgard sometimes did) separate from management. After all it was often management's function to 'beat up' the agent and promoter on behalf of the artist! How could that be insured in those circumstances? He further questioned whether a very busy agent, booking dozens of acts, would have the time and energy to devote to full management of one individual artist. Fair enough. Nonetheless, realising how much I depended on Paul at the time and how instrumental his input had become in moving things along in all directions, I was happy to agree to expand the situation and we signed a management agreement.

It was summer by now and I was still in demand as a folk singer so I was booked to play at all the big Irish outdoor folk festivals. Macroom, Lisdoonvarna and Ballisodare came and went. I appeared solo at them all. Asgard and I began talking about an Irish tour later in the year with a full band. I started thinking about who to ask to play. Paul McAteer had a day job and didn't want to tour so I started looking elsewhere. First on the list was the Meeting Place. Some of the greatest players in town appeared there. Jimmy Faulkner was an incredible guitarist, both acoustic and electric. Fran Breen periodically played drums with the Floating Dublin Blues Band and I loved his style. James Delaney on keyboards stood out, as did Tommy Moore on bass. I started talking to them and we agreed to meet later in the year and rehearse for some shows.

Now the summer was drawing to a close, the plan at WEA (we now had a definite album commitment) was to record a single first, 'Crazy Dreams', preferably in London, and follow up with an album in early 1981. It was suggested that, as I hadn't begun rehearsals with the Irish band yet, I should use London musicians. I agreed to try it out. By a circuitous and coincidental route (the details of which escape me now) it was suggested that John Wood produce the single.

John Wood had been the engineer all those years ago on the first Johnstons' album back in 1967. Sound Techniques – the studio in Chelsea's Old Church Street where we had recorded then – was the suggested recording venue this time too. While it had been over a decade since I'd worked with John, and there was maybe a faint whiff of 'a past I'd left behind' about the association, I was relieved that I was not walking into the unknown and felt I could deal with whatever came up.

A date for recording was set: 11–12 September. The plan was to record three songs, an A- and B-side and a spare song as an insurance policy. 'Crazy Dreams' was the agreed choice as A-side. We picked a new song I had just written called 'Something in the Atmosphere' as B-side. 'Night Hunting Time' was the insurance.

Paul Charles put a band together: Peter Van Hooke on drums; Mark Isham on trumpet and flugelhorn (both with Van Morrison's band); Mo Foster on bass; Billy Livsey on piano; and Bryn Haworth on slide guitar.

These were all top players on the London session scene. Billy went on to play on records by Tina Turner (notably on her huge hit 'What's Love Got to Do With It?'), Pete Townshend, Gerry Rafferty, Cliff Richard and Leo Sayer. Mo Foster played with Phil Collins, Ringo Starr, Cher, Jeff Beck and Gerry Rafferty among countless others, while Mark Isham went on to be one of Hollywood's most successful film music composers. This was a major leg-up for me, an unknown in this world. I felt lucky and nervous.

The recordings went well. All the basic tracks went down easily. Despite my inexperience working with a bass and drums rhythm section, I got through the 'who follows who' dilemma successfully and for the most part felt I was in control of my music. All the players seemed to like the material and were full of encouragement and respect. Only downside was I didn't particularly get on with

John Wood. I found him gruff, impatient, arrogant and dismissive. Still, job well done, we said our goodbyes and I went home.

After a few days I felt the 'Crazy Dreams' mix could've been better. Through Paul Charles, I contacted John Wood and discussed my reservations. I asked would he consider remixing that *one* track?

A flat 'No' was the response, 'I'm off on me holidays.'

That was that. Fair enough, I guess, if a little brusque!

Undeterred, I took the mix to Dublin engineer Brian Masterson in the recently opened Windmill Lane Studios. Brian had mixed my *Welcome Here Kind Stranger* record and I admired his capabilities. We sorted the problem out in an hour or so. I stopped fretting.

The single 'Crazy Dreams' backed with 'Something in the Atmosphere' was released in Ireland in October to coincide with my first Irish tour with a band the following month, promoted by none other than my former Irish booking agent, Gerry Harford. Nice that we found a way to keep working together after my move to Asgard.

All the guys I had talked to earlier in the year were on board plus Arty McGlynn. I needed Arty, not just as a great player but as a good friend with vast experience in bands and for gelling with other musicians. I was still insecure about what I was taking on. Never a bandleader, I wasn't practiced in balancing the day-to-day employer–employee dynamic. I welcomed Arty's reassuring presence as a buffer between any potential personnel problems and me.

'Crazy Dreams' entered the Irish charts on 9 November 1980 and remained there for seven weeks. The tour was a success with sell-outs everywhere. We did an extra date in the Sportsman's Inn in Dublin on 9 December. I remember it well because that morning I got a call at home from a journalist asking had I anything to say about John Lennon. I had no idea why someone was calling me till I heard him say John Lennon had been shot dead in New

York the previous night. What a shock. The gig that night was a rollercoaster of emotions both for the band and audience.

The new year had hardly arrived when I was thrown into preparations for the recording that became *Hard Station*. Over the final months of 1980 I'd had many phone calls with Hugh Murphy. Now that an album deal with WEA was in place with a budget allocated, he was on board as producer. He came over to Dublin to see Windmill Lane studios and meet with engineer Paul Thomas. We discussed song arrangements and musicians and, while he was generally happy with my Irish players, he suggested that his wife, the keyboard player Betsy Cook be involved.

Betsy was a brilliant player and musician and the thought of having her involved was very attractive. I also wanted to have something new and fresh to look forward to and Betsy had played at the highest level. Of course, if I went in that direction, it meant I wouldn't be using James Delaney who had toured with me. After a long discussion, I accepted that Hugh too needed someone on board he knew well who'd be inspirational, professional and dependable. What's more, Betsy loved the songs and had loads of ideas about how to record them. She was also a great backing singer. This was the deciding factor.

It was difficult telling James, whom I admired and still do, but as I learned many times over the next few years, nothing in the music business stays the same. Change is often exciting and a creative necessity. The rest of my touring band formed the nucleus of the studio band: Tommy Moore on bass, Fran Breen on drums, Jimmy Faulkner and Arty McGlynn on electric guitars.

I was finally a songwriter, though it was a strange and varied collection I was preparing to record. It was pointed out to me later by 'professional' songwriters that two of the songs, 'Crazy Dreams' and 'Cold Cold Night' didn't even have choruses but were just a series of verses! That must've come straight from my years in folk music where the song was, in the first place, a story. Choruses seemed a commercially driven extravagance I had yet to acknowledge the importance of.

We started recording *Hard Station* in late January 1981. There followed the most intense period of work I had experienced in my life to date. Somehow, all my previous projects in studio, while important, seemed one step removed from the core of my being. Now, at this stage of my life, and with a bunch of songs that expressed a part of me I had never revealed before, indeed a part that I was only discovering with each day, I began to feel pressure in a very different way. Everything was new. The technical way Hugh worked in studio, the length of time it took to set things up, the endless sound checking all began to frustrate me.

First and foremost, I was a live performer and I found it hard to conserve my nervous energy until it was time to record. I couldn't understand why we would spend a quarter of an hour listening to Fran banging one drum or deciding which of *three* different microphones would work best on Jimmy's amplifier. But that was how it was recording a rock band in those days. A record was going to be around forever. Let's get it right! I had to put up with it.

I was often exhausted too. At home in our three-bedroom house, Colm, now almost two, slept in his cot in one room with Mary. Sarah, aged three and a half, was in the small bedroom. I would come in sometimes after midnight and crash in the spare room stepping over my old Akai reel-to-reel machine.

It took ages to get my mind to shut down after the intensity of the day and for sleep to come. Often, however, Sarah would wake up at 3 or 4 a.m. and I would have to take her into the bed with me for the rest of the night. There was no other way to do it. Mary had more than enough on her plate with Colm. I would frequently arrive in studio feeling I had hardly slept at all. Not a good way to start what was going to be another demanding day.

It wasn't all pressure, of course. I still remember the excitement of hearing 'Nothing but the Same Old Story' come together. The way we decided to record it was that I would play the song structure on acoustic guitar just like a live performance with bass, drums and Betsy on piano. The vocal would go down later. Last would be the electric guitar.

I had written the piano part some months previously and sent a tape of me playing it in my own amateurish way to Betsy. Her interpretation of it on the day was stunning. As I was driving the basic track along silently singing the words to myself, her piano playing in my headphones almost brought me to tears of joy. The authority, musicality, passion and sensitivity she brought to the recording later helped me to do one of my best-ever vocal performances. Jimmy Faulkner's electric guitar overdub made the song soar on high. We knew we had something special here.

There were of course difficulties. I was struggling with the need to make creative and final decisions about the music. I had a flashback to me in boarding school where I was a slow-enough learner. I was the kind of student who when asked a question would know the answer at a deep level, but it would take some time for that to come to the surface and a kind of panic would set in. So it was with my burgeoning music. The problem was that Betsy Cook was a forceful personality and she had strong and definite ideas about what should be played when and where or what sounds the keyboard (which she owned!) should produce. We called them synths (synthesisers) in those days. We clashed many times as my fear of my baby being taken away from me asserted itself: 'This is my music, Betsy, even if I'm incoherent at the moment. If you want to make your own music, go off and do it somewhere else' kind of thing! Pathetic really, I know. Betsy was just being her natural, maybe pushy, but very talented self, which brought a lot of magic to the record. But the struggle was very real and caused me deep anguish quite often.

'Busted Loose' and 'Cold Cold Night' went on tape easily. 'Night Hunting Time' was a departure. Probably the first time I had ever employed a click track to lock down the rhythm. I had started it at home on an Arp Odyssey mono synth. It sounds very Spartan now and lacking some core percussion to nail it down, but it was early days in the synth era – I was just learning.

'Dancer in the Fire' remains one of the highlights of the record. Again, it was a piano arrangement I had written a year before, but nervous, as I still was about my piano playing, I turned it over to Betsy. I'm glad I did. Her playing on this is dazzling, full of class and way better than I could have pulled off.

In spite of the success of the London version of 'Crazy Dreams' the previous year, there was something about it that bothered me. It was too lightweight or something, the tempo too fast, too much bippity-bop going on in the drums. I found myself going back again to listen to the demo version I did in Keystone way back in December 1979. There was a languid lope to that recording that was the perfect vehicle for the song's lyrical sentiment and I knew I preferred it.

Rather than try and record it yet again, we decided to use the original demo recording and build on it. We transferred the eight-track multi to the Windmill Lane twenty-four-track machine. We kept the acoustic guitar, drums and vocal and added another great piano track from Betsy, electric guitar and synth from me and bass from John Drummond. That has been the established version of the song ever since.

I took a break of a couple of days in the middle of the record. As if there wasn't enough pressure to contend with between parenthood and the ongoing recording, we moved to a four-bedroom house on the other side of the city in Deansgrange. The moving date was slap bang in the middle of the recording. The day of the move I woke in a panic. Sarah, who'd woken up crying around

4 a.m., was asleep in the bed beside me. The whole family was still in bed and there was a house-move lorry outside the door. The day was a surreal blur. We'd just the rest of that day and the next to make sense of the new place, then it was back to studio.

We started off again on 'The Road to the Promised Land', which took a different shape to that of the Keystone demo. It moved from being a Memphis thing to the Caribbean and a grass-skirt/steel-drum feel emerged. That was probably the biggest surprise on the record. I played the core keyboard part on Wurlitzer with lots of atmospheric and rhythmic overdubs on synths from Betsy and me. Arty played this rock-solid electric guitar groove that made you want to shake your booty big time. The background voices from Betsy were heavenly. Tommy's bass and Fran's drums completed the smiley picture. After we finished, I felt I'd been given a gift from above.

Last to come was the title track 'Hard Station'. The song melody and chord structure were based on an earlier piece of music I had written back in 1979 to accompany a radio ad campaign for the Irish language. I always liked the shape of the tune and it kept coming back to haunt me in the following year. Dublin was in the throes of the major early 1980s recession. I started writing words, putting myself in the situation of someone who was struggling to keep head above water in the savage downturn, someone who had done some time and who was now looking to put it behind them and move on. What came out became the song 'Hard Station'.

The recording came to an end. We started mixing and then the problems started. 'It's time to let go, Paul!' We'd been working crazy hours. I wasn't sleeping and by now was exhausted. I was so far inside the trees that I couldn't see the wood at all. Every single squeak on a bass drum pedal I could hear as loud as the lead vocal. Perspective went down the tubes and, I know now, I went tempo-rarily insane. 'This is too loud ... that's not loud enough. There's too much reverb on this … not enough on that.' But the die was cast. Studio time ran out. I had to grit my teeth and get on with it. Shame, after so much great work from writing to final recording, that this paranoia cheated me of even a basic sense of satisfaction in what I had achieved. It wouldn't be the last time.

I got together with artist, Johnny Devlin, who had also done the artwork for *Welcome Here Kind Stranger* to discuss the album cover. By this stage I knew it was going to be called *Hard Station*. Johnny came up with a radical idea, which we went ahead with, to do a painting of Tara Street train station in Dublin with all the people transformed into Subbuteo figures, some standing, some knocked over, the idea being how fragile, powerless and vulnerable we all were in this dreadful economic downturn.

The record came out in May and was critically very well received. WEA Ireland put some money behind it, and it began to get airplay and sell. I did some more Irish gigs with the studio band minus Betsy, who'd left after the recording. James Delaney magnanimously agreed to rejoin even though he hadn't been part of the record.

That same month we were asked to do BBC TV's *The Old Grey Whistle Test*, which Paul Charles set up. That was a big break in the UK. We flew to London and, sharing the show with Jim Capaldi late of Traffic, I sang 'Crazy Dreams' and 'Busted Loose'. On 25 June the Stag Hot Press annual music awards voted 'Crazy Dreams' the best single of 1981. The previous week *Hard Station* went to No. 1 in the Irish album charts – I guess not everyone shared the artist's opinion that it was deeply flawed.

June saw me once more at the Macroom Mountain Dew Festival sharing the bill with Elvis Costello, the Undertones, the Pretenders, the Blues Band, Scullion, Q-Tips, the Rhythm Kings and Sniff 'n' the Tears. Great times and a great festival. But things were to change very soon.

Paul suggested I look for separate management in North America. He was quick to acknowledge that it was an entirely different market and would require on-the-spot attention. He got on well with Bill Graham, the well-known concert promoter based in San Francisco. Bill's company also managed Van Morrison and Santana, and Paul had been booking both acts in Europe, so there was an ongoing good relationship in existence.

Paul sent *Hard Station* to Bill's office. They loved the album; it was tailor-made for the market they operated in, and they immediately expressed interest in managing me in North America; they even paid for my flight and hotel so I could meet them and discuss things. Paul Charles was already in LA at the time and joined me in San Francisco for the meetings. It was early July. I met the Graham people, Mick Brigden and Nick Clainos. Bill himself was in New York and it was arranged that I would meet him on my way through, as I was heading home. Everyone was enthusiastic about the album. They were even talking about Santana recording 'Night Hunting Time'.

San Francisco was a dream-like trip. I left for New York on a slightly confused high. I didn't feel part of what was going on, like it was happening to someone else. I met Bill in his apartment overlooking Central Park. This is the legendary Bill Graham. Everyone in rock music knew who Bill Graham was. He was very courteous, 'I hear my people want you to come on board,' he said.

'Oh, so it's just your people and not you personally, is it?' I hear this voice from inside.

'They tell me you've made a great record,' he says.

'Oh, so you haven't heard it yourself?' the voice goes on.

I'm spooked. Who is this idiot pretending to be me? My face is hot. I'm suddenly looking for ways to puncture the balloon. My head feels like it's in a tumble dryer.

The meeting lasts about fifteen minutes but the vast majority of what is said I don't really hear and certainly can't remember. I now know that, at that moment, I was overwhelmed by a deep fear, not of success as such, but of the demands it would make on me, though none of this inner terror was apparent on the surface. It wouldn't be the last time I was similarly afflicted.

On the plane home I tried to imagine how it would all work. The more I thought about it the more I felt it was mad and would only really work out if I was prepared to move lock, stock and barrel (the whole family) to the US. But I wasn't even prepared to move to London, which was the more obvious and logical place for me to be. The time difference alone between Dublin and San Francisco would have made regular daily contact difficult. After a week's reflection, talks with Mary, and Paul Charles, I decided against it. It was a lovely dream, but the real world interrupted the reverie. The internal disrupter slunk back to his lair, satisfied for the moment.

I now had a deal with a major record label, the Asgard booking agency was looking after my live work and Paul Charles was managing me. But in a strange move at the time, Paul seemed to have second thoughts about the management aspect of our relationship. With hindsight I guess he was enthusiastic about my prospects from the beginning, and in the absence of management, he assumed the mantle until he decided that it would probably be better for me in the long run that the two functions be separate, as my friend and accountant Ozzie Kilkenny had initially advised. He would continue to be my booking agent, however – a specialty role in itself.

At the time, he had close relationships with successful artist management companies in London. One of those was Damage Management, who looked after the affairs of Dire Straits, then already a globally successful band. Paul now went one step further in helping me by giving *Hard Station* to Damage Management supremo Ed Bicknell. Ed liked it and before long it reached the ears of Mark Knopfler, Dire Straits leader, who felt the same and started to talk it up. Bicknell's deputy in Damage Management, Paul Cummins, at the time the band's tour manager, heard the record too and fell in love with it. It was serendipitous that Cummins was ready to expand his role in the company and looking for an act of his own to manage when *Hard Station* fell into his lap. He and Paul Charles got to talking and they decided to come to Ireland together to see me play. I knew nothing about this. I guess Paul Charles didn't want to jump the gun in case things didn't work out. The next gig that was ahead of me was with the Irish band at the Lisdoonvarna festival over the weekend of 10 July.

I had just come off stage at Lisdoonvarna after what had been a difficult set. Things had fallen apart in the keyboard department on 'Night Hunting Time' causing an awkward hiatus in the gig that took a while to resolve in front of a waiting audience. I didn't think we had played well and I wasn't feeling sociable when Paul Charles met me at the bottom of the off-ramp with another man I didn't know.

He introduced me to Paul Cummins. It was a stiff encounter. When I don't enjoy a gig, I never like to meet people immediately afterwards until I've come back to myself and got a bit of perspective. I didn't know who he was and why he was there. He seemed to have enjoyed the gig, however, and he stayed around our backstage area and chatted amiably to the band and me. He talked about the album and how much he liked it and after a while mentioned he was from Dire Straits' management.

I took Paul Charles to one side and asked him what was going on and why was Paul Cummins here. He said, 'He wants to manage you.' It was all very confusing. Paul Charles was managing me, or so I thought. Why, was he now seemingly facilitating someone else to do the same job? It was all very weird.

As the weekend continued, I was spending more time with Paul

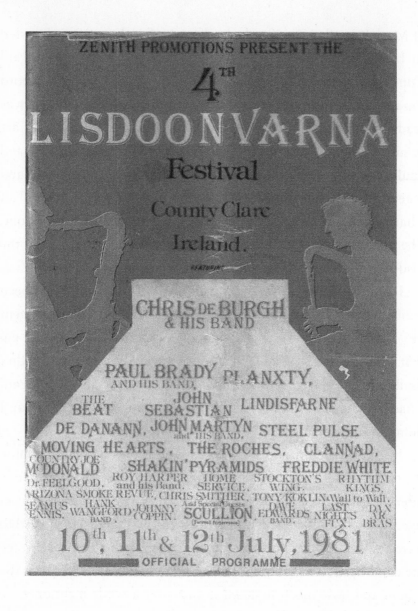

Cummins. He opened up about wanting to manage me. I was giddy with it all; it didn't seem real. Cummins was staying at a hotel in Ennis. When he got back to his room, he discovered he had been burgled and £700 had disappeared. He seemed unconcerned. I was amazed at his sangfroid. I would have been foaming at the mouth. The current value in today's money (2022) is around €3,000. Most impressive. If he had planned to dazzle me with the prospect that I could soon be so rich under his management so as to not really miss that kind of money, he did a good job.

I was left to think things over but it didn't take long to make up my mind. This was a major opportunity for advancement. I'd be an idiot to turn it down. Paul Cummins came across to me as honest, trustworthy and genuinely a fan who wanted to make things happen for me. Further, it seemed he was in a position to do what he said he could do. I called him up on the Monday and said yes.

Things moved at breakneck speed in the second half of 1981. In those six months I signed a world-wide publishing deal, changed record labels, put a new UK-based band together, did some London shows and toured Ireland.

So far, *Hard Station* was only on release in Ireland. Cummins approached WEA/UK with whom my deal was signed. My agent Paul Charles had a contact there, Dave Walters, and he liked the album. WEA were of course aware of the album's success in Ireland, and we weren't expecting any problems; here was an artist with top-class management, a booking agency, a chart-topping album in his home country and plans to tour. What's not to like? But that's not how it happened.

In a development that became a common feature of most record companies at the time (and would blight the careers of many artists), the 'supporting-executive-has-moved-on' syndrome asserted itself. Dave Walters had left the company and, in his place, a new man, with the unlikely name of Tarquin Gotch, took his place.

In a move that again was common in those days, Gotch said he didn't want to release *Hard Station* as it was an old album, and I should record a new record straight away. It's a kind of ego thing, an 'I don't want to be involved with something I didn't start, that wasn't my creation' is what the motivation typically was. It happened all the time in the record business. It was not what I wanted. After all I had put into the record, the thought that it was now going to be binned and not heard by anyone outside Ireland was unacceptable. I said no. The result was that I ended my relationship with WEA. Cummins and I started looking in other directions.

By a stroke of luck, a Dutchman called Freddy Haayen, who had a record label in New York under the Polydor umbrella called 21 Records, had heard *Hard Station* and fallen in love with it, especially the track 'Busted Loose'. Freddy was at the time managing and producing the well-known Dutch band Golden Earring and he liked up-tempo rock songs. He said he wanted to release *Hard Station* worldwide. Sweet vindication.

Now however, my previous paranoia about the album reasserted itself. It had never gone away. For some reason, I felt the original mix lacked 'punch' and 'dynamism'. In retrospect I know that my exhausted state at the end of the original mix coloured my opinion – 'How could it be any good if I was so wrecked finishing it?'

I raised the issue of a remix. This was not an uncommon thing in those days. As technology advanced, people were forever feeling they could improve a record. Freddy, probably feeling the same, said yes. And in late 1981 I went into Startling Studio in Surrey, England with Hugh Murphy and Steve Lipson to remix the record.

The house, Tittenhurst Park, where the studio was located, was the former home of John Lennon, and in fact Ringo was living there at the time, having bought it from John. The film of John singing and playing 'Imagine', which we are all familiar with, was made in the main room of the house and the white piano was eerily still there. The remix took about four days. I enjoyed the process a lot. It was there I wrote 'Helpless Heart'.

I'm sitting here inside this stranger's place
and time is racing by

The stranger was Ringo Starr, who genially put his head round the studio door from time to time to hear what was going on. Everyone, including Freddy Haayen, liked the remix and I finally put my paranoia to bed. Finally? I had yet to learn that the temporary insanity I'd been cursed with when finishing *Hard Station* was episodic and contingent on the rollercoaster of emotions and doubt that accompanied creating a new piece of work in a studio where deadlines reigned and a whole team of people were 'on the clock' to complete that vision. Pretty much every album I subsequently made, up until the time I built my own studio in the 1990s and I could take my own pace and produce myself, saw me, at one point or another in the process, losing my grip on reality.

Was I alone in this? Many artists I've spoken to confess to the same ailment. To this day people who know and love *Hard Station* argue about which mix is the better one. I can't decide. I was too close to it all. The first is more organic, the second a bit slicker. In the end, I made both versions available on my website. Let people make up their own minds.

I spent a lot of time in London over late summer 1981. I met Mark Knopfler and Dire Straits bass player, John Illsley several times in August. We'd go out to dinner with Paul Cummins if they were free. We'd frequently end up back in Paul's apartment in Pimlico, having a few beers and listening to music. A record we all liked at the time was *Pirates* by Rickie Lee Jones. American artists like Todd Rundgren, the Fugs, Frank Zappa and the Mothers of Invention got played a lot too, as did Peter Gabriel and Steve Winwood, and a British band Paul knew some members of – Sniff 'n' the Tears. Mark and John were welcoming and inclusive. I began to feel part of the family.

Freddy Haayen invited Cummins and me to meet him in New York later in the year to discuss a plan for the global rerelease of *Hard Station* on 21/Polydor. The album had come out again worldwide and was receiving a fair bit of attention. Radio stations across the US were playing 'Crazy Dreams' and 'Busted Loose'. All kinds of promo tricks were happening. One Californian radio station, KTIM from Marin, even produced little circular pin-on badges: 'I Heard Paul Brady on KTIM!' The record was favourably reviewed, talked-up and in the end sold respectably well, though it didn't set the charts alight.

At the meeting we also began speculating as to who might produce my next album. I had already written a lot of new material: 'Helpless Heart'; 'Not the Only One'; 'The Great Pretender'; 'Steel Claw'; and from ages back the song that didn't make the *Hard Station* record, 'Trouble Round the Bend'.

Mark Knopfler also happened to be in New York at the time. The Straits album *Love over Gold* had just come out and he was out there doing promo. Cummins and I went to see him in an apartment he was renting overlooking Central Park. He had already heard the demos of my new songs and liked them. Out of the blue I heard him offering to produce my next album. It came as a surprise. I was unprepared for it.

What happened next is hard to explain. I felt a panic attack coming on. One side of me felt giddy but another came up shouting, 'Mark is too strong a personality, he'll dominate you and you'll end up making his record!' It was a very strong feeling and it overcame me. I didn't want to be dominated and I felt viscerally that's what would happen if we worked together. There was also the thought: where was Mark going to get the time to do this? His new album was just released and there would undoubtedly be loads of work and touring ahead. Had he really thought about what this would mean? I didn't want to be rushed into recording an album in double-quick time just to fit in with somebody else's schedule. All these thoughts rattled around. Like at the meeting with Bill Graham, I did my best to hide what was going on inside

and said, 'Thanks Mark, I'll think about it and get back to you.'
The internal disrupter was rubbing his hands in glee.

Cummins and I left. In the corridor, walking to the lift, I looked
at him and said, 'Dunno what came over me there but I don't think
I want to do this.'

Cummins seemed strangely excited and said something like,
'Don't worry. Do what you feel is right,' or words to that effect.

I have to say that this was entirely going on inside me and I had
no basis to assume my fears were justified. Recently, when I asked
Mary about that period, she said she'd thought I was mad and had
made a mistake, though at the time she said nothing. Perhaps I was
mad. But that's what happened. What I was looking for probably
didn't exist – a super-talented recording engineer with a total love
of my songs and loads of creative ideas as to how to record them,
who'd roll over and not be in the least bit upset if I refused to take
any of those ideas on board.

Cummins told Mark a few days later that I didn't want to do
it. In the end I decided to co-produce with an engineer and we
went with the guy who had recorded, among others, the Straits'
new *Love over Gold* album and Bruce Springsteen's *The River*. His
name? Neil Dorfsman. To give him his due, Mark Knopfler in no
way took it personally and never held it against me in the future.
Maybe he was actually relieved!

Back in London, Paul Cummins started looking around for
players to put together a band. He knew the London scene well
and before long I was rehearsing for some shows. I played the Half
Moon Putney, Woolwich Tramshed and the Golden Lion in Ful-
ham with a band including some great local musicians: guitarist
Steve Simpson, Irishman Dave Quinn on bass and drummer Jamie
Lane.

Asgard had set up an Irish tour in October. The band for that
were all based in London with the exception of Dubliner Fran

Breen who had played on *Hard Station* and in all my Irish bands. An eclectic mix of people – Durban Laverde from Argentina on bass, Richard Brunton on electric guitar, Betsy Cook on piano and keyboards – joined me on a fourteen-date tour that took us all over the country from Donegal to Cork, ending up in the National Stadium Dublin.

25

DIGGING DEEP

As if I hadn't enough of 'perfection', just after New Year 1982 I went to London to rehearse for the recording of what became the album *True For You*. After a week in town, we arrived at Ridge Farm Studios in the countryside outside the village of Rusper in West Sussex on the evening of 10 January. With me were a bunch of musicians that Paul Cummins had drawn together. Betsy Cook again, drummer Jamie Lane from Sniff 'n' the Tears, Fermanagh man (now Cornwall resident) Dave Quinn on bass, guitarist Phil Palmer, percussionist Julian Diggle, and recording engineer and co-producer Neil Dorfsman.

It was zero degrees and we trudged through three feet of snow up the drive. The main farmhouse was warm, but the outbuildings, where the studio and accommodation were, maintained authentic Dickensian temperatures. The beds were covered with old-fashioned eiderdowns that weighed a ton. You'd go to bed with your clothes on plus an extra sweater and two pairs of socks. Ice formed on the inside of the windows at night. The studio itself was in a converted barn, a space the size of the tundra, impossible to heat.

After good rehearsals we were, we thought, reasonably well prepared for the recording. But before long I was rediscovering how difficult the process was for me. I always knew what I didn't want, but what I did want was harder to define. I found that Neil, while a great engineer, hadn't a lot to offer me in the production department, so I was thrown back on myself to make decisions all the time. It took several albums before I could get on top of that indecision, that feeling that it was hard to leave a song behind.

Highlights of the first week were 'Not the Only One', 'Steel Claw' and 'Trouble Round the Bend'. The rhythm section of Jamie, Dave and Julian slotted easily into place, and it wasn't long before Phil Palmer was showing his genius. His solo at the end of 'Only One' is still one of the most beautiful things I've ever heard. Betsy was a wizard on the keyboards, Hammond organ, synths and electric piano. Her take on my music was always interesting, quirky and different.

Unbeknown to me, the decision to leave my singing till the end, till all the backing tracks were recorded, would prove to be a mistake. It was common to do that in those days, put the vocal on last, but by the time that all came round (ten days later) I was so stressed and exhausted I couldn't find my voice.

Another error was not to have sung the songs on stage before going into studio. That way I would have realised that the keys I picked were at the very top of my register. No problem, in fact good, when the excitement and adrenalin of live performance is running through you. But, tired and stressed in an empty room with just me, a set of headphones and a mutely expectant Neil Dorfsman, the Beast, as I call the animal that has always powered through me in live performance, didn't turn up on cue. The keys I'd picked were a little too high and it was too late to do anything about it. We weren't going to go back and redo the tracks. I found I was struggling trying to sing 'Steel Claw' and 'Not the Only One', songs I'd normally stroll through. That freaked me for a while.

We carried on. We had to. Peter Veitch added the eerie keyboard that introduces 'The Great Pretender' and the great sax player

Mel Collins came in for that song and 'Let it Happen'. 'Dance the Romance' was a gas to record. Paul Brady doing dance tracks? Yeah! But we were running out of time at Ridge Farm with another act due in.

We packed up, left the cold behind and ended up in Oxford Street's Air Studios where I recorded 'Helpless Heart' on a 9ft Bösendorfer piano, the biggest piano I'd ever sat down at. It's amazing the myriad of challenges that making a recording throws up. Used to playing smaller, unresponsive keyboards all my life, I had developed a touch that was more like a percussionist to make the keys sing. But this baby was a monster, and the slightest touch of my fingers produced this huge sound that frightened the life out of me. Of course, if I had a day or two to play the thing, I'd have been at home in it but, time is money in studio land and that was an unattainable luxury. Yet again I was forced to realise that, in real life, I couldn't always play the music I heard in my head.

I was glad to get to the end of it. It's a strange thing but, while this was the most difficult record I had made to date, three of the songs were covered by other artists later and were extremely successful for me: 'Helpless Heart' (Phil Collins, David Crosby, Maura O'Connell, Johnny Logan); 'Not the Only One' (Bonnie Raitt); and 'Steel Claw' (Tina Turner and Dave Edmunds). I've met several people over the years, whose opinions I normally respect, who swear it's their favourite album of mine.

On 4 March, while I was still in the UK finishing up the album, I signed my first publishing contract with Rondor Music. Damage Management had negotiated the deal. Stuart Hornall from Rondor Music Publishing had fallen in love with *Hard Station* the year before and in particular 'Crazy Dreams'. As part of the agreement, I got, for the time, a good advance against future royalties of £20,000. But in case anyone thinks we splurged or celebrated, we were seriously in the red after a couple of years of inward investment in my new direction. I had a bank overdraft and negative balance of IR£19,000. Ozzie Kilkenny negotiated that one. Ozzie would become more and more important and helpful to me in the years to come. We lodged my new cheque and went out to treat ourselves to a modest dinner and an even more modest bottle of wine.

By mid-1982 the family and I were well settled into our new place in an estate called Meadowvale in the parish of Deansgrange in South County Dublin. We were the last house on the road and by dint of how the overall estate was designed, we luckily had that bit more space than the other houses. That left us fully detached, whereas the others were terraced. The previous owners had built an extension that increased the downstairs area of the house. We were in a cul-de-sac with a decent sized garden and a large public green space just the other side of our end wall where the local children played football and adults jogged or walked their dogs. So, it was a great place for our kids to grow up. Safe on the street too, as there was no through traffic. Pure suburbia.

We started looking for schools. Sarah was three, so with four being the take-in age in Ireland, we needed to work fast. The closest school, in fact, just the other side of the green space beside us, was Kill O'The Grange Church of Ireland school. I hadn't practised Catholicism since I quit boarding school. Mary, also born Catholic, was not a churchgoer either. The school's particular religious orientation was not high on our agenda. Our main issue, helped by my own positive experience of mixed-gender primary education, was that we'd find a school that took boys and girls. Kill O'The Grange did that. Church of Ireland schools in the Republic of Ireland naturally favoured admitting children from the Protestant community. But if there were spaces left after that demand was satisfied, then they were happy to take other children. We were fortunate at the time in that the school had a shortage of new entrants and risked losing a teacher. So, Sarah, although not yet four, was accepted and started the following September. Over the summer our kids started to make many friends on the road. There was also a good-sized front room, actually a converted garage, in our new place. There I set up my home studio and installed the piano from our old house. We felt lucky to have landed on our feet.

I started writing new songs. In the first months came 'Walk the White Line' which to this day I regret not having called 'Back to the Centre'. 'Back to the Centre' was the hook-line at the end of the chorus, whereas 'Walk the White Line' was just a background vocals refrain. 'Back to the Centre' is also what everybody called the song when they'd shout it out at gigs. I even called the album *Back to the Centre*. 'Follow On' came next, then one of my favourite songs, 'Wheel of Heartbreak'. I had just got a new keyboard, a Yamaha DX7, the first of the affordable new digital ones. Digital? What on earth was that? 1s and 0s? Algorithms? For a serial analogue guy like me, this was all very confusing. How can numbers end up as sounds (and even pictures)? But the sounds were exciting. They suggested fresh musical and emotional landscapes, manna to a budding lyricist and composer. 'Wheel of Heartbreak' was the first song I wrote on the DX7. The sonic environment I set that tune in when I recorded it was probably a little grandiose given the words, but I sure had fun driving around in it.

Around that time, I heard from my publisher that the American band Santana had recorded 'Night Hunting Time' from *Hard Station*. It was going to be released on their new album *Shango* that August. My first-ever cover.

Santana was managed by the Bill Graham office. My abortive trip to San Francisco the previous year had borne fruit after all. I was thrilled and my nagging self-doubt was quietened by the knowledge that someone else wanted to sing one of my songs.

On 7 May 1969, Taoiseach (the Irish prime minister) Charles Haughey had introduced a law allowing tax exemptions for painters, sculptors, writers, poets and composers on earnings gained from works of 'cultural merit'. Haughey was a well-educated, urbane and sophisticated man who enjoyed the company of artists of all disciplines. He had a strong attachment to the historical cultural legacy of Ireland. His frequent soirées in his beautiful house on the northern outskirts of Dublin regularly included those from the artistic community. Aware that Irish literary, musical and to a lesser but significant degree, visual culture was highly respected on the world stage, he came up with the idea to make Ireland a recognised cultural haven for artists worldwide and presumably thereby increase the country's visibility and attractiveness to inward investment. After all, we didn't make cars or aeroplanes, produce stunning wines, design internationally coveted clothing. But most had heard of William Butler Yeats, James Joyce, Samuel Beckett, Van Morrison even. Irish folk music too had begun its inexorable global expansion in the shape of the Clancy Brothers and the Dubliners in the early days, soon followed by a plethora of younger groups including my own former band, the Johnstons and Charlie's own favourite, the Fureys.

How all this was meant to translate into fiscal growth was never explained but no one objected at the time. Over the next decades many artists and writers did come from abroad to live in Ireland for extended periods of time: English novelist Frederick Forsyth; Australian Booker Prize winner D.B.C. Pierre; French writer Michel Houellebecq; Scottish author of *Trainspotting* Irvine Welsh; English songwriters Elvis Costello, Joe Elliott (Def Leppard) and Sting; Scottish songwriter Donovan; and many more.

My now accountant and former band member Ozzie Kilkenny called me up during the summer of 1982 and said he was applying to the Irish Revenue on my behalf for the artist's tax exemption status. Ever since Dylan, songwriters' works were increasingly being considered 'works of art'. My album of the previous year had been well received by the critical press and not just from inside Ireland. Songs like 'Nothing but the Same Old Story' and 'Hard Station' had been singled out as having a significant musical and lyrical quality and a particular social and cultural relevance. Ozzie insisted that this made my work as meritorious as any of the previous successful applicants and equally deserving of being favourably considered. I asked, was it not just for foreign writers? The prevailing assumption among us Irish artists at the time was that this was only a legal ploy by Haughey to show himself off as a patron of the arts and that it was only on offer to famous artistes from outside the country. Ozzie said that wasn't the case and he duly applied.

Six months went by with no reply from the authorities in Dublin Castle, where the relevant tax department was situated. Ozzie's office got back to them eventually to be told that it seemed Mr Brady wasn't on the 'list of well-known people'. I was right. This exemption wasn't meant for the 'mere Irish' at all, but solely for big names in the world outside. What was even more ridiculous was the fact that the decisions about what was deserving of cultural merit (or not) were being made by civil servants.

Ozzie, already a force to be reckoned with in the Dublin financial world, 'went bananas' and within a month or so, after some blistering meetings and exchanges, I was included on this exalted list. This development changed my life and the life of my family. I would also say that Ozzie's interventions here directly, or indirectly, led to many more 'mere Irish' artists being granted deserving status within the law.

To be clear, this tax exemption only applied to the proceeds of the individual's *published* works – something which has often caused confusion for those outside the music business. For a novelist, composer, poet or songwriter this meant publishing royalties alone. It didn't mean that a songwriter who was also a recording artist and performer (there are many songwriters who aren't) was free from tax on earnings from their concerts or record sales. Those activities were still taxable at normal rates. These subtleties have often caused confusion in the minds of people outside the music business.

There are two types of copyright in the recording of a song/piece of music. The first is the copyright in the words and music of the song that is owned by the songwriter and controlled by a publisher that the songwriter employs to manage and administer the exploitation of the song. The second is the copyright in a sound recording of that song, that is, the 'record', usually owned by whatever record company has paid for the making of the record, hiring the studio, musicians, technicians. I can be the singer Paul Brady who makes a record containing five songs I wrote myself and five songs by other writers. When that record is bought and paid for, a certain negotiable portion of the net retail price of the whole record is due from the record company to me as singer/named artist (according to the terms of my recording contract). In addition, statutorily under international copyright law, the record company has to pay a further portion of this retail price to the writers of the songs on the record via their publishers.

Paul Brady therefore has two separate revenue streams: firstly, as the singer/named artist on a record he makes (on which earnings he pays Irish tax) and secondly as a songwriter, for which he is paid a royalty on the five songs he wrote (of which earnings are tax exempt up to a ceiling figure, above which Irish tax is also paid). The proceeds of the other five songs go to the other songwriters (who may or not even be Irish residents and whose taxability depends on where they live). It is solely the proceeds of Paul Brady's five songs that are exempt, up to a ceiling, from Irish tax.

For me this can be a significant amount of tax savings if a song written by me ends up on a record by an artist that sells huge quantities. It further engenders serious tax-exempt income if that song is played a lot on radio or TV worldwide or is attached to a big movie soundtrack.

26

RORY GALLAGHER, PHIL LYNOTT AND U2

Early 1982 I had a postcard sent to me, addressed to my booking agent. It was from Rory Gallagher. It had come from Switzerland where he was touring. Rory had just heard *Hard Station* and liking it a lot, decided to send me a card and tell me.

I was blown away. I wasn't close to Rory having only crossed his path a few times while I was in the Kult and he in his band Taste in the mid-1960s. He had since gone to London from where he conquered most of Europe in his comparatively short life, while I had turned left into hardcore Irish folk music for most of the 1970s. So, it was a lovely surprise and gave me a big shot in the arm at the time.

Next thing I heard from my agent that Rory was coming to play Ireland at Punchestown racecourse in July of that year and he'd like to hook up, hang and maybe we'd do something together? As the day approached, I heard that Phil Lynott was set to come too, and Rory asked could we all do something on the gig. It was getting exciting. *Hard Station* might not have topped the charts worldwide, but it had got noticed in (for me) the right quarters.

The day arrived. I drove down to Punchestown. We met backstage and talked about how we were going to do it. We had decided beforehand I'd sing three songs: 'Mercury Blues', a song I suggested from a David Lindley record that Rory was familiar with, and two of my own songs from *Hard Station* that Rory loved, 'Busted Loose' and 'Night Hunting Time'. Phil was going to play bass and not sing. Rory's bassist Gerry McEvoy was happy to take a break.

The place was packed. Rory didn't play Ireland often those days and this visit was a must-see. Phil and I came on in the middle of Rory's set. My adrenaline was sky high. I started 'Mercury Blues' too fast but it settled and found a good groove. I looked around and saw Phil and Rory grinning and having fun, so I relaxed and got into it. By the time we got to 'Busted Loose' we were cruising. It was a really hot day. I was sweating so much onstage that my glasses slipped off and landed in the middle of the monitor speakers at my feet. Not the coolest thing, but I was feeling no pain and having a total blast. The crowd loved it. Somewhere on YouTube there is a bootleg audio recording of the performance. It sounds as exciting as I remember it.

© Colm Henry

On 8 October 1982, I had just returned to the city from the funeral of the legendary uilleann piper, Séamus Ennis in the Naul, North County Dublin. I didn't want to leave. There promised to be one of the sessions of all time somewhere and the only way to join in was to wait around and see what developed. It was a day to be there. But *True For You* was not long out and I had agreed to do a live interview on the Dave Fanning radio show in the late afternoon in Montrose, other side of the city. So, after a pint in the local in Naul, I reluctantly dragged myself off and drove back into town.

I was still slightly buzzing with the alcohol when I arrived at RTÉ (this was when it was legal and socially acceptable to drive after a pint). In the studio I found that I was sharing the 'panel' with Bono and the Edge, from a new Northside band called U2. Fresh from the graveside of Séamus Ennis, those names alone were enough to raise my folkie hackles. I had recently done a TV show where they had also performed, and I wasn't overly impressed. There was a lot of hype in the local music columns about this mystical band who lived together in some mythical village of the mind – Lypton Village it was called. There was something about the whole picture that irritated me. It was as if all that showbiz 'image' bullshit, 'style over content' glam, posing crap that had sickened me in the excessive 1970s and sent me deep into hard-core traditional music had come back again. They had previously given a few interviews that came across to me like they thought they were above the rest of us mere mortals. There was a whiff of 'the saved', the 'we know something you don't' about them which frankly, based on their initial gawky output and posturing, I didn't think was accurate. I thought they were just another 1980s 'haircut' band with more attitude than the facts warranted.

Now, arriving in from the funeral of one of Ireland's musical giants, where I was surrounded by legend after legend in the traditional music world and with the tongue loosened by the pint, I found myself inclined to have a go. Bono was, even then, seriously alpha male and liked to talk. His conversation model was everything that the trad camp eschewed. It all seemed ridiculous and pompous to me at the time and every fibre in my slightly inebriated body was inclined to burst the bubble. I heard myself truculently demanding of them, what was this oul' guff about an imaginary Lypton Village and what did they think they were doing out there anyway? I can't quite remember what was said, but there seemed a slight faltering in Bono's gallop, a chink in the armour. Honour was satisfied. All was right again with the world. The proper order of things had been restored.

The conversation veered off into something else, the interview ended and at the time I never thought much more about it. Dave Fanning, interviewer on the day, remembers it well and on several occasions over the past decades at this or that function, when the drink has been flowing, he has laughed at the memory and congratulated me on my put-down of the Hueys as U2 were often called.

But I knew what really happened that day. I regret it ever since. I was slightly drunk, short-sighted and my alpha-male ego was feeling aggressive; now I believe it precluded any development of a close relationship with a band and a man (Bono) I grew to admire and appreciate. No, I am not proud of being one of those at the time who were mistakenly convinced U2 would never happen.

27

PRIDE AND PROGRESS

March 1983, I get a phone call from my agent Paul Charles. Eric Clapton is coming to play Dublin for three nights in the National Stadium the following month and his manager Roger Forrester has just called up and asked would I support him.

Eric is one of the biggest acts in the world. How had he come to know of me? I find out that it's Albert Lee, another guitarist I admired then playing in Eric's band, who turned him on to *Welcome Here Kind Stranger* and later *Hard Station*. Big surprise. I never expected my folk record to cross musical boundaries in that way. I'm thrilled to bits. Like every other rock-music lover I knew, I loved Eric's playing, his music, his melodic sense, his tone. As a teenager in Strabane back in 1966 I'd bought many of his records from the great *John Mayall & the Bluesbreakers* record to Cream's *Disraeli Gears*. I'm in one way delighted with the honour but in another quite conflicted.

I've spent the previous decade struggling to increase my stature in Ireland. By 1983 I have reached national prominence. An alumnus of the already legendary Planxty, and with the success of the *Andy & Paul* album, *Welcome Here Kind Stranger* and *Hard Station* I'm established as a headlining act. Over the previous couple of years, I've twice headlined at this same venue with my own band. I'm on the way up. Am I now to go back to being the support act ... even if it's to the great Eric Clapton?

This surge of defensive pride is one I recognise; my mother in me, familial, well-meaning perhaps, the unintentional saboteur of dreams. I can almost hear her voice in my head, 'No one's going to put me down! I'm as good as anybody.'

I sleep badly, knowing I must give my answer in the morning. By 6 a.m. I'm awake. I know what I will do. Here is an opportunity on a plate, an acknowledgement of my worth by a talented, globally successful artist. Time to swallow my pride and walk into the unknown. Who knows where it might lead?

Over the three days I do the shows solo. I enjoy it. Once onstage all the previous angst disappears, and instinct takes over. The audience response is warm and enthusiastic. I'm well looked after by Eric's crew. After the shows we repair to Barberstown, a castle in Kildare jointly owned by Eric and his manager, Roger. Mad nights with many of the locals continue till the early hours. There's a piano. Eric and his band are happy to join in the impromptu session. And I was considering not doing this? The fun is only starting.

The morning after the Dublin gigs, 17 April, Roger says they'd like me to continue opening the show on Eric's European tour. It's a fantastic opportunity but it means I only have a couple of days to prepare for it as the next gig is in Bremen, Germany just three days later. Again, it means being away from home for weeks which is going to be hard on Mary and the kids. But it has to be done.

The great thing about being a solo artist on the tour is that I'm looked after as one of the family. Normally a support band has its own crew and transport and has to make its own arrangements regarding travel and accommodation. But my deal is that, in addition to a nice gig fee, Eric's party will look after my hotel, and I'll travel with his band. It's just one extra hotel room and one seat on the tour bus. Easy. Eric's minder Alfie takes me under his wing and makes me feel at home. Even better, on several occasions where the distance between shows is large and there is a day off, Eric rents a Lear jet for the band members, and I'm invited aboard. I'm included on all the communal meals on tour. I stay in the same class of hotel room as the band. It's pure luxury and I take to it like a duck to water. The band (Jamie Oldaker, Duck Dunn, Chris Stainton and Albert Lee) are supportive of me and often stand in the wings to watch my set.

It's a challenge performance-wise. The halls are big, capacity from 8,000 up to 14,000. I'm introduced from the sound desk. I run on and go straight into 'Busted Loose'. For any support act it's tough but for a solo performer it's the hardest. The hall is filling up, people are wandering around looking for their seats and talking among themselves. Nobody knows or cares who you are. Loads are still out in the bar area. You're just this little speck on the stage. You feel so small. I get to play 'Helpless Heart' on Chris Stainton's piano. Then it's 'Nothing but the Same Old Story', 'You Win Again' and 'Crazy Dreams'. I give it all I have and just concentrate on the few hundred rabid music fans clustered at the front, so they can be close to Eric's band when he comes on. Bit by bit, I get their attention and milk it for all it's worth. Sometimes I feel I'm getting nowhere, then I see a friendly face smiling at me, grooving and willing me on. I lock onto that individual and just sing for him or her.

It's a strange thing. Years later I'll meet people on my own tours who'll say the first time they saw me was opening for Eric Clapton and this was when they became fans. It's a mystery, the effect of a performance, the sound of a voice and where it leads. I'll never understand it.

The tour goes on. I become adept at making my thirty minutes count. I change the set list order, the choice of songs, learn a few bits of whatever language they speak and talk a little to the people. By tour's end I'm afraid of nothing and make an earlier and bigger impact with each night. Eric and the band compliment me on the way I'm taking control.

We get a week off in the middle and I go home for a much-needed break with Mary and the kids, but then it's back to business. In the five weeks between 20 April and 23 May we are in Spain, France, Germany, Switzerland, Holland and the UK. The UK leg is at the end. The highlight is the four nights at Hammersmith Odeon. By then I'm accepted as part of the family. Eric regularly invites me into his dressing room after the show with whoever are the guests of the night.

At these London shows, the great and good of British rock royalty turn up backstage. Roger Waters of Pink Floyd and his lady, Sting and Andy Summers, Ian Stewart, the Stones' piano player, Robert Fripp and Adrian Belew on the guest list, many more. It's fun being a fly on the wall, watching how they all relate to Eric, all these massive egos circling around each other, doing the backstage shuffle. They're not quite sure who I am. Probably didn't arrive till the support act was over. I feel privileged to be present. Billy Connolly and Pamela Stephenson come in. Billy says he loved my set. He remembers me from the Johnstons when we were both on Transatlantic Records.

The last night in London is my thirty-sixth birthday. Everyone is being extra nice to me in a kind of structured way. I'm suspicious. After the show Alfie takes me into Eric's room. Patti Boyd is there with Eric. There's a cake. Everyone starts singing 'Happy Birthday' and I blow out the candles. Patti presents me with an old vintage toy – a dog that has a coin in its mouth that ends up in a barrel when you push a button. Cost a packet probably. I'm surprised and touched. I get loads of hugs and feel wildly happy. What a birthday.

We finish up, as Eric always does, with a one-off special gig in Guildford Civic Hall close to his home in Ewhurst, Surrey. That becomes a blast and a half. In Eric's dressing room before the show Phil Collins introduces himself to me. Says he's heard my album at Eric's place, and he likes it. Justin Hayward of the Moody Blues turns up. I'm feeling quite at ease with all these mega-stars now. No longer tongue-tied. Lots of security tonight, promoter Harvey Goldsmith's people, Eric's people and the Civic Hall staff. They're expecting loads of liggers tonight as the band, crew and Eric are all bringing their significant others, wives, girlfriends, mums and dads. I've bought a case of thank you Champers for the crew and distribute it.

I'm doing only twenty minutes tonight. It goes well. Chas 'n' Dave are also supporting and follow me. Then it's Eric and his band followed by a grand finale with Phil Collins and Jimmy Page joining in. Eric comes to me before I go on and asks me not to do 'You Win Again' in my set as he wants me to come up at the end and do it with the whole band and guests.

When the time comes, and I'm called on, I run out and blather a bit to the crowd and I'm off. Everyone lurches in and it's rocking. It's surreal to turn round at one point and nod at Jimmy Page to take the solo. He's all into his Zeppelin shapes and gyrations. He takes off and plays a blinder. Eric grinning encouragement at me. Unbelievable.

I finish and I'm making to leave the stage and Eric grabs me and shouts at me to stay. He heads into 'Irene Goodnight'. Chas 'n' Dave join in. I end up singing the chorus with Eric, the two of us on the same mic. Smiles all round, then suddenly the crew arrive on stage spraying everyone with Silly String. To see Eric and Jimmy trying to solo with their guitars covered in goo is hilarious. Chris Stainton at the keyboards with his head mummified with the stuff. Mad. I'm in heaven for a few minutes fronting a line-up of the greatest players on the planet. Lucky boy, me. Everyone heads to a chaotic backstage with more security than concert participants. Then it's talk of the after-show party at Eric's place.

The last gig at Guildford followed by a party at the house is by now a tradition with Eric. It's a tight affair. I've three guests from London, Steve Brickle, his date Beverly plus Sarah Schwartz (the girlfriend of Dave Stewart, a concert sound engineer I've worked with who is off working with Dire Straits). I bump into Patti Boyd and she says straight up, 'You can't bring three people with you, Paul; just your *girlfriend*.'

Sarah and I laugh.

When Patti moves off, Sarah says, 'I'll drive.'

It's a no-brainer. Now all we've got to do is find the place.

Roger says to follow him in his big silver Mercedes. Harvey Goldsmith tails behind us. Off we go. Miles and miles, little country lanes, Beatrix Potter signposts and village greens. This is the hidden England, Home Counties, stockbroker belt, money screaming from every gilded gate. I'm winding down now, helped by a little end-of-tour toke.

We're there. Torches flashing in the dark, Alfie and Nigel directing traffic, checking occupants. No crashers getting in here in a hurry. It reminds me for a split second of the Brit Army night-time checkpoints in Northern Ireland (only for a split second).

We park along the driveway. Rhododendrons? Hard to see. On we go, walking up the drive till we come to the house. It's fantastic! All lit up, many people already there. It looks like something out of Hollywood. Wish I could see it in daylight.

In we go. Extensive hallway with a long table filled with cold delicacies. Kitchen off to the right. It's a catered job and very professional too. Oodles of wine. Hot bites too – prunes wrapped in bacon and skewered. Nice. Barbecued kebabs, dips, salads, strawberries half-dipped in molten chocolate. Talk to Harvey

Goldsmith for a while in a corner. He's quite affable and friendly. Lots of people here I don't know. Local neighbours? Relatives? There's Eric's mum, a little old Cockney dear talking to Alfie. Sarah's disappeared off talking to someone. The din, the raucous laughter and loud talking becomes too much. I decide to wander. Find this beautiful sitting-room at the bottom end of the house. No one there. Exquisite furniture, paintings. PIANO. Sneak over to it. Everyone else is at the other end of the house. Start to play. Getting the feel. Nice instrument. My 'Road to the Promised Land' starts coming and I'm singing. The toke has really hit in now and I'm in my sweet spot. Did someone come in? Vaguely aware of a presence. Keep on playing. Suddenly this acoustic gut-string guitar starts. Plays with me ... Good! ... knows the chords ... who is it? ... Never mind. Keep on going. Don't want to break this spell. Finish off, turn around. Good God. It's Eric. Don't know what to say, so start singing again. It's the only thing I can do. 'Dancer in the Fire'. It's good. I'm on form. Solo comes. He's got it, plays the syncopation bit, amazing. I move over to where he's sitting and pick up a Martin acoustic that's lying on a chair. We keep on playing. 'Bobby Magee' for God's sake, where did that come out of? I'm singing away. People now starting to drift in. Staring. I'm totally into it. Eric is beaming. Takes a solo. People not sure what to make of this. Eric's mum asks me to sing 'When Irish Eyes Are Smiling'. It's a hard one to get out of. I plead drunkenness. Thankfully the notion recedes. Eric's mum is about to leave. Eric asks me to sing 'The Lakes of Pontchartrain'. Big panic looking for a capo. Eventually one is produced. Sing it. Eric plays. He's right there. Knows it inside out. I nod to him to take a solo. Beautiful. Asks me to sing 'Amerikay'. I figure out it's 'I Am a Youth Inclined to Ramble' from *Welcome Here Kind Stranger*. He knows that too. Plays along. God, I'm flying now and fuelled with the drink.

Things start petering out. Eric is tired, as am I. It's been a very long day. Breaking up now. Goodbyes in the kitchen. Squeezes and hugs from Patti. Find Sarah and off we go. She has to pick Dave up at the airport at 11 a.m. I fall asleep in the car. Don't know how she manages it, but she drops me off at my gaff in London at around 5 a.m. This is one of the best nights of my life.

Only now do I look back and realise how lucky I was to be invited to step up to this other level. Indeed, the tour was just the beginning of a long friendship with Eric. The following year he played beautiful soulful guitar on the recording of 'Deep in Your Heart' for my album *Back to the Centre*. Later I played tin whistle on 'Broken Hearted' for his album *Pilgrim*. At several of my London gigs over the next decades he arrived unannounced and came to say hello after the show. At my Lifetime Achievement celebration in Dublin's National Concert Hall in November 2015 he sent a congratulatory video of him and Ed Sheeran singing my song 'I Will Be There' from my *Spirits Colliding* album. To my surprise that duet recording then appeared on his 2016 album *I Still Do*.

Discussions progressed between Roger and Damage Management about whether I would continue to open for Eric on his upcoming US tour. Word was that the US promoter was unhappy with a 'solo act' as support. The venues were large and he wanted a band. At the same time, we were discussing the idea of a Paul Brady band tour of the US later in the year with Freddy Haayen of 21/Polydor – my new label.

None of this came about. In the case of the Eric tour, this was understandable. However, the toing and froing with Freddy was just another episode in the sorry saga of major label politics – something I encountered often enough in the next decade.

The ridiculous thing from a current perspective is that while Freddy is jostling with his major label backers through a succession of musical chairs-like 'ins and outs' of executives, he's hmmming and hawwwing about whether it would make more sense for Paul Brady to make a video rather than tour America – the video age is upon us; MTV is the new God.

It's scarcely credible now but the cost of making a video in those days was in the same ballpark as supporting a three-week live band tour of the US. Videos cost tens of thousands of pounds for an average one from an up-and-coming director. The big ones, say Michael Jackson's 'Thriller', released later that year, had an obscene budget of $900,000. Nowadays, people make respectable videos on their phones and GoPros.

In the end, Freddy fell out with someone higher up the food chain and Paul Brady became just some collateral damage in the ongoing 'Lanigan's Ball' of the record business. *True For You*, my follow up to *Hard Station*, died in America and I can't even remember now if it was released or not.

I was beginning to blank out the behind-the-scenes record business machinations – it was totally beyond my control. Besides, a new development was taking place. Dire Straits asked me to open for their upcoming tour of Europe, 12 June–23 July, starting in Holland and moving on through France, Spain, Italy and Yugoslavia (as was). Obviously, my success as support act on the Clapton tour had an influence. But it was further evidence that Mark Knopfler hadn't taken my decision to spurn his offer to produce *True For You* personally. There would be many more instances of his magnanimity and generosity in the years to come.

Things weren't plain sailing for me management-wise, however. With hindsight it's obvious, though it wasn't to me at the time – I was very much second fiddle. Dire Straits were the main concern, and their considerations were paramount.

When they were on tour, as they had been since late-1982, in the UK, Australia, New Zealand, Japan, Germany and Austria, my manager Paul was on the road with them all the time as tour manager. That was a full-time job and one that was demanding on him, emotionally and time-wise. I was only getting to speak with him once or maybe twice a week, often at crazy times and on bad lines. That was not enough with all the stuff that was going on with me, the record company and touring-wise.

Okay, of course this was understandable, given that Dire Straits were the biggest band in the world at the time. But I felt alone at the time with the waning relationship with 21/Polydor alongside the discussions about 'touring the US' versus 'making a video'.

As the 1980s progressed, this happened again and again but I learned to put up with it. It wasn't going to change. The advantages of being attached to Damage Management outweighed the disadvantages, didn't they? Beneficial things came my way that otherwise wouldn't. But as my own difficulties with my recording career continued through the 1980s, I couldn't help feeling, fair or not, that some of this was because management wasn't being proactive enough in my direction. This was unfortunate as it caused me (and probably Paul Cummins too) great pain.

28

TOURING WITH DIRE STRAITS

On 12 June 1983 I joined the Dire Straits tour of Europe as support act. They had been touring the *Love Over Gold* album since the previous November, so they were a well-oiled unit. All were very welcoming of me right away. I relaxed into things.

The band was extended for this tour with the addition of Hal Lindes on guitar and Tommy Mandel from New York on keyboards. It was the *Love Over Gold* album tour. Mel Collins on sax also featured on some songs every night. By now, having experienced three weeks on the road with Eric, I was match fit and knew what I had to do.

We spent the week in Holland and the following weekend we hit Paris. We played four nights in the huge Palais des Sports and the following week Mary joined me for a few days; a big change from the time she visited me in New York when I didn't have the money for a postage stamp.

The tour was a well-run affair, no Lear jets mind, but comfortable buses and high-end hotels. We ate well too. On days off there'd be a communal feast with the best of food and wine. On gig days the backstage catering was first class.

Dire Straits' audiences adored them. I spent nights side stage after my own set figuring out the basis for this attraction. There was, of course, the brilliant musicianship of all in the band, Mark's guitar and Alan Clarke's keyboards the centrepieces. But in those days Mark was no singer. (Though in recent years he has developed a lot in the vocal department with a warm and pleasant voice.) He talked his way through the songs in a Dylanesque monotone. The musicality of it all, apart from his stunning guitar solos, was in the lush sonic landscapes they created, providing a vast emotion-laden backdrop to what were well-written stories about things and people the audiences could immediately relate to. The rhythm section was a large part of it too, with John Illsley and Terry Williams solidly underpinning it all. The whole affair was a masterful and rare confluence, at the right time and in the right place, of many influences from blues, country, rock, the European chanson tradition and classic pop. It went on to make them, for a number of years, the biggest rock band in the world. I was lucky to share in all that.

When we left Zagreb in mid-June we had a few days off before the Straits' Irish visit. I flew home for a well-earned rest, as much as was possible with a six- and four-year-old in the house.

At the weekend I retraced my steps of the previous year, rejoining the band for their only Irish gig at Punchestown Racecourse. The tour finished the following week in London with a night in the Dominion theatre and two in the Hammersmith Odeon.

Just as I thought it was time to go back to my own world, an opportunity arose that was too good to pass up. Just two months after I had realigned myself to being Paul Brady headline act, I got a call from Paul Charles to say that the Everly Brothers, who were on a worldwide reunion tour after many years apart, were big fans of mine, especially my recording of 'The Lakes of Pontchartrain'. Don Everly asked would I open for them in London's Royal Albert Hall later that month and sing that song? Memories of Gregory Donaghy and me, aged ten, singing 'Wake up Little Suzie' and playing our guitars from Santa at our school term-end party came flooding back. The first record I ever had as a thirteen-year-old, a 78-rpm shellac disc from my uncle Tommy's record shop in Lisnaskea, was their 1960 smash hit 'Cathy's Clown'. I had always been a fan of their close harmonies and musical heritage. Now they're fans of mine? I was thrilled to be asked. I said yes.

On the day I wasn't entirely on my own. In the Everlys' band of the night was my old friend, guitarist extraordinaire Albert Lee, who had first brought my music to the attention of Eric Clapton, indeed that very same song that the Everlys now wanted to hear. It was great to hook up with him again just months after we parted company at the end of Eric's April tour. I am indebted to Albert. His passing my recordings around touched so many bases in the mid-1980s. That interest and generosity of spirit on his part is still making the most unexpected and magical things happen for me. Thanks Albert.

Later in the year I went to Germany to promote *True For You* with my band in Hamburg and played the famous German TV show *Rockpalast*. The band personnel had fundamentally changed by now. As I came up to the end of the Dire Straits tour in early summer and was planning to do more of my own shows, I'd had a conversation with their drummer, Welshman Terry Williams. I told him I was looking around for musicians. Terry and I had got on well on the tour. He was a fan of my more 'rock-' type songs like 'Busted Loose' and songs from my current record, 'Steel Claw'. I in turn had long loved his earlier incarnations with Dave Edmunds, Nick Lowe and Billy Bremner in the 1970s band Rockpile, and his playing with Dire Straits was superb. I asked him did he know any drummers that might suit me. He asked when I was planning on touring. I told him it would be later in the year. His immediate response was, 'I'll do it!'

I was surprised. Of course, the Straits big world tour was over, and Terry was free for the foreseeable future. What a turn-up. I was so excited and immediately went looking to fill out the band. Manager Paul Cummins approached guitarist Phil Palmer who had played on *True For You*. Phil was delighted to play. The final line up was Mickey Feat on bass, late of David Gilmour's band (and later Van Morrison) plus Hammond organ and keyboard player Kenny Craddock formerly with Gerry Rafferty's band and soon to be musical director for Van. What a line up.

We drove to Hamburg from London. Early December, bitterly cold. We finally got there and did a pretty good gig to a responsive crowd. More than thirty years later a video of that concert *Paul Brady Live at Rockpalast* came out on DVD as part of an archival series of the iconic German TV music show that lasted several decades.

In January 1984, I worked on the soundtrack Mark Knopfler was writing for *Cal*, a film about the current Troubles in Northern Ireland adapted from the book by Bernard McLaverty. Knowing of my long involvement in Irish traditional music, Mark wanted me to bring that dimension to the project.

I added mandolin and tin whistle to several of the tracks. The ensuing combination of ethnic and contemporary sounds made for a record that was well received and continues to be played today. On a recent 2019 weekend vacation trip to Catania in Sicily, it was a pleasant surprise to hear it as the background music on the top deck of the hop-on-hop-off city tourist bus! The film, directed by Irishman Pat O'Connor, starring Helen Mirren and John Lynch, went on to win several awards including Best Actress for Helen Mirren at the Cannes Film Festival of that year.

Over the 1980s, Mark continued his love of Irish folk music and, mixed with his Geordie heritage, it became a strong influence and a big part of his self-expression in later recordings. In the mid-1990s he approached me about a project that led to his first solo album *Golden Heart* after Dire Straits was dissolved. Wanting to have an Irish flavour on several of the songs, he asked me to source a band of great Irish players for an upcoming recording session in Dublin. I contacted my old friends and colleagues: Seán Keane, fiddler with the Chieftains, Dónal Lunny on bouzouki, piper Liam Óg O'Flynn and accordion player Máirtín O'Connor. They were all interested in being involved. We contributed to three tracks on that record: 'Darling Pretty'; 'A Night in Summer Long Ago'; and 'Done with Bonaparte'.

Mark had been generous with opportunities for me once again.

29

TINA TURNER

Late in 1983 another opportunity appeared on my horizon. The great American soul singer, Tina Turner, finally left her husband Ike after years of abuse. She had been taken over for management by Australian, Roger Davies. Roger also managed Olivia Newton-John, a major global star at the time.

Ed Bicknell, the other half of my management team, was friendly with Roger and one night out to dinner together, they were talking about his new signing. Roger asked Ed if he had access to any songs that Tina might record for her first record under his care. Mark Knopfler had just written a new song 'Private Dancer' that Roger had already heard and liked but he needed more. Ed happened to have a copy of my current album *True For You* in his briefcase and he passed it over, suggesting that the song 'Steel Claw' might suit Tina.

Next day, Roger called Ed. Tina loved the song and planned to record it. The only thing they wanted was to change the lyrical setting of the song from Europe to the US (there was a mention of the Spanish tourist resort Benidorm in my version, and they felt no one in America would get that). I agreed. I was thrilled when I heard the news, not because I expected it would mean great sales; Tina, at the time, was at the bottom of a long downhill slide in popularity after the bad years with Ike and a career confined to the Chitlin' Circuit in America. I was delighted because I was a fan of her voice and performance. Back in the 1960s, in Rockhouse, I had sung several of her songs and had sadly watched her star wane.

A few weeks later Ed sent me a cassette of her recording of 'Steel Claw'. I loved it. It was ballsy and real. She'd got right into the spirit of the song and sang it like she loved it. I spread the news among a few close musician friends, and then kind of put it on the back-burner, well used to that old music business mantra 'hurry up and wait'.

A week later I got a phone call from management to say that, after listening to the whole new Tina recordings closely, Roger decided it was all too old-fashioned stylistically- and production-wise. They were binning the entire project and starting again with a different producer and songs.

I was devastated. I thought her recording of my song was great. Over time, however, I just put it down to sod's law – if shit can happen, it probably will. This was the 1980s. Everyone was looking for 'new' sounds.

I got on with things. I had an Irish tour to do, and I'd just had a spurt of writing that resulted in a bunch of new songs. 'Wheel of Heartbreak', 'Walk the White Line', 'Deep in Your Heart', 'Airwaves' and 'To Be the One' came out in quick succession over the next few months. I'd also done some more work on a yet-unfinished song called 'The Island'. Plenty going on.

I had put the whole thing behind me when along comes another phone call. The Tina camp are indeed binning the first recordings, finding new songs and producers *but* they're keeping just *one* song from the previous batch. And that song is? 'Steel Claw'. Unbelievable. Further, they had amassed some seriously commercial songs like Graham Lyle and Terry Britten's 'What's Love Got to Do with It', Ann Peebles' 'I Can't Stand the Rain', Al

Green's 'Let's Stay Together' and of course the title track, Mark's 'Private Dancer'.

The re-recording of my song was produced by John Carter, known just as Carter. I was disappointed with the new version. It was too fast, too frantic and the spirit of the song kind of got lost. I preferred the tempo of the original and thought Tina's performance was more real and engaging. But I knew it was a massively lucky break to get onto the record.

The album was released in May 1984 and was an international success, topping the charts all over the world and going on to sell more than twenty million copies. It changed my life. I will always be grateful to Ed Bicknell for his intervention. It wasn't the last time he waved a magic wand in my direction.

In April that year, as I was doing loads of gigs with a band, we decided to record a live album in London. The Half Moon in Putney on the south side of the Thames was a long-established and very popular music venue. I had played there several times and stuffed the place, so it seemed sensible to do the recording there.

Nowadays you can record an entire orchestra into ProTools on a laptop via a simple USB cable from a digital live sound desk. In the old days you had to hire a truck (like the Rolling Stones mobile studio) that would drive up to the gig and park outside. On board would be a couple of engineers and two huge reel-to-reel analogue tape machines with cables and wires snaking into the venue and onto the stage. It was a big deal and very expensive. Normally for a live album you'd record two or three gigs to have a few options of each song. But not being flush, we went with just one.

We had a full house that night too and with striking originality called the record 'Full Moon'. Made up of a mixture of songs from both *Hard Station* and *True For You* the album has a raw and energetic feel to it as the songs found shapes different from the original studio versions in the hands of some of the best players on the scene at the time.

The band was the same one that played the Rockpalast in Hamburg the year before except that Ian Maidman had replaced Mickey Feat on bass. Ian and I would go on to form a close friendship and productive musical relationship for many years to come.

30

BOB DYLAN BECKONS

There were lots of phone calls bearing good tidings that summer of 1984. Next came one from my booking agent Paul Charles to say Bob Dylan was coming to London's Wembley Stadium on 7 July for a gig as part of his European tour and wanted to meet me. I was flabbergasted. What was all that about?

I flew over to London and after the usual fuss collecting AAA passes, I went backstage into a stockade of hi-end caravans. I wandered around for a bit, chatted to Eric Clapton who was due to get up and do a spot with Bob; we hadn't crossed paths since the after-tour party at his place a year previously. Van Morrison and Carlos Santana were hanging too, both also due to make an onstage appearance.

I already knew former Stones guitarist Mick Taylor (now in Dylan's band) and we chatted some. I told him Bob had asked to meet me and he took me over to his caravan. I was shown in on my own and Bob and I met and shook hands. He thanked me for coming, asked me to sit down and said he really liked the way I played and sang 'The Lakes of Pontchartrain'. Could I show him how I did it?

I asked him to pass me his guitar. I told him I used an unorthodox 'open' tuning. I proceeded to tune it that way and started to play. He watched carefully for a while and asked could he try it. We swapped the guitar between us a few times as he tried to learn it. He'd give a stab at something and ask was that right and, seeing he hadn't quite got it, I found myself lifting his fingers on and off the guitar neck and putting them back in the right spots. He was laughing and enjoying himself. After about ten minutes of this, Chrissie Hynde wandered in unannounced with a bawling child in her arms and that was kind of that. What a day. I never expected that morning I'd be shifting Bob Dylan's fingers around the fret board of his guitar that afternoon.

He then said he was playing Slane Castle in Ireland the next day, and asked would I be there? I said I would. So, we parted company. I flew home that night after the gig and went to bed in a daze.

Next day Mary and I drove the thirty miles to Slane where we had backstage passes sorted; quite who'd sorted them I can't recall, though it was probably through Paul Charles, who was also at the Slane gig.

We were wandering around in the backstage area when a large tour bus arrived. I figured it was the Dylan party as he wasn't there yet. Checking it out, I saw someone waving out the window in my direction. I looked closer. It was Dylan. I turned round and looked behind me (as you do) to see if he was waving at someone else! But when I turned round again, he was definitely waving at me and gesturing that I should come over to the bus. I wandered over. He got out and immediately minders started directing him to his caravan. He motioned me to join him. Mary stayed back with some friends.

I went with him to his caravan and we started talking again about Pontchartrain. We had hardly begun however when, incredibly, a very drunk, totally out of it, woman journalist came clattering in the open door of his caravan and started stumbling around and blithering at us. How she got that close is a mystery, but the upshot of it was that Dylan freaked, got up and made to leave the caravan with me following him. That put an end to our second meeting. I still am amazed at how 'your wan' got through all the security.

31

BACK TO THE CENTRE

In February 1985 I went to England to record the songs that went on to be the album *Back to the Centre*. Having done two albums with musicians in studio right from the start and remembering the pressure to make decisions too fast (I only had these guys for a short while) I thought I'd start the next album on my own and bring in other players as I needed them.

I decided to go back with producer Hugh Murphy whom I'd worked with on *Hard Station*. Hugh and his wife Betsy Cook, who had so memorably played on that album, were living in rural Buckinghamshire where Hugh had a recording studio attached to the house, Birdland. The deal was that I stay there as well.

It was a bitterly cold winter and we were snowed in for most of the time I was there. What I didn't realise before I arrived was that Hugh and Betsy were on the verge of a separation. This situation cast a pall on proceedings. We three were thrown together all day, every day. It became claustrophobic. The tension was exacerbated by Betsy's not being initially involved in the recording, difficult, since she was around most of the time. I needed space to formulate my own thoughts and ideas. Betsy's natural exuberance and can-do personality tended to see her jump in from the beginning and want to take over. Nothing wrong with that in principle, but it just didn't suit me and I'd made that clear in advance (time enough to involve her when the song structures were solid and established).

I started recording three songs there: 'Wheel of Heartbreak'; 'Deep in your Heart'; and 'To Be the One'. But after a couple of weeks of building arrangements around machine click tracks and keyboard parts like Lego blocks, I felt I was getting nowhere. It was the 1980s. We were all obsessed with the new generation of keyboards and midi sequencers. What I still failed to realise was that my instinctive talent was as a live performer. The best way to record my songs was to get a performance from me *unfettered* by some rhythmic structure outside of myself. It could be a solo per- formance with me playing guitar or piano, or one with a band that followed the rhythm I created as I played. The essential thing was that every addition to the musical arrangement should be overlaid on my original performance rather than building a finished struc- ture and trying to fit me in at the end. What we were doing was dismantling what didn't need to be dismantled and then trying to put it together again brick by brick just so we could 'control' the eventual result. Everyone in the recording world was doing that at the time. But for me it was mad.

In the end I pulled the plug on Birdland. Following consulta- tions with manager Paul Cummins and the then record company, Polygram, I moved to Utopia Studios in London to finish the record. Wanting to get back to a more 'live' way of recording now, I brought in Ian Maidman as co-producer.

Since recording the live album *Full Moon* the previous year, I had formed a close bond with Ian. After a try-out overdubbing Swedish drummer Ole Romo on two songs started at Birdland, 'Wheel of Heartbreak' and 'Deep in Your Heart', we decided to use the musicians from my touring band the previous year, Phil Palmer, Kenny Craddock and Liam Genockey, and we recorded 'Follow On' and 'The Homes of Donegal'.

'The Homes' was a song that was always around as I grew up. Written around 1955 by Donegal man, Seán McBride, it was originally recorded in 1960 by Bridie Gallagher, affectionately known as the Girl from Donegal. It became a huge hit in Ireland. Bridie went on to have a long and successful career worldwide, in her day selling out the Royal Albert Hall, Sydney Opera House and New York's Carnegie Hall.

I always loved the song. It reminded me of being a happy kid on summer holidays in Bundoran. One day in late 1984, home alone in Dublin, I found myself pacing up and down with my guitar, singing it and throwing it around feel-wise. Bridie's original recording was an 'old-time waltz' but I found myself rocking it up in a kind of slow, bluesy shuffle. I started to get excited about the possibilities.

When I later introduced it to the band in studio they loved it and it soon took the shape that led to the album version. With backing vocals from Loudon Wainwright, Phil Saatchi and Ian, and with me playing the tin whistle, we were all transported to the North-West coast of Ireland for the afternoon. This recording became more popular than I ever imagined. To this day it's hard to get away with not singing it whenever I play to Irish people the world over.

'Walk the White Line' and 'The Soulbeat' were next to come from a quick session in Surrey Sound Studios. Then it was back to Utopia for 'Airwaves' featuring a young Larry Mullen from U2 on drums. Larry and I had shared the stage on a charity gig in Dublin a few weeks earlier and had talked about doing something together. Probably unaware of my earlier on-air grumble with his band mates Bono and Edge, he came up trumps and now turned up to play on a track. It was exciting to hear him enjoying himself in the driving seat.

We had almost come to the end of recording when I thought of asking Eric Clapton to play on 'Deep in Your Heart'. There was an aspect to his playing that reminded me of Gheorghe Zamfir, the Romanian master of the pan pipes. Eric was a fan of his. We had discussed the similarities between Romanian flute music and the blues back when I was touring with him in 1983. Sometimes in an extended solo onstage, Eric's blues improvisation sounded to me like it was from that same East European place and not just the Mississippi Delta, the universality of music perfectly displayed. The melody and chords of 'Deep in Your Heart' had a similar Zamfir loneliness to them that I felt sure Eric would get. He loved it. We booked an afternoon session in the Townhouse, in London's Shepherd's Bush, and he blew us all away with his contribution; a gorgeous instrumental colour that totally suited the mood of the song. Later Mitt Gamon added a soulful harmonica that rounded off the recording. There was just one more mountain to climb before the record was complete – a new song called 'The Island'.

32

'THE ISLAND'

'The Island' had been germinating in me since the Maze hunger strikes back in 1981. By then the situation in the North had deteriorated further. With the death of Bobby Sands and nine other prisoners over the summer, the IRA campaign of violence had increased. People were becoming more and more polarised. I wanted to write about what was happening but felt conflicted and nothing would come out.

Since the first IRA campaign of the mid-1950s I'd had this ambivalence about the justifiability of violence in achieving political ends. My own forebears had suffered the disadvantages resulting from the discriminatory practices of a system in Northern Ireland that favoured a dominant unionist population determined not to give an inch. My family on both sides had a long tradition of wanting to see the end of British misrule in Ireland. But as the violence spiralled out of control in the 1980s and showed no signs of achieving anything but wholesale misery, I began to lose faith in the old arguments and to see the cult of death as a perversion. Violence begot more violence and became an end in itself. In an extension to my long-held belief that society evolves from the inside out, that is, from the way one single person changes in how they relate to another, I saw the power for change that ordinary people, or an ordinary couple for example, could wield by simply loving each other.

The musical community in the South was polarised too, with many in the traditional music camp supportive of the Provisional IRA campaign. It almost came with the territory. With so much of Ireland's historical troubles mirrored in songs, some great songs too, it was inevitable that sentiments would rub off and influence how people looked at the contemporary scene. But I felt that many in the Republic were seeing things in a way which was too black and white. It was easy for people, some of whom had never even been in Northern Ireland, let alone been brought up there, to have strong opinions about what to do and how to do it.

I might have changed direction musically in the recent past, but I still had friends and deep contacts within folk music in Ireland. There was a lot of discussion, and many assumptions were made. One day I got a phone call from a well-known musician whom I admired and had often played with, asking me would I perform at an upcoming concert to support the hunger strikers. But I felt that in the South, support for the hunger strikers generally meant support for the IRA campaign of violence too. There was no middle ground, it seemed. I said no. The silence at the other end of the phone told its own story. In the months to come, many friends and comrades drifted apart, never really to trust each other again. It was a sad, sad time.

I'd had the music of 'The Island' for a long time, many years. I had been toying with a tune on the piano that kept coming back to me again and again. Something about my father's love of singing those old Mexican Spanish songs, 'La Paloma' and 'La Golondrina', had nestled in me ever since I used to accompany him in my early teens in Donegal.

Out of me now came this big blowsy piano melody like a slowed down tango. I loved it and, despite its exotic provenance, I knew it was going to be the perfect musical vehicle for what I wanted to say about what was happening in my country.

But it was proving really difficult to finish the words. I'd tried for ages and kept binning my attempts. Every time I wrote a line, the other conflicting voice inside me would say, 'But, Paul, you can't say that ... are you forgetting this ... and that ... and what about the other?' My existential confusion and natural inclination to see all sides in an argument was overwhelming. What did I actually really want to say and how did I want to say it?

I still was nervous about playing the piano in studio and so I'd taught the arrangement I'd written to Kenny Craddock, a beautifully assured and sensitive player. We decided to record it live with me on headphones in an isolated vocal booth so that there'd be no leakage of any other instrument into my vocal mic. I'd sing what lyrics I'd written to date and was happy with, and come back to it later when I'd finished them.

We went at it and as I heard Kenny's beautiful rendition developing in my headphones I was overcome with an emotion so strong I almost couldn't sing. When Phil Palmer began his acoustic guitar solo, I just didn't know how to go on. I sang some makey-upey words on the last verse so Kenny had a structure to continue playing to and suddenly it was over. It was a profound moment. Everyone in studio knew that something special was happening. But I needed to finish it.

I asked them to run the recording again and as I sang once more over Kenny's piano I heard myself singing words that didn't yet exist 'and teach them dying will lead us into glory'. Where did that come from? Some instinct then told me to just get out of the way, keep singing and let what wanted to come through, come through. I was exhausted afterwards. I couldn't listen to it for half an hour. Then, when I went back to it and heard the words 'these young boys dying in the ditches is just what being free is all about' I was shocked. This was not what I believed or wanted to say ... till I heard the irony in my voice and realised the character in the song was expressing my own ambivalence, my sense of powerlessness and resignation in a perfect way. I felt giddy, ecstatic and freed from a burden. More than thirty years later, this is still one of my most loved recordings.

Popular as 'The Island' became, it was initially controversial and rubbed many people up the wrong way. I was, on several occasions, verbally abused in public, mostly in pubs where alcohol had loosened the tongue. I was physically assaulted in a South Dublin music venue by one of our freedom fighters from the North who accused me of 'turning my back on my own'. My one-time colleague Christy Moore wrote, recorded and released an enigmatic and lyrically rambling song entitled 'Tyrone Boys' containing a thinly veiled reference to me in the chorus 'Away from the island where Tyrone boys dream of loving on the strand', entirely missing the point of my song. My island was never Ireland but a mythical island of the heart and mind.

The iconic stature of the song these days was contributed to by Dolores Keane's great recording of it three years later on her album *Lion in a Cage*. Her stunning performance which totally 'got' the song, brought it to a whole other audience for which I'm very grateful.

33

PRIMITIVE DANCE

On the back of his proven talents as leader of Dire Straits, plus the fact that he had written the title track of Tina Turner's global smash album *Private Dancer*, Mark Knopfler was chosen to be one of the producers on Tina Turner's follow-up album. I was surprised, pleasantly, when I got the phone call from him to ask had I any songs for the new Tina album.

I was in London in early 1986 staying with my friends Peter and Iris Pimm in Shepherd's Bush when the call came. The story was that Tina was in town. The time to throw my hat into the ring was right now, this morning.

I had recently written a new song 'Paradise Is Here' and done a rough home demo of it, but I didn't have it with me. Of course, this was before the digital age. You didn't just call up and ask the engineer to email an MP3. If you didn't have a cassette, you didn't have it.

What I *did* have with me, however, and I can't remember why, was a cassette of the backing track of this demo with no voice. That was pretty useless. I thought about it for a minute and knew what I needed to do. It was mid-morning on a bright sunny day. The Pimm house was empty except for me. I turned on their house sound system and put my cassette into their player. Like every self-respecting pro musician at the time, I had my own portable cassette recorder with me. After a couple of attempts to try and get a reasonable balance through my headphones, I played the backing track over the house speakers really loud and sang along with it, recording the combination into the tiny on-board mic of my own cassette recorder. The result worked in a crude but strangely effective way. The cassette signal compression rendered the sound almost like a radio track and while it was rough, it had a kick and certain charm to it.

I called my management and told them the situation, that I was happy to present the song myself if Tina was happy to see me. Word came back that she was in residence in Holland Park and was happy for me to come round.

Holland Park was relatively close to where I was staying in Ellerslie Road, right opposite the QPR football ground. I took a cab into the leafy opulence of a totally different world of mansions behind high walls and gates with cameras, announced myself to the voice on the intercom, and was shown in to a large reception room, 'Wait there please. Tina will be here shortly.'

About five minutes later the door opened. This smallish lady wearing a dressing gown and slippers came in. At first I didn't recognise her without the trademark wig and high heels. Her hair was short and naturally frizzy and she wore no make up.

While I was still getting over my initial surprise, she greeted me quietly and warmly and after a few moments of small talk, she said, 'I hear you have something to play me?'

I started to make excuses that what she was going to hear was not a professional demo, but was in fact a very rough thing altogether.

'Carry on,' she said.

I took out my cassette player and played the recording. It sounded agonisingly awful to me over the tiny speaker. I couldn't wait for it to be over. When it finished, she asked to hear it again. Strangely it began to sound better the second time around.

'I identify with the lyric,' she said, 'and I like the melody. Leave it with me?'

After what felt like a long wait, I heard that 'Paradise Is Here' was going to be recorded by Tina in Air Studios, above Oxford Street, produced by Mark Knopfler. I later attended the overdubs session and it sank in that, thanks to Mark, I had another Tina Turner cover. The album was *Break Every Rule*, released September 1986.

In late 1986 I began recording for the album *Primitive Dance* in Dublin's Westland Studios. Recording engineer was Tim Martin. I asked Ian to produce. Moving on from *Back to the Centre*, where he came in at the latter stages to take over production, I felt really close to him musically; he seemed to understand instinctively where I was at as a writer and singer and wouldn't always just be listening to the songs as to whether or not they'd primarily be hits. Not everyone agreed with my choice. The record company were 'iffy' and my publisher Stuart Hornall wanted the record to sound more commercial.

I knew I was moving away from the daytime radio sound. My antipathy to the pressure of being commercial was getting stronger. I didn't want that atmosphere to infect the recording. This was partly the reason I decided to record in Ireland again for the first time since *Hard Station* in 1981. It was harder for the record company to 'drop in'.

The band, mostly put together by Ian, included: Tim Goldsmith on drums; Ian on bass, piano and electric guitar; a new discovery on keyboards, Steve Fletcher, who would go on to be my favourite player right up until the present day; Mick Bolton on Hammond organ; and Geoffrey Richardson on a kaleidoscope of instruments from electric guitar and viola to ukulele and kalimba. Maestro uilleann piper, Davey Spillane, popped in one day to wail and rail on my new recording of 'Eat the Peach', a song I'd written with Dónal Lunny, first recorded the previous year as the title song to an Irish film of the same name about two out-of-work brothers in the Irish midlands who decided to build a motorcycle wall of death as a hoped-for money spinner. Finally, Bill Whelan arrived with the cream of Dublin's horn players to play his arrangements of 'Don't Start Knocking' and 'The Soul Commotion'.

We went over to London in January 1987 to add more ingredients, beautiful background vocals, sweet harmonica, Mark Knopfler topping it off with a gorgeous performance on nylon strung guitar on 'The Game of Love', a song about how hard it is to make love really work.

Then it was back to Dublin in February to finish off. That led to one of the outstanding highlights of the record as Clannad's Moya Brennan came in to duet with me on 'The Awakening' and 'The Game of Love'.

'The Awakening' came out of a growing interest I had in meditation following on from a long-term build up of stress over the previous couple of years. I wasn't meditating in a religious sense – I had long ago given up on organised religion – but by employing a simple physical technique of slowing my consciousness down and listening to whatever came up from the depths when I shut the world out. It's amazing how, by removing myself from my own reality and just letting life happen without me, even just for half an hour, I feel a part of something else, something vast. It has helped me to stop blaming myself for where I am and where I'm not and gradually accepting life as it is. This relaxation technique was crucial in all that I aspired to do from then on and still is a major defence mechanism for me against the curved balls life throws.

As I got deeper into 'The Awakening', I knew I had made a connection with what I took to be my spirit, and I felt I now had somewhere to go, a presence inside I could totally trust when I was under pressure. Moya's ethereal voice seemed to complement this celebration of the power of the cosmos perfectly.

'Paradise Is Here' is another song that came out of my interest in spirituality. Now that Tina Turner's version had been released I wanted to record my own. I'd been reading *Beyond Violence* by the mystic, Krishnamurti. One of his beliefs was that there was no such thing as the future. There were just events, the moment, the present. Whatever one is doing *right now* was in fact the so-called 'future'. We were the creators *of*, rather than created *by*, events. In hindsight it was perhaps a stretch to apply this theory to a romantic relationship but at the time it made perfect sense to me.

> *Paradise is here, it's time to stop your crying*
> *The future is this moment and not some place out there*
> *Tonight I need your love, don't talk about tomorrow*

The chorus of 'Steal Your Heart Away' was melodically a variant of an old Irish traditional tune from the North of Ireland called 'The Verdant Braes of Screen'. The music of the verse came out of my love for Stevie Wonder and black soul music in general. Lyrically it was for anyone who felt locked out of a relationship. Running the gamut of every emotion from plaintive entreaty to downright rage, it sure was exciting to record.

The groove and tune for 'The Soul Commotion' came to me during a band soundcheck somewhere in England. My testament to the redemptive and transformative power of music, it's one that I still enjoy singing and playing. The album came out mid-1987. Straight away I went into tour mode. On the personal front, a highlight of the year was a joint birthday party with my long-time friend and colleague from Rockhouse back in the mid-1960s, Ozzie Kilkenny. Mine was on 19 May and his was on 23 May. We were both forty. Ozzie had moved into the stratosphere in the interim. Now a mega-successful accountant to the stars including U2, Bob Geldof and a host of others, he was fond of the grand gesture. As we lounged at his beautiful home in South Dublin's Killiney, a shout went up from the assembled guests. We all looked skywards to see a small single-engined aeroplane towing a massive banner over the city with the legend 'Ozzie Kilkenny and Paul Brady are 40 today'. Mad. As it happened, Oz owned the plane too.

34

'PARADISE IS HERE'?

Saturday, 30 May 1987, I'm at the Tina Turner concert at the RDS Showgrounds in Dublin, standing up at the sound desk with Roger Davies her manager. Already I've had the success of my song 'Steel Claw' on her big comeback album of 1983, *Private Dancer*, and she's just covered another song of mine 'Paradise Is Here' on her current album *Break Every Rule*. So, I'm kind of automatically extended an invite to her gig.

It's a beautiful late spring day. Tina is at the peak of her career and the place is jammed. At one point during the concert, Roger turns to me and says, 'D'ya wanna get up with Tina?'

Total surprise. I know she's singing 'Paradise' in her set. That's what he must be talking about. I'm freaked at the suggestion. This is off the cuff. There's been no rehearsal and I'm sure Tina knows nothing about it. Plus I'm out for the day, expecting to relax and enjoy myself, slightly high as I sometimes am at gigs to get into the music.

'Will she be okay with this?'

'No problem!' Roger says, 'Let's get up there'.

We get down from the sound desk and make our way slowly through the crowd. People start to recognise me, and I'm being pulled here and there by punters wanting to say hello. Thankfully it's before the upsurge of the 'selfie'.

Tina's on the last verse of 'Let's Stay Together'. She looks nothing like the petite woman I saw in her dressing gown and slippers in Holland Park. Now, in nine-inch heels, extravagant wig and body-con dress, she's in full command of the stage. A goddess, whose party I'm about to gate-crash. Too late to stop now.

The song ends. Tina catches sight of Roger stage-side; he points at me and does a 'holding the mic' gesture. Next song on the set list is 'Paradise'. She kinda looks slightly confused. None of this has been planned. I feel a push in my back and I'm out there walking towards her.

Instinct takes over. By now the crowd sees the dynamic has changed and begin to notice me. First cheers that become a roar. One of our own out there with Tina! I'm there beside her and she's definitely panicky, but already gathering herself. She doesn't know me that well. Last time I saw her was in her living room playing my crappy demo. Now we're standing in front of 30,000 people, all waiting for the duet of a lifetime. We've never performed together. The band is bemused.

'What are we gonna do?' I hear her say.

Quick as a flash I go, 'You take the first verse, I'll take the second and we'll both sing the chorus.'

Already the band has started the intro. I feel an adrenaline rush and I know this is going to be great. It is. Off it goes. We're singing our hearts out. The band is into it. She relaxes when I start to sing. She has her arm around my shoulder in the choruses and the crowd is loving it. I'm in heaven. A totally surreal moment in what, to me right then, seems like a totally surreal career.

Later, I'm talking to an English music biz ligger backstage, and he says, 'Hey, man, that roar when you got up. We're finking it was Bruce fahking Springsteen or somebody!'

Nothing like an Irish crowd digging one of our own.

Later still, we're all at dinner in Bray. I begin to feel paranoid.

© Paul Bell

Mary and I are across the table from Tina and it all seems awkward. Maybe she didn't enjoy being put upon like that? It was a strange thing for Roger Davies to do. Anything could've happened. If I had been Tina, and that intervention had been foisted on me, I might have been pissed off, no matter how well things went. But Tina was upset because, after our duet, there was an incident in the front of the crowd where a girl was hurt in a crush and things got messy. The girl was fine, but it really got to Tina and spoiled her enjoyment of the gig overall. Shame that one of the most magical days in my life ended on a slightly paranoid note. Note to self: 'That's the oul' weed, Paul. Bites you in the ass when you least expect it!'

As 1987 came to an end I began to feel that confining myself to playing live with a band was closing off a number of avenues in the live-performance arena. Glastonbury, Roskilde in Denmark and the Cambridge Folk Festival were great, and we did an enjoyable month-long tour of UK finishing up in London's Hammersmith Odeon, as it was then called. An Irish tour in September saw my home profile continuing to grow too. But it was costly to keep together and I found myself with long periods of time where economics dictated that I wasn't playing live. I missed being on stage. I also wanted to get back to writing, which was hard to do while the band dynamic dominated my creative energy.

I'd had a couple of nice experiences playing solo which gave me a fresh taste for it. In March I performed solo, singing 'The Island' at the London Palladium as part of a concert to benefit Amnesty International called The Secret Policeman's Ball. To share the stage with Joan Armatrading, Chet Atkins, Peter Gabriel, Bob Geldof, Jools Holland, Nigel Kennedy, Mark Knopfler, Yousso N'Dour, Lou Reed, Loudon Wainwright and Jackson Browne was a singular honour. The icing on the cake was to play guitar as a duo with Jackson Browne on his song 'El Salvador'.

My newfound delight at the success and comparative ease of my once-again solo status sent me out on the road for a twenty-five date nationwide Irish tour in February and March of 1988 that included the Belfast Opera House and five nights in Dublin's Olympia Theatre. Audiences flocked to the shows – clear evidence that a lot of my followers preferred me solo.

Then that August, I was asked at short notice to headline the Rose of Tralee festival in Kerry, filling in for Christy Moore who'd had to cancel because of illness. After a dodgy start to the set-up proceedings, which included borrowing a grand piano from a big house on the Lee estuary and, to the amazement of passers-by, transporting it to the marquee on a forklift truck, I enjoyed the gig and gleaned more evidence that my strength as a solo performer had not diminished.

I decided to put the band on ice for the next year or so and concentrate on writing and performing solo.

That same year, I also took up scuba diving. It had been years
since diving off the board at Roguey or swimming in Shene Pool
with my dad and uncle Gerry, but now my mind moved more and
more to those memories, moments of leisure and enjoyment in Bundoran as a kid. That summer 1988 I passed my open water tests
and became a two-star diver; I could travel anywhere in the world
and dive. Over the next couple of decades after many dives in Irish
waters I found myself underwater in Egypt, Hawaii, Australia's
Barrier Reef, Malta, Cozumel in Mexico, Cape Verde, The Azores,
Gran Canaria, Grand Cayman and Antigua in the Caribbean.

35

TRICK OR TREAT

Despite my increasingly jaundiced attitude to the record business, a new development in 1989 drew me back in again. Though signed at the time to Phonogram International (under the PolyGram conglomerate) another in-house label of theirs, Fontana, started to show interest in me. Londoner David Bates, who was at its helm, was a fan of mine and was friendly with my management. After some meetings where he suggested putting me together with a close friend of his, Gary Katz, long-time producer of Steely Dan, I got excited again.

I'd been a Steely Dan fan forever, even while I was in the Johnstons back in 1972. In New York back then I had heard their first hits 'Do It Again' and 'Reelin' in the Years' and bought their first album *Can't Buy a Thrill* when David Palmer was still in the band. This was music I loved. My own song 'Dancer in the Fire' from *Hard Station* owed a lot to their music.

Bates suggested I send Gary Katz some home demos of recent songs. I sent him 'Nobody Knows', 'Blue World', 'Trick or Treat' and 'Don't Keep Pretending'. Katz got back straight away. He really liked them. When he started talking about recording in LA and putting together a band including the drummer Jeff Porcaro, keyboard wizard David Paich, electric guitarist Mike Landau, and Freddie Washington on bass, I was hooked. Paich and Porcaro were also members of another favourite band of mine, the iconic Toto. These guys were the cream of American contemporary music. I didn't give much thought to the commercial possibilities of this pairing yet, but I realised it was a musical opportunity to work with the best. I wanted it. David Bates agreed the budget. We were all set.

It took a while to pull together, busy as all these players were, but finally on 10 November 1989, I flew to LA to begin recording what became the album *Trick or Treat*. Gary Katz flew in from New York, engineer Wayne Yurgelun from Nashville and we all stayed at a cool hotel in Studio City, each of us with our own rental cars. Mad really, and typical of the excesses of the record business then. We'd all meet for breakfast then each drive in our own car to the same destination and back again that night. Environmentally crazy by today's standards. LA was still shrouded in smog in those days. Of course, this was all going on the recording budget tab – my money eventually.

We started in the famous A&M recording studio in Hollywood and after a week moved out to the Village Recorder in Santa Monica. In the beginning it was hard to pull together musically. Most of the songs' rhythm tracks I had programmed at home on an Atari computer using Steinberg Pro24 software and a Yamaha RX-5 drum machine and we were using these programmes as a basis over which to record the real drums and bass. This was in the early days of digital 'sequencing' and the software I had was primitive. Subtle feels like 'swing' and 'shuffle' were impossible to replicate on the machines of the day, at least the ones I could afford at home. Jeff Porcaro found it particularly hard and chomped at the bit for some time until I wisely let him have his head and things started to come together.

Freddie Washington was due a couple of days later, so the great bassist Jimmy Johnson started us off. We began with 'Soul Child', a song I wrote in a dark period six months earlier, then an impassioned call out to a temporarily lost inner guiding voice. When the track was cut with Porcaro on drums and Jimmy stomping through the undergrowth, it sounded more like a celebration of some indomitable beast. Mike Landau's soaring guitar would have called any wandering spirit home.

'You and I' followed, a song I earlier wrote in anger at the insulting treatment of Garret FitzGerald, the Irish Taoiseach (our prime minister) and the people of Northern Ireland by the then UK Prime Minister, Margaret Thatcher, in her notorious 'Out. Out. Out.' press conference, 19 November 1984, 'Out' being her response to the three possible options to bring politics forward in our country:

A unified Ireland was one solution. That is out. A second solution was confederation of two states. That is out. A third solution was joint authority. That is out.

The cheek of her. A few years later, Cliff Richard expressed a desire to cover the song. For one reason or another it never came about, but it certainly had nothing to do with Maggie's outburst being the inspiration. I never told him.

'Blue World', now with Freddie on bass, was my two-finger riposte to the increasing demands from the extremist political classes in Ireland that the role of artists, songwriters and poets should be to mirror and support their take on how to resolve the Northern Ireland problem. No thank you.

'Solid Love' was one I wrote for my then eleven-year-old daughter Sarah who was suffering school bullying. It ended up with a kind of Toto feel to it, unsurprisingly.

'Don't Keep Pretending' was a tough one to crack. About an imagined clandestine love affair destined never to develop the way the singer wants, the demo had a hybrid feel, the melody almost 'country' but rhythmically with a kind of Latin pop groove. A mad combination but ending up strangely legitimate. Years later at home I picked up an acoustic guitar one day and began to sing it again. What came out was an old-fashioned country waltz. Maybe that's what it was all along. I'm forever amazed at the secret mysteries of music. I feel sometimes like a song is a specific individual and that I have a wardrobe full of wildly differing outfits to clothe it. Why not put a country tune to a Latin groove?

The writing of 'Nobody Knows' was a strange experience. The picture in my mind, before a word appeared, was of the Beatles performing 'Get Back' on the roof of the Apple building back in January 1969. At the top of their fame with Savile Row's lunchtime workforce gawking admiringly from below, it was an outrageously confident gesture that symbolised their power – seductive to any aspiring artist. My imagination drifted to another scenario where a mythical artist 'Johnny' was on the same rooftop, the only difference being that now there was no one watching from below. Was the lyric my subconscious at work dealing a reluctant farewell to the idea of being accepted as a massive rock/pop icon worldwide?

> Johnny's got high expectations
> He's gonna rise
> Everyone knows that Johnny is ready
> He's ready to fly
> Up on the rooftop he turns to the crowd
> No one is waiting
> No one is there

I knew the song would be about the precarious nature of fame and success, how we may have our life scripted out on paper only to find it adds up to nothing like the plan. Why? Nobody knows. As I wrote, Elvis came to mind. I fought it for a while. 'You can't use Elvis, Paul.' I had a disdain for songwriters that dropped famous names or peppered their songs with words like 'radio', appealing to the DJ's ego and thereby getting a play. But the ignominious way the great Elvis departed this world had stopped us all in our tracks. I knew, that as an example of the unlikeliness of events, it was one of the most prominently lodged in my generation's collective memory. He had everything any of us could want. Where did it all go wrong?

Next along came the words 'Nobody knows why Rubin had to fight.' What was all that about? The wrongful murder conviction of the boxer Rubin Carter that Dylan had also written about in his song 'Hurricane'? I played with it for a while, but it took me no further. Then Rubin turned into Ruby. What? Ruby who? Maybe Jack Ruby? I ran with that. Despite countless books and documentaries about the Kennedy assassination, we're all still in the dark as to exactly why Jack Ruby shot Lee Harvey Oswald. What was he hoping to hide?

I stuck with Jack. It's strange, but I've often found as a lyricist that the first thing that comes up from the depths is a vowel sound, in this case 'oo'. It's like the muse already knows the word has the 'oo' sound before it gives it up as an actual word. In this case 'Ruby' took precedence and the song was complete. Bringing it back to Elvis, I asked, 'Who could see heaven and not want to stay?' Is universal adoration and acceptance heaven? I didn't believe that anymore.

Looking back now, although a lot of the music on *Trick or Treat* is up-beat in tempo, the themes of the record are of loss, loneliness, vulnerability and the struggle towards acceptance, sadness even.

On a day off recording, I'd been speaking on the phone to my dear friend and colleague Maura O'Connell in Nashville. She suggested I call up LA bassist James 'Hutch' Hutchinson who, she said, liked my music and was a lover of, and an authority on, Irish music in general. Hutch was then (and still is) one of the great American bass players; at the time he was in Bonnie Raitt's band. We spoke and he invited me to come to a concert in the Santa Monica Civic Auditorium that Friday where Bonnie Raitt, Jackson Browne, Ry Cooder and David Lindley were playing at a benefit. Thanks to Hutch, that was where I met Bonnie for the first time. I had been a fan of her work since my time with the Johnstons in New York in 1972 and had bought her record *Give it Up* back then. Following her upward trajectory through the 1970s and as her star temporarily waned in the 1980s, I was in love with her voice and music. She had recently made a comeback with a record, *Nick of Time*, and was at the beginning of what became an even bigger spell of nationwide success.

We got on really well. She was familiar with my previous recorded output and was a fan, particularly of 'Not the Only One' from my 1983 *True For You* album, saying she planned to record it. Remembering how I'd felt after messing up that recording by picking too high a key for my voice, this was some 'get out of jail' card. A rush of self-absolution overcame me. I found myself asking her would she duet with me on the song 'Trick or Treat' that we were in the process of recording right then. We made a date for her to come to the studio a couple of days later.

On one of the nights back in my hotel after a day in studio, I found myself in the bar having a nightcap to level off my adrenalin. Apart from a couple of Japanese businessmen it was just me, solitary, at the bar. The bartender was a woman in her late twenties, her back to us mostly as she dusted liquor bottles and tidied things up. I was feeling loquacious and tried to engage her in conversation with my usual killer line, 'How long have you worked here?' Immediately her response was, 'Oh, I don't really work here, just a temp waiting for my screenplay to be accepted.'

How silly of me. Here I am in LA. Everyone is either in the movie business or trying to be in it. I went to my room and started messing around on an acoustic guitar.

> *You dust the bottles on the bar counter*
> *You're writing screenplays on the side*

Ten minutes later a song had taken shape. It was raw but fully there. Next day Bonnie was due in studio to duet with me on 'Trick or Treat'. We had a ball singing it and afterwards, while we were decompressing in the studio, she asked had I any other songs. She was getting ready to record again and was looking for material.

'Well,' I hesitated, 'I actually wrote one last night ...'

'Last night?' She was taken aback. 'Can I hear it?'

'Well, there's no recording of it yet.'

'You could sing it.'

I picked up the guitar. I could hear the harmony on the chorus

> *These things we do to keep the flame burning*
> *And write our fire in the sky*

When I was finished, she asked what it was called.

'Luck of the Draw,' I said.

'Sounds like an album title,' she ventured. And so it became.

The following year, Bonnie's new album *Luck of the Draw* appeared including my new song and 'Not the Only One'. It went on to be her biggest-selling album worldwide, winning three Grammys and reaching the No. 2 slot in the US Billboard charts.

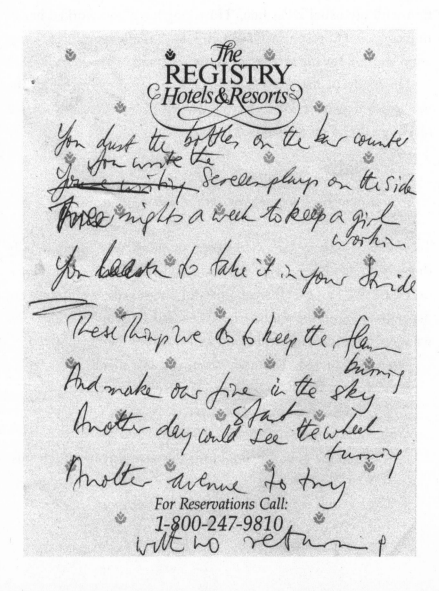

'Not the Only One', released as a single, also reached No. 2 in the Adult Contemporary charts. My luck as a songwriter was holding.

Gary Katz told me we were winding up in LA and moving east to Bearsville Studio in Woodstock NY. It was all the same to me, all new, and I didn't really care where we recorded so long as the band came too, which they did.

The weather was a change. We went from endless Californian sunshine, where each morning I'd have a swim in the outdoor hotel pool before studio, to knee-deep snow and freezing temperatures.

In Bearsville, we took on 'Can't Stop Wanting You', and some more guitar work on 'Blue World' from Mike Landau. I recorded 'Love Goes On' with difficulty. Once more I was back saddled with a piano arrangement I'd written that I found a challenge to play. The more I tried, the worse it got. David Paich helped out by offering to play a supportive keyboard part along with me.

I started listening to him, forgot what I was playing myself, and suddenly it was done. Stop thinking, Paul. Just play.

I went home for Christmas 1989. It was great but unreal to be back in domesticity after all the momentous stuff I'd been going through over the past few weeks. Sarah and Colm were twelve and ten now and growing up fast. Mary was holding the reins and handling the by now frequent periods of single parenthood better than might have been expected.

There was always that little dance as we all tried to find space for me on my return. Stressed and travel weary, I wasn't above expecting more attention from Mary than was reasonable in the circumstances. But in time the tensions dissipated and 'normality' returned. My parents came down from the North as usual and, in spite of the added pressure that sometimes came with these visits, Christmas and New Year passed off well.

In early January 1990 I went back to the US, this time to New York City to finish recording and begin mixing the album. One of the final additions saw Elliott Randall, he of the iconic guitar solo on Steely Dan's 'Reeling in the Years', coming in to lay down a beautiful solo on the title track 'Trick or Treat'.

The recording completed, Grammy-winning engineer Elliot Scheiner was drafted in to mix. That's when the trouble started. As had happened with every album to date, I entered my customary period of temporary insanity. Having been immersed for a couple of months in every tiny detail of the arrangements of ten songs, I ended up unable to see the wood for the trees. I'd have this aural picture as to how each track should sound, but it was never going to be possible, no matter who was mixing the music, that I was going to be happy with everything I heard. Worse, it wasn't long before I realised that my opinion didn't count for much. It turned out that David Bates, the record company supremo, also had definite opinions as to how 'my' record should sound. Unlike my previous records where, for better or worse, I was the final arbiter, it was clear that he considered this 'his' record. I had a major fight on my hands.

Bates had this thing about the lead vocal on all the tracks being too loud. He wanted it buried in the overall mix with the result that the listener had to struggle to hear the words. He said this was what daytime 'radio' wanted. This was total anathema to me. To me the vocal was everything. I'd always loved the sound of the older records where the voices of Elvis, Frank Sinatra, Nat King Cole, Ray Charles were the loudest thing in the mix. Coming, too, from a decade in Irish folk where the story was paramount and the words 'the thing', I couldn't accept this. But Bates was not giving in. Unknown to me, he'd call up producer Gary Katz in New York and told him to go back and remix this and that according to how he heard it.

Other engineers were brought in to do different mixes. Neil Dorfsman, my nemesis from the *True For You* album was one. That was a path I did not want to retrace. Bruce Lamcov another. Wayne

Yurgelun, the original recording engineer, ended up mixing a couple of the tracks. I was extremely unhappy and becoming more and more disillusioned with the record business and my place within it.

Whatever about my own difficulties with perspective at the point of delivering a record that was going to be there forever, it did not suit me that anyone else should make that final decision on what was my own life's work. Though I didn't see it then, this conflict would contribute to the ending of my relationship with 'major' record labels.

The record was critically well received on both sides of the Atlantic with 'Soul Child' and 'Nobody Knows' getting most initial attention while the title track, the duet with Bonnie Raitt, one of their biggest stars at the time, got a fair degree of airplay in the US – I performed it on the David Letterman TV show. I did an NY photo shoot with the 'celebrated' Deborah Feingold. She was the rudest, most arrogant photographer I ever worked with. She treated me like I was a piece of shit on her shoe.

In January I made a video for 'Soul Child' in London. I did promotional trips to the UK, Holland, Germany, Italy, the US and Canada in the first half of 1991 talking to endless people, many of whom hadn't even bothered to read the bio or press release before I got there.

In March and April, I played Ireland and UK with my band which (at the time) included all Irish musicians: Robbie Brennan on drums; Tony Molloy bass; Anto Drennan on electric guitar; and Trevor Knight and Mick Bolton on keyboards. The Irish tour included Cork City Hall on a strange night when there was a power outage that delayed the gig by more than an hour. Only problem was I had a film crew from the UK ready to shoot the show. In the end it all worked out with a raucous crowd well-watered by an extra hour in the pub. The long-form video, called *Echoes and Extracts* was released later that year.

In July I toured Canada and the US with the same band. The gigs were great, but the enormity of the task ahead revealed itself, particularly in the US. I did a 'showcase' solo gig in a place called the Blue Willow in downtown Manhattan. Alain Levy (head of Universal worldwide, then called Polygram) was there, along with the top brass of the New York office including the NY Mercury CEO Mike Bone and a plethora of breathless young record company types. I did my short set to muted response, everyone looking at the big cheeses to gauge how to respond.

I went to dinner afterwards with producer Gary Katz whose comment in response to my query about how I'd done still reverberates in my head. He thought for a while then said, 'Right now, Paulie, they're trying to decide whether to even put you in for the race.'

I mean, for God's sake, I was forty-four years old and trying to break through the US pop business. They must've thought I was ancient.

A couple of weeks later my main supporter in the US label, Mike Bone, was fired. That was basically that. In the record business, if you're fired it's the kiss of death for the acts you signed too. Countless artists suffered from the 'revolving door' attitude to record company executives. *Trick or Treat* was gently led back to the stables.

36

SONGS AND CRAZY DREAMS

I continued to remove myself from the music business outside Ireland. Fortunately, my success with others recording my songs paid the bills. We started having family holidays in Portugal, France and Spain and I spent time diving. I became addicted to the underwater world.

I allowed myself to enjoy one-off projects that didn't play into the US scene. In early 1992 I went to Norway to guest on a TV programme hosted by a Norwegian star of the time, Lynni Treekrem. Lynni was a popular folk-rock artist with her own TV series. A huge fan of my songs, she eventually recorded four of them: 'The Island', 'Road to the Promised Land', 'Follow on' and 'Steel Claw', all with lyrics in Norwegian that she herself translated.

At home my horizons were expanding too. What if I had space to build a studio of my own? One that was close but separate to the house? I thought of all the studios I'd recorded in, the clock dictating the creative process. I thought of all the times away from Mary and the kids. What if the studio was part of the day-to-day life?

We spotted a place in Sandyford on the south-eastern edge of the city in sight of the Dublin mountains.

It was an unusual house, built on an acre (a lot in Dublin) but with an unconventional design. With lots of glass and archways, the builder must've been fantasising they were in Spain. I loved it. Though it felt like we were in the country, it was still only a twenty-minute drive to the city centre. The size of the garden meant that I could build a separate studio in time.

The record company now thought that, after a decade as a songwriter with five albums of my own songs, it was a good time to put together a compilation, a mini 'best of'. David Bates suggested that it would be an added attraction if all the songs were remixed.

Remixing was the mantra of the times. Granted the recording industry technically had changed a lot since the 1970s and there were all sorts of new production techniques on offer. (Some would say it had changed negatively. The early days of the new 'digital' recording in the 1980s produced a sound many thought brittle and lacking in warmth.) A London-based mixing engineer, Simon Vinestock, was found and the one thing Bates insisted on was that I stay away from the studio and let him get on with it – my new approach of trying to distance myself meant I didn't object.

I was rewarded for that decision. The project turned out well. We called the record *Songs and Crazy Dreams* and, surprisingly to me, it turned out to be one of my most popular and successful records, bringing me a whole new audience previously unfamiliar with my work. My existing fans too reacted very well to these fresh new versions of songs they knew well.

All this change didn't stop me from performing. I was very busy in 1992 with a three-week nationwide UK band tour in May and a solo trip to East Coast, US in November. Shows in London's Dominion Theatre, Belfast Opera House and Dublin's National Stadium followed. My collaborations with other artists too brought some lovely times this year, onstage and off. A highlight was duetting with Bonnie Raitt at Wembley Stadium on my song 'Not the Only One'. We'd come a long way from that moment in LA where she told me she was ready to record again.

It was nice to hook up again with Eric Clapton at the Wembley gig (Clapton was co-headliner with Elton John on the day) and to hang with Curtis Stigers, who's been a good friend and sometime collaborator ever since.

The weekend was capped by being Bonnie's date at a lunch party in Elton's palatial Windsor pad the day after the gig. I sometimes joke in certain company that I was once in Elton John's bedroom. But it is in fact true. In the middle of pre-lunch drinks Elton and Bonnie were talking about a famous painter they both knew. Elton had a couple of his paintings; would we like to see them? We followed him upstairs to a massive room with a bed the size of a tennis court and there on the wall were the said works of art. Truth can be stranger than fiction.

37

SPIRITS COLLIDING

My profile in Ireland was high again after the success of *Songs and Crazy Dreams*. In April 1993 I won Best Male Irish Artist at the Irish Recorded Music Association (IRMA) awards. It showed how commercially successful the album was. As an organisation of the major record labels, the IRMAs didn't give out awards unless they made money.

I was spending my time writing. I had written a lot of new songs by mid-1993 and as *Songs and Crazy Dreams* had run its course, I felt the urge to make another studio album. This time, however, I decided to make it in Ireland with my own crew and musicians. Much as I admired Gary Katz, I'd had enough of the big budget album. I now wanted to record at my own pace and closer to home. David Bates, realising too that spending zillions on a record didn't always translate into massive sales, acquiesced, and told me to get on with it.

I contacted Shea Fitzgerald, Dublin musician, singer and song-writer, who had a good grasp of the techniques of recording and asked him to come on board as co-producer. Shea and I had worked together before and had co-written the song 'The Soulbeat' on my *Back to the Centre* album back in 1985.

We decided to get out of Dublin and booked a couple of weeks at Sulán Studio in Ballyvourney, County Cork. The record developed organically. My idea was to play a lot of the songs on acoustic guitar first then overlay percussion as required.

I recorded 'I Want You to Want Me' and 'You're the One' with just me on guitar and Jimmy Higgins on bodhrán. The recordings felt great. I also had good demos of 'Trust in You' and 'Marriage Made in Hollywood' – a song I'd written with writer, actor and then husband of Bonnie Raitt, Michael O'Keefe.

A new direction developed when I heard that Béla Fleck, Roy Wooten and his brother Victor from the US band, the Flecktones, were coming to Ireland on their way to play at the Montreux Jazz festival in Switzerland. I'd known them all for several years and loved the way they played. I asked them would they do a little detour for a couple of days via Ballyvourney to play on the record. They were happy to oblige and with their arrival, the record really began to take shape.

We put the final shapes on 'Trust in You', 'Marriage', 'You're the One' and 'Just in Time'. I went back to the original home demo of 'The World Is What You Make It' and we started building on that too. Everything was feeling just right. I was delighted. I'd gambled on asking them to come.

We finished up in Ballyvourney as the Flecktones moved on and after a break of a week or so we restarted in Bow Lane studio in Dublin. There we recorded 'Help Me to Believe', 'I Will Be There' and 'After the Party's Over' and started the final vocal and instrumental overdubs. I had completed 'Love Made a Promise' except for some backing voices. A new up and coming family group, The Corrs, came in to sing on 'Just in Time' and that was that as far as the recording went.

The final song on the record, 'Beautiful World', had a strange genesis. It began in Nashville in the early 1990s at a party in the house of John Prine and his Irish partner, Fiona. There was music and singing all evening. The mood was celebratory. At one point

John approached me with his guitar, played a series of notes, (about ten in total) and with a grin said, 'What can you do with that?'

'Play it again?'

He did. In my best casting director's voice I said, 'Can you leave it with me?'

We laughed, and in minutes had forgotten the song.

Six months later, back home, I had just bid farewell to a bunch of friends we'd had round for dinner and as I often did at happy times, I sat down at the keyboard. From nowhere, the tune John had played me at the party back in Nashville came back into my head and now was suggesting itself as the first line of a verse.

Imbued with his spirit, I started to develop the melody and began to write lyrics in what I imagined was the style of John Prine. In about ten minutes I had not only a completed song, but a good recording of it, just me on keyboard.

Next morning, I sent it to John saying, 'Does this remind you of anything?'

In a few days he called me and said, 'Hey, Paulie, here I was, having not written a song all summer and along comes a song I wrote I didn't even have to write!'

We laughed our heads off.

The fact is John was indeed co-writer of the song since without his series of notes to me all those months ago it would never have existed. There are a hundred ways to co-write a song. That's part of the magic of it.

As it happened, that late-night after-dinner recording of 'Beautiful World' was what ended up as the last track on *Spirits Colliding*. John recorded his own take of it on his album *Lucky 13*.

Mixing the record brought on the usual disagreements with record company boss, David Bates. Shea and I had mixed in Bow Lane, but Bates didn't like the result. Eventually the album was mixed in London by Mick Glossop. He did a great job.

Spirits Colliding came out in April 1995 with 'The World Is What You Make It' as the first single. The song was chosen as the theme song of *Faith in the Future*, a popular UK ITV sitcom at the time that ran all over the English-speaking world from 1995–8, which drew more attention to the album.

They say a manager/artist relationship is like a marriage. Mine with Paul Cummins had its ups and downs. In the beginning all was great. Paul is a very generous and soulful man and he opened up his world to me. All of this was new and exciting. He was very personable and easily developed good relations with my record company, publisher and booking agent. From his years in tour managing all sorts of bands, he knew loads of musicians in the London area and in the first couple of years, in effect, he put together the various bands I worked with. He let me stay at his place when I'd come to London, which was often and for extended periods in those days. I remember fondly the many nights Mark Knopfler and John Illsley (Straits' bass guitarist) joined us socially. We'd all end up at Cummins' place in Pimlico listening to the latest records and talking into the night. A happy time. But things changed.

It's ridiculous now I look back, but I was insecure at the time, feeling rejection from the area of the music business I was aimed at, constantly needing support. Things improved between us when the Straits stopped touring and we soldiered on, but by the early 1990s I felt we were going round in circles. I think Paul was feeling the same. He worked hard for me and must have been as frustrated as I was at the lack of forward movement within the UK mainstream record business and radio. He had his own issues and problems to deal with too, in his personal life and with the management company. Things started deteriorating in a significant way in late 1994 ending up with us separating in 1995. It was painful in the extreme, particularly as it coincided with the end of my relationship with the record company who'd finally decided Paul Brady was not UK pop chart material.

We were an extremely complex pairing. We'd worked together for almost fourteen years. Many great things happened through my association with him that wouldn't have happened otherwise. I'm grateful for that and there's no ill will. The real reason we separated is probably connected to what I've mentioned earlier, that all through our association I was being aimed at a marketplace I was unsuited for and it eventually became too hard on both of us.

38

THE CASTLE

Through a narrow window we can see only part of the sky,
and not the whole vastness ... of it.

Krishnamurti

The parting with Paul Cummins left a sizeable void in my confidence,
my sense of where I was going, even of who I was. It gradually hit
home that for several years I had been drifting, in denial about what
now seemed obvious to me, that continuing to let myself be defined
by success, or lack of it, in the commercial record business was limiting my prospects, blighting my career even. I needed a major change
of direction, a fresh roll of the dice.

The old Irish phrase 'The Lord never closes one door but opens
an apartment block down the road' never seemed truer when in July
1996 I found myself invited to be part of a week-long gathering
of songwriters at Myles Copeland's fourteenth-century Chateau
Marouatte in France. Financed by a conglomerate of publishers
including my own at the time, twenty-five writers were similarly
invited from all over the world to collaborate and co-write songs.

This came at a perfect time. Stepping back from the record
business was something completely new and challenging. I had
never professionally co-written before, in fact previously didn't feel

comfortable with the concept, fearing that the songs would be formulaic and lack emotional integrity.

With only a few exceptions, all the songs on my previous albums I'd written on my own. Those few I co-wrote were very organic and individual creations and not designed to be covered by anyone else. I was nervous too. Would I be able to do it?

Songwriting on your own is hard but at least there's no one telling you it's wrong to say this or that, or that the musical suggestion you just made sucks. But, knowing it was a privilege to be included and ready to try a new direction, I said yes and found myself flying into Bordeaux, catching a train to Angoulême and being picked up in a minibus with a load of people I'd never met and driven through rural France to a massive mediaeval chateau like in a fairy tale.

We were welcomed and shown to our quarters, either a modest room in the heart of the castle or a tiny garret in one of the four corner turrets of the building. I never knew how the accommodation was parcelled out, whether those who had been there before got priority or whether it was drawn out of a hat, or what. I didn't really care. In the four times I went there over the next couple of years I found myself billeted in a wide variety of different rooms each of which had original features, antiques, tapestries and art.

There was a coordinating team made up of employees from the contributing publishers. The deal was, each morning, as we'd all meet for breakfast in the huge central dining room, we'd be told who we were to write with that day. Most times you'd be partnered with two others, occasionally just one. The expectation was that the various teams would repair to their preselected workrooms, each with a keyboard and guitar provided, write a song and produce a completed demo of it by that evening.

To do that there were rooms converted into recording studios where a team of musicians including drummers, bass players, keyboardists and guitarists, contributed to the recording of the demos.

It was a scary prospect on the first morning, sitting across a room with two total strangers and a blank page. All the participants were experienced and already varyingly successful songwriters, some also successful artists. But the majority would've been backroom writers who co-wrote all the time and whose output was mostly recorded by other established artists.

Mainly they were American; from Nashville, Los Angeles or New York. Some were British, one or two from continental Europe or Australia. I was the only Irish person. There were a few who, like me, were performing singer-songwriters and who only wrote on their own.

Songwriters often say co-writing is a bit like sex on a one-night stand. Who makes the first move and what form does it take? Typically, I'd start to play something on the guitar or keyboard and hum a tune, or I'd have a scrap of a lyric and maybe I'd tentatively throw in a thematic idea. Someone else would join in or suggest a topic they were thinking of. It's a kind of sorcery and it all depends on the mercurial collective energies and positivity of the participants. Like sex too, sometimes it's awkward and precarious or even silly. You feel vulnerable, at least I did initially. It involves trusting that the others share your need to make something beautiful. If it's working, and individual talents are running free, something starts to grow in mid-air and in a frenzy of collaborative urges and outpourings it becomes tangible and a definite thing. Suddenly there's a song that didn't exist an hour ago and will be there forever. A bit like a baby, it's the closest this writer will ever come to giving birth.

I began to love it and found I was good at it. The discovery that this didn't involve the whole of my inner being became a liberating thing. Up to now I had been restricting my creative output content-wise and stylistically to some subconscious notion I had of myself as a performing artist. I'd avoid musical areas and lyrical subjects that I didn't feel fitted in with that notion, that image. I think, in a way, this might have come from my years in the folk world where the concept prevailed that songs had to 'mean' something, be true to some historical context, human struggle for advancement or at the very least deal with some real and burning personal ideals or emotions. Now that I was involved in making something that wasn't necessarily an expression of my deepest inner self, I found myself bursting with musical ideas in styles I was fluent in, that somehow as a writer I had ignored or considered 'not for me'. I'm not saying that everything I wrote on my own up to that point was pregnant with 'meaning' or burning with emotion all the time. But I tended not to be able to finish a song I was writing unless I identified with the message or emotion in a direct personal way. Now at the Castle, as we called it, I was engaging with the ideas and emotions of others and able to look at an emerging work from a distance. That all these people were very skilled and successful writers helped me to relax into the process and allow myself to be led in directions where the destination wasn't yet clear to me. I found myself being pleasantly surprised all the time at the things that would surface.

It was at the Castle that I first met Carole King. Early on in my first visit I was put together with Carole and Mark Hudson, another successful US writer and record producer who had worked with, among others, Aerosmith, Ringo Starr, Ozzy Osbourne and Harry Nilsson. Mark co-wrote the Grammy award-winning Aerosmith hit 'Livin' on the Edge' in 1993. Carole, of course, was already a mega-legend in the world of songwriting.

I was in a slight daze as I faced the two of them and had to pinch myself a few times. But as I sat at a keyboard, I found myself playing some kind of figure and groove which caused the others to smile and get excited. Strangely I wasn't intimidated and settled into the process naturally.

That first morning we wrote 'Monday Without You', which went on to be covered by Carole herself on a subsequent album *Love Makes the World* and by the girl band Wilson Phillips (daughters of Beach Boy legend Brian Wilson and John Phillips from the Mamas and Papas). Over the next few years, I wrote several more songs with Carole, including 'Believe in Me' that I recorded and 'I Don't Want to Be the One' recorded by Trisha Yearwood.

In my various visits to the Castle I wrote twenty-five songs in total. In addition to Carole King and Mark Hudson, I wrote with artists Belinda Carlisle, Mark Everett – known as 'E' (leader of the band Eels), Conner Reeves, Debbie Petersen of the Bangles, Beth Nielsen Chapman, Jill Sobule, Angelo Palladino and a bunch of songwriters who were super-talented but not really known outside the songwriting fraternity. Three of the songs I wrote there, 'Minutes Away, Miles Apart', 'Travellin' Light' and 'Try Me One More Time', I recorded on my own subsequent album *Oh What A World* in 1999. It was a remarkable time, setting me on a whole other path that freed me from the stultifying grip of the record business. It changed my life.

Away from music, our kids were growing up fast. Sarah, after finishing secondary school in 1995, worked for a year at Polygram Records in Dublin 'doing everything': helping with album launches, running the company's Britannia Music Club, working in sales, assisting in marketing and manning the reception. She spent the next couple of summers, firstly in Boston working in the National Park Service and in a bar at weekends, then in London with an Irish-owned ad agency. Sarah came home to Dublin to start a four-year degree course in '97 which took her to Provence for a while. Hopped back and forth to UK for work each summer and she finally settled there after completing her degree in 2000.

Colm turned seventeen in 1996 and was playing a lot of hockey. He quickly developed as a player and was an established regular in midfield for his school Newpark. They won the Irish schools competition that year – the only time Newpark won that competition since. Going on to play with local clubs Avoca and later Pembroke, and for the province of Leinster, he was capped several times for Ireland under 21s in the European Championship in 2000 and played against England, Scotland, Germany and Japan. Hockey contacts led to a couple of extended trips to Holland and New Zealand in the late 1990s. New Zealand in particular cast its spell on him and some years later he would eventually move there. Always interested in music, he took to the guitar and in a short time made great progress. Despite this talent, he chose software development as a career after degrees at Dublin Institute of Technology (BSc) in 2002 and Trinity College Dublin (MSc) in 2004.

39

NOT-MAKING-AN-ALBUM

My live shows were continuing apace and the songs I wrote at the Castle were starting to bear fruit. I started to feel like making another album. It had been three years since *Spirits Colliding* and I had at least a dozen new songs I wanted to get out there.

Of course, with no record deal, I had no idea how I was going to do it. The record business was still flourishing in those days before the existential challenge brought on by the onset of Napster and the plethora of illegal digital downloading platforms that followed. While I had ceased wanting a deal with a 'major', there were a load of less high-pressure alternatives signing acts with a viable career and ready-made audience who weren't necessarily aiming at the top of the charts.

It became clear too that since I was no longer on the radar of my former label Mercury/Fontana (a division of what is now Universal) my entire recorded back catalogue, which they still controlled ... my life's work to date ... was now at risk of disappearing into 'nowhere land' where nothing would be done to promote it or even make it available. This was a regular occurrence with acts that had been dropped by a label and not something I was happy to accept.

In a mad coincidence my lawyer who, all those years ago, had negotiated my side of the original recording agreement with

Mercury/Fontana was offered the job of CEO of the parent company, Universal UK. I contacted him to ask about the future of my catalogue.

'Not sure what you mean, Paul,' he sounded guarded.

I asked about the possibility of them giving me back my records now they were no longer interested. I said to him in a humorous, mate-to-mate conspiratorial way, 'Don't we both know someone who can help make this happen?'

His reply cut me to the quick. 'Paul,' he said, 'I think you may possibly be overestimating the extent of my power here.'

Poacher turned gamekeeper in one fell swoop. I was devastated and really pissed off.

Though Damage Management was no longer officially representing me, I had remained friendly with the company supremo, Ed Bicknell. My booking agent Paul Charles suggested I talk to Ed about the problem. After all, Damage's main act, Dire Straits, was on the same label. Ed was sympathetic and equally upset that the man I had recently paid good money to as my legal representative was now refusing to look positively on a situation coming out of that very same contract he had negotiated on my behalf.

As it happened, Dire Straits, after a decade and a half at the top of the global entertainment ladder, had reached the end of their life too and had recently broken up, and, as all record companies do in that situation, the label wanted to have a final payday by releasing a best-of collection. Ed told me he was going to stick it to the new CEO on my behalf at a meeting they had set up to discuss its Christmas release. Ed actually got off on the cut and thrust of artist management/record company power play. I was in the London office with him at the time and just as the meeting was about to begin, I sneaked up the stairs a bit, just out of sight but within earshot.

'Before we even talk about the Dire Straits' release, there's one condition we've to agree on,' Ed was firm.

'What?' the CEO said.

'Give Paul Brady back his catalogue.'

Stunned silence.

'You're joking.'

'No. I'm not.'

The dance went on a little longer but eventually (and sensibly, given the diametrically opposed financial implications) it was agreed. I felt giddy sitting on the stairs, terrified I'd give myself away with a cough or a laugh. It was an incredibly generous thing for Ed Bicknell to do and I've never forgotten it. A few months later, I got back the rights to my work and once again, my life was changed.

Of course, I still had no management.

The next few years saw me go through a dizzying succession of managerial and recording situations as I tried to find a way to exist and develop as an artist in a business that seemed unable to know what to do with me and as a result, unwilling to accommodate me. It was not a lot of use having acquired the rights to my back catalogue if there was no one to help me make it available.

Then out of the blue came an offer from the Rykodisc label in the person of Englishman, Ian Moss, CEO of the UK branch of the company. In 1998 I had begun a management relationship with Anne-Louise Kelly. Anne-Louise had worked for several years with Principle Management (U2's management company) and now with a young family had left to pursue other interests that weren't, she hoped, so full-on or high-pressured. As she discovered a year or so down the line, however, there was a big difference between being an important cog in a big wheel where someone else made all the crucial decisions and now having to make those decisions herself and be solely responsible to the artist for the outcome. Furthermore, her former clients U2 were in the lucky position that the world lined up to have access to them. My situation wasn't so easy. I think that came as a shock to her. She was principled and took the role seriously. The load became too great though and she bowed out after a year or so. I was back to managing myself again, though I was lucky to retain Anne-Louise's talented assistant Liz Devlin in a quasi-managerial role where I made the decisions and she helped to bring them into effect.

The Rykodisc relationship was initially productive. Ian Moss was a big fan of my music and in early 1999 he decided to remaster my entire back catalogue and release a 'best-of' from the 1970s through to the 1990s called *Nobody Knows*. That was a success, selling well.

But the songs I'd co-written in the Castle were still fresh in my mind and although I was not-making-an-album, I set about recording one or two songs in my studio in late 1997. I even got a professional engineer, Richard Rainey, to help put a shape on 'Sea of Love', 'I Believe in Magic', 'The Law of Love' and 'Minutes Away, Miles Apart'.

But these were one-offs. Sporadic recordings. Today, given technological advances, this isn't unusual. Some might say the instinct to record one single song now and again was prescient, but in late 1990s the business model ran along the lines of 'choose ten or so songs, record, mix, release as full album'.

This is exactly what I was *not* doing – I had bowed out of all that commercial pressure where creativity was hostage to deadlines and profit. However, when Richard Rainey understandably took up an offer to be the engineer on a long-term project, I felt a stab of regret. Why? After all, I was not-making-an-album.

I forgot about recording for a while. I went to the US to do some gigs and collaborate on other projects, and I developed songs that were embryonic or needed fleshing out and co-wrote some entirely new ones including 'Believe in Me' in Carole King's project studio in LA.

This was the fifth time I had written with Carole since that first session in the Castle. The anticipatory thrill of working with her hadn't faded five songs later. In fact, I still had to do a hefty amount of self-talk to get through what they now call imposter syndrome, 'It's just another songwriter, Paul. Same as you. Nothing out of the ordinary.'

It didn't work all the time. As sometimes happens with co-writing, a song doesn't get completed first day. This was the case with 'Believe in Me'. But later, at home in Dublin, I started to write the lyrics. Carole and I finished it up via fax, phone and email.

Other songs emerged during the time I was not-making-an-album. 'Good Love', for example, co-written with jazz afficionado and record-producer Bob Theile. I had never worked with Bob before and found him gracious and enabling. 'Good Love' was one of those songs that 'fell out' before we had time to think too much. Similar to the Carole King song, we finalised the lyrics later over fax, phone and email.

Often a co-written song was the beginning of an enduring relationship. For example, my relationship with Bob brought forth an unusual collaboration several years later. He became the music supervisor on the hit US TV series, *Sons of Anarchy*, and asked me to sing the vocal on a remake of the Rolling Stones' 'Gimme Shelter'.

The instrumental track, by his band, the Forest Rangers, was sent to me in Dublin. I recorded my vocal and added a mad tin-whistle. It ended up as the song over the credits on the final episode of the second series. It is one of the most-listened-to Paul Brady recordings on Spotify.

Stranger still was when American composer, Jonathan Bepler emailed me in 2000. He was writing the musical soundtrack for the third episode in a cycle of films by the American visual artist Matthew Barney entitled *Cremaster* named after the muscle that connects the scrotum to the male body, or, as the writer of a subsequent review in *The Village Voice* said, 'Named for the muscle that turns your nutsack into a walnut when it gets cold.' Part of the film referenced the involvement of Irish labourers in the 1928 construction of the Chrysler Building in New York.

Bepler confessed to being a fan of the Irish traditional music resurgence in the 1970s, in particular *Welcome Here Kind Stranger* and *Andy Irvine & Paul Brady*. He needed some Irish colour in his score, so he and Barney asked me to become involved as a singer and appear in the role of maître d' of the Cloud Club – the legendary lunch club on the 68th floor of the Chrysler Building.

To say this turned out to be one of the strangest side roads I took in my career to date would be an understatement. After several weeks of toing and froing on email and phone with songs and lyrical ideas, I landed in New York early January 2001 and was immediately cast in character. I was driven downtown to have a 'short back and sides' in a traditional Russian barber's shop. Next up was to be measured for the maître d's tuxedo. What followed was a week of filming the most bizarre set of scenes I could ever have imagined.

Barney's style is confrontational and *Cremaster 3* went on to inspire wildly contrasting opinions from Jonathan Jones in *The Guardian* saying it was '… one of the most imaginative and brilliant achievements in the history of avant-garde cinema …' and *The Village Voice* noting that '… for all their production design and performance bedazzlement, the *Cremasters* display the rhythmic excitement of congealed goo. Their montage develops through a ponderous ping-pong movement that mistakes flat-footed deliberateness for hypnosis.'

Make your own mind up. I was left numb-struck and uncustomarily speechless. I was still stuck for words at the film premiere. A year after that, my surreal role as maître d' became a live act, singing tenor vocals for 'Song of the Vertical Field' in a concert in New York's Guggenheim Museum. Matthew Barney today remains one of America's most celebrated avant-garde visual artists.

40

OH WHAT A WORLD

But back home in the summer of 1998, despite my involvement in a wealth of creative projects, a sense of restlessness emerged. By October the restless evolved into a sense of urgency. What had changed? Then it dawned on me: nothing had necessarily changed; it was about completing what I had already started. These sporadic recordings, the abundance of songs I'd accumulated over the past three years, it was clear what I had to do. I had to make the album. Or in other words, finish the album I was not making.

I got to work straight away. Alastair McMillan came in to engineer the recording. My restless energy now had focus. String arrangements, would they work? I called Fiachra Trench whose orchestrations I had admired for years and asked him would he get involved. That was one of the most enjoyable periods of the record. Fiachra and I threw the music around and talked about what 'suit of clothes' we'd put on which song, stuff like that. The magic he came up with expanded the emotional impact of the songs, made me look at them in a new way. As the album progressed, Greg Wells, Anto Drennan, Percy Robinson, Rod McVeigh and Linley Hamilton came into the mix. And in a wonderful and serendipitous turn of events, long-time friends and fellow travellers, Ian Maidman (bass guitarist) and Liam Genockey (drummer and percussionist) visited from London and put their touch on the songs.

Soon the list of ten or so songs for the album began to take shape. Four songs: 'Minutes Away, Miles Apart', 'The Law of Love', 'Travellin' Light' and 'Try Me One More Time' all written at the Castle, would be on the album.

The two songs 'Believe in Me' and 'Good Love' written with Carole King and Bob Thiele respectively would also be included. That left five or so more songs to choose out of the fifty songs I'd co- or self-written over the past few years.

I'd been to Nashville a couple of times. The perceived image of Nashville is that all the musicians are into country. The reality is that a large proportion aren't. Gary Nicholson (whom Bonnie Raitt introduced me to) was one of those musicians. His original hometown was in Texas where he'd absorbed a lot of blues, R'n'B and what I call southern soul.

But like many musicians he was living, writing and performing in Nashville and so, it was there in his studio in Nashville, years before I had even conceived of this new album, that we wrote 'I Believe in Magic'. In the typical way of things now, I wrote the answering vocal lyrics at a later stage in Ireland. 'I Believe in Magic' was added to the list of possibles.

'Oh What a World' was a joy to write as it was in partnership with the great Will Jennings, citizen of the world, bon viveur, Francophile extraordinaire, southern genl'man, beat poet (I like to think), not to mention writer of countless hit songs over the past few decades. Will came to my studio in Dublin in the summer of 1996. For a while I thought we were going to have to write through the medium of Creole French. But soon I was discovering that his gift for, and love of, words was the same in any language. Somehow a New Orleans funeral band kept coming to mind when I recorded this song.

'The Long Goodbye' also had its genesis in Dublin. Ronan Keating from Boyzone (at the time) came by one afternoon to write.

'Any idea what we might do?' I said.

'Well,' Ronan thought for a second, 'on the way over, this title popped into my head "The Long Goodbye".'

Sometimes a strong title is all it takes to get me going.

We got stuck in and it came together quickly. I loved it. Later I did a demo of it which I liked so much I decided I really wanted to record this song for real. Then I realised I already had. Apart from adding strings and a little Hammond organ, what you hear on this record is the demo. If it ain't broke, don't fix it.

There were two songs I wanted to include that I wrote on my own. I had the music and lyrical idea for 'Love Hurts' as far back as 1992 when I had been in Norway on Lynni Treekrem's TV show. During rehearsals for the show, I had found myself playing what became the guitar part to 'Love Hurts'. Later that night in Norway the broad outline of the lyrics came, and over the following months I finished it.

'Sea of Love' came a couple of years later. Struggling with the perennial artistic dilemma of trying to balance the need to be alone, live dangerously and be creatively alive alongside the need for domesticity, family, love and affection, I was enjoying casting 'love the enricher' in the role of 'love the destroyer' (or suffocator). The music came in one go while I was staying with a friend in Los Angeles. The lyrics came later.

> *Frightened to go, frightened to stay*
> *Frightened that our lovelight's fading away*
> *Somebody tell me how a man survives*
> *With his body and soul livin' separate lives.*

Apart from a couple of weeks in November when Philip Begley was at the controls, Alastair stayed with me till we finished the record in late 1999. He assumed co-producer's role and it became apparent how much of himself he was bringing to the record; how indispensable his input was.

We went to London in June 1999 to record a session with Lascelles Haughton who brought together singers from the London Tabernacle Choir to sing on six songs. Angelo Palladino sang and former Rolling Stones guitarist Mick Taylor played slide guitar on 'Travellin' Light'. Ren Swan came in from London to mix in my studio in July and by Christmas 1999 we were done.

Oh What A World was a change in direction for me. Of the eleven songs, all but two are collaborations written in lots of different locations in the period from 1996–9. Musically speaking, they all come from very different places. Each one inhabits a world of its own. In songwriting, sometimes you're hot and it comes in a rush and there's a lot of you in the song. Other times, the writer you're working with is on a roll and you stand back and watch it happen, nudging it here and there like a midwife, bringing someone else's baby home. Sometimes it's even-stevens.

Any way is fine with me as far as writing goes. Singing is another thing, however. For me to want to sing a song, I really need to have a strong emotional connection with it, to feel I am the person in the song or perhaps the person it's being sung to, even if it's just in my imagination. The ones I chose to put on the record in the end were the ones I put most of myself into lyrically and musically.

41

THE PAUL BRADY SONGBOOK
AT VICAR STREET, OCTOBER 2001

My booking agent Paul Charles started talking to me about doing a retrospective series of concerts. He had been speaking to promoter Peter Aiken who booked Dublin's premier club Vicar Street and who had just seen and enjoyed a recent gig of mine. Both men agreed it was time to put together an event that would acknowledge the impact I had made in Ireland over the past couple of decades. After all, by now (late 2000) I'd been on the go successfully for over twenty-five years with a large body of work already out there. It was maybe time to look back and try and make sense of it all.

'How should we do it?' I asked. 'How many shows?'

'Let's do a month,' says Paul Charles.

'You're joking!'

I knew I'd been well regarded in Ireland since back in the 1970s, and to some extent was part of the current musical fabric of Ireland from traditional music through to my own songs. But a month in a 750-seater venue, as Vicar Street's capacity was then, seemed pushing things. I was sceptical.

When Paul suggested I invite some of the many artists that I'd worked with in the past to play with me, I got even more nervous.

Over the years I'd been lucky to work with a plethora of great artists and songwriters, many better known globally than me. But I've always had a thing about not wanting to be seen to be climbing up on other peoples' backs to get ahead.

I thought about it for a good while.

There were more meetings with Peter Aiken. Both he and Paul Charles emphasised that the respect and affection accorded to me from a multitude of artists was real and genuine and that I was being unnecessarily scrupulous with regard to approaching them.

The more I saw their optimism and positivity about the project the less I worried. In the end I agreed to do it on condition that the guests would not be officially advertised beforehand. That way I couldn't be accused of profiteering from my 'famous friends'! In a strange way that actually added to the mystique of the event, as we will see.

We decided to do twenty-three shows, taking Mondays and Thursdays off. As I wanted to show all sides of my past musical journey, the first thing I planned was to apportion six nights where I'd tip the cap to my traditional music period with Planxty and Andy Irvine in the 1970s. In a throwback to the 1978 concert I did in Dublin's Liberty Hall to celebrate the launch of my first album *Welcome Here Kind Stranger*, I decided to invite all the musicians who had played that night: Andy Irvine, Dónal Lunny, Liam Óg O'Flynn, Paddy Glackin and Noel Hill, to join me again. Matt Molloy was off with the Chieftains somewhere and couldn't make it. We called ourselves the Liberty Belles in memory of the original concert.

For the rest of the month, I planned to bring my regular band of several years in from the UK: Liam Genockey on drums, Ian Maidman on bass and electric guitar, and Steve Fletcher on keyboards. Leslie Dowdall, the great singer from Dublin of the now defunct but still revered group In Tua Nua, rounded off the band on vocals. To expand the sound, on several of the nights we were joined by a horn section featuring a selection of the greatest players in the country: Richie Buckley on tenor sax, Derek 'Doc' O'Connor on tenor and piano, Linley Hamilton on trumpet and Annie Whitehead on trombone.

I sat down to think of who else I might ask to join me, and a long list quickly appeared. I decided to push the boat out and see what happened. We'd around ten months to pull it together – not a lot of time in the global music business – all these major artists were often booked at least a year in advance.

I first approached old friend and colleague Bonnie Raitt not actually expecting she'd make it, living in San Francisco as she did. She immediately accepted, providing we could work around her existing dates.

Over the next couple of months I had confirmations in principle depending on precise dates from: Mark Knopfler, Van Morrison, Sinéad O'Connor, Curtis Stigers, Maura O'Connell, Moya Brennan (Máire Ní Bhraonáin), Mary Black, Ronan Keating, Brian Kennedy, Gavin Friday & Maurice Seezer, Brendan Bowyer, Altan, Eleanor McEvoy, Tim O'Brien, Arty McGlynn, Sharon Shannon, Paul Cleary and the Hothouse Flowers all of whom eventually made the journey.

Eric Clapton, Phil Collins (who had recently produced David Crosby's version of my song 'Helpless Heart') and Tina Turner all expressed a desire to be there but regretted that their schedules were already full. Phew!

Then the fun started. To pull together more than twenty different international artists' schedules was a Herculean task. If we had known how hard it was going to be beforehand, we might have baulked at the prospect. No sooner had we begun locking individual artists into specific dates, a couple of weeks later a request would come in, can so and so change from the 10th to the

12th? And so on. All the out-of-town artists had to have accommodation, so if we changed the appearance date, we also had to change the flights and hotel dates and hope that other artists didn't mind being asked to move their already confirmed dates. It was a logistical nightmare. I owe a huge debt of gratitude to agent Paul Charles and my assistant at the time, Liz Devlin, for stepping into the breach and handling all the endless grief that inevitably ensued.

Next came the rehearsals. For just my own and my band's material plus the Liberty Belles' gigs, we had an intense period of work in advance of the shows. For the shows themselves, while we knew in advance what songs our guests would sing, the only time we could actually run through them and rehearse was at the soundcheck in the afternoon of each particular gig. In many cases we had never performed together before, which was a big challenge. That meant everyone was at work from early afternoon till the end of the show that night.

It was mad and exhausting. Already in my fifties and carrying the can for the success of the entire month, I still don't know how I managed to do it. One strategic move was to put a pull-down bed in my dressing room where in the period of an hour or two between the day's soundcheck/rehearsal and the gig, I'd crash out in a half-sleep/half-meditation state. It was a lifesaver.

The event took off the first week of October with Curtis Stigers as guest. Curtis and I had known each other from the mid-1990s when we had shared a TV show in Dublin around the time of his first big hit 'I Wonder Why', which we sang again now.

The highlight of the evening had to be a Paul Brady–Curtis Stigers duet on 'Arthur McBride'. 'A life-long ambition to sing this with Paul!' said Curtis who acted the role of the sergeant in the song. A great start to the month.

Later that week Sinéad O'Connor came in and we duetted on 'The Lakes of Pontchartrain', 'Dreams Will Come' and her own song 'In This Heart'. I was delighted how our two very different and distinctive voices blended. The crowd adored it and Sinéad had a good time.

At the first weekend I reverted to my 'folk' self with the first of three nights with the Liberty Belles. Much to my amazement, all these gigs were selling out. Word got round that something special was going on in Vicar Street.

Rumours abounded that Bonnie Raitt was coming in and someone had 'leaked' that Van Morrison and Mark Knopfler were due to appear at some stage in the month. The thing was, nobody knew which night as we hadn't advertised the guests, so the event began to take on a mystique: 'Who's appearing tonight?' kind of thing, all of which started to build and eventually became the hallmark of the month. People started flocking to the shows, many coming back for a second time.

Week two began as a Nashville night with long-time Nashville residents Maura O'Connell and Tim O'Brien joining the band already augmented by guitar wizard Arty McGlynn. Wednesday was definitely girls' night – what a thrill to be on stage together with three of the greatest female singers of the day: Maura O'Connell, Mary Black and Máire Ní Bhraonáin.

Eleanor McEvoy, composer of one of the most popular Irish songs ever 'A Woman's Heart', was the special guest on Friday. Looking splendidly pregnant and singing and playing guitar, hers was one of the most perfectly judged performances of the month. Guests Paul Cleary, Altan, Sharon Shannon, Shea Fitzgerald and the Hothouse Flowers raised the roof on their respective nights.

Week three saw the return of the Liberty Belles for three more traditional-music nights plus a couple of nights with just my band and the horn section.

Week four saw the big guns arriving in force with Van Morrison and Brendan Bowyer arriving on the Tuesday. When Van was starting out in the early 1960s with the lowly Monarchs Showband in Belfast, way before he formed Them, Brendan was already huge in both the North and the South as lead singer with the Royal Showband. When he heard Brendan was set to sing, Van was delighted and the two shared many stories before the night was out. Brendan had just recorded a new album featuring my song 'Follow On' and Van's 'Bright Side of the Road', so the plan was for Brendan to sing 'Follow On' and then to duet with Van on 'Bright Side of the Road'.

The audience loved Brendan Bowyer; such is his unique combination of shyness with charisma. Then it's Van and straight away everything moves up a couple of gears. The man's energy is amazing. Van and Brendan traded lines and verses and vocally had a real go at each other, which brought smiles to both their faces and roars of approval from the audience.

Brendan left to huge cheers and then Van and I took up with 'Irish Heartbeat' and Van's 'I Will Be There'. Derek 'Doc' O'Connor left down his tenor to take over the piano for this song. What a talent he is. Van seemed to enjoy himself more and more and by the time he went off, the place was going nuts. Brendan comes back again for 'The World Is What You Make It' with Van returning at the very end to join me on the Ray Charles classic 'You Don't Know Me'. A beautiful night.

Next night's guests were Gavin Friday and Maurice Seezer. They had been a team for some time and were fresh from a run in the Tivoli Theatre as part of the Dublin Theatre Festival. Gavin, who started out in the late 1970s with the Virgin Prunes, probably Ireland's most outrageous art-rock band of the period (and since) has always impressed me with the breadth of his musical interests and his dramatic performances. Maurice provided the musical muscle to their unique pairing. A surprise was in store. Gavin's rendition of 'Nobody Knows' was much slower and more theatrical than my original. It showed a whole other side to the song and the audience was genuinely blown away.

Friday's guest, Mark Knopfler, arrived in the early afternoon from London and immediately got into the Vicar Street spirit. Gracious and accommodating, he slotted into the proceedings seamlessly. Mark's and my long association since 1981 meant he was familiar with a lot of my songs and his request that he 'play on as many as possible' promised a special evening. Joining the band on 'Nothing but the Same Old Story' his guitar immediately lent a warmth and poignant edge to one of my best-loved songs.

'Baloney Again', the beautifully poised musical short story of the plight of black people in segregated US, from Mark's then new record *Sailing to Philadelphia* came next and the trademark Knopfler vocal and guitar sound filled Vicar Street with joy. Now things were set to go up a gear as the stage began to fill for 'Done With Bonaparte' from his *Golden Heart* album. Dónal Lunny on bouzouki, Liam Óg O'Flynn on uilleann pipes and whistle and Ciaran Tourish on fiddle slotted in and the scene changed to the Russian front during the Napoleonic era with a spirited rendition of another great song.

On Saturday of the fourth week Bonnie Raitt was my star guest. Her first song was my 'Not the Only One', a hit for her in the US from her Grammy-winning album *Luck of the Draw* named after the song I played for her when we first met. That was the song that sealed our friendship. And here we were, friends and collaborators for over a decade now, we'd worked together on countless occasions, from singing on each other's albums, to writing together, to playing on each other's shows both live and on television.

Next up, a rendition of our duet on 'Trick or Treat' from my album of the same name. Bonnie is a consummate performer and a wonderful singer and guitar player. A legend in her own land. It's rare enough to see her this side of the ocean and the audience rose to the occasion giving her a great reception.

Entering the final week, it's the home strait now and the shows keep getting better and better. The guest tonight is Belfast's Brian Kennedy with a new album out including a song we wrote together called 'Call Me Old Fashioned' which we sing for the first time in public. On it goes with 'The Island', which I dedicate to my mum and dad, Mollie and Sean, who are in the audience. Brian reappears to share verses on 'The Lakes of Pontchartrain' then it's everyone on again for 'The Homes of Donegal'. One of the special nights.

Second last night, sadness, yet relief that it all went so well, that the gargantuan effort is almost over. Tonight's guest is Ronan Keating who by now has left Boyzone and is a successful solo artist. We sing the song we co-wrote in my Dublin studio, 'The Long Goodbye', and it's a satisfying moment to realise the song together, live in Vicar Street. Twenty-two gigs down, one more to go.

Last night – 31 October 2001. A huge party is planned for after the show with loads of guests turning up to send us off. The band is playing its heart out tonight. Ian, Steve, Liam and Leslie have made this a wonderful month. No better musicians and none more fun to be with. Total respect to them for slotting in every night with a huge variety of styles and content without one complaint from a guest artist, indeed compliments all round. The set and the month end with 'Steel Claw' and 'Arthur McBride'. There follows the mother of all parties. Around midnight a session starts in the bar next door. The backdrop is a huge video screen showing footage of the past month's gigs. Tour sweatshirts are passed around. I finally leave for home at 5.30 a.m. A fitting end to an amazing month.

42

TV SERIES

If I thought things were going to get dull post the 'high' of a month-long gig I was mistaken. After the success of the Vicar Street season, I was approached by Julian Vignoles, senior producer at RTÉ TV with an idea about a series based on my work. The plan was to film enough material to make six programmes using the title of the Vicar Street gigs *The Paul Brady Songbook*. The venue was the recently restored Marlay House, a big old stately home built in the late 1700s in Marlay Park and now owned by Dublin County Council.

We all piled in there for two weeks in July 2002 with a big camera crew, catering, make-up, wardrobe, the whole deal. I brought over my core band from the UK: Ian Maidman, Liam Genockey and Steve Fletcher, augmented by many of the players from the previous October in Vicar Street. Mary Black and Curtis Stigers came back in to sing with me. The Vicar Street brass section of Annie Whitehead, Linley Hamilton and Richie Buckley were there for most of it as was Leslie Dowdall on vocals, Ciaran Tourish fiddle, Shea Fitzgerald on mandolin and a one-off visit by one of my favourite guitar players, Anto Drennan.

As we were kind of doing a TV version of the Vicar Street sessions career retrospective, I had Andy Irvine and Dónal Lunny come in on some of my traditional Irish songs. We mixed the audio and edited the visuals in September and the episodes, featuring more than thirty of my best-known songs, were broadcast weekly on national TV over a six-week period in October and November. A DVD of the entire series accompanied the broadcast.

One surprising development happened during the filming. Part of the production style was to interview the band members to garner their feelings about what was going on and to reminisce about our long association together. While watching the rushes one night, I heard bass player Ian reveal that he was transgender and had always felt female in a male body. It was of course a great surprise. I had worked with Ian since the mid-1980s and apart from appearing in a few beautifully outrageous sequined stage outfits from time to time, there hadn't been any obvious harbingers of what was now being revealed. This was very early on in the now widely publicised transgender acceptance reality, and it took some getting used to. Ian has subsequently been officially recognised as 'trans' in the UK and for the last decade and a half has lived a fulfilled live as Jennifer and remains in a relationship with her long-time partner, trombone player Annie Whitehead. These days it's hard to remember her as anything other than the stunning musician and wonderful woman she is.

It was a very successful and enjoyable project, well-received by the public. The only downside came a few years later when I decided I'd like to revisit the footage with a view to using the material in a more expanded way. A lot of the song performances in the TV series were edited and incomplete, intercut, as they were, with contextual and interview footage. In a rapidly developing media world where visual content was becoming more and more essential, I wanted to have access to the original unedited material so I could re-present full versions of the songs in other ways. But when I approached the producer Julian Vignoles to talk about it, he revealed, to my horror, that RTÉ had wiped the entire two weeks' recording so they could save money by using the tapes again. I was totally shocked and incandescent. It was well known in the artistic community that RTÉ had been guilty in the past of the mass erasing of many iconic audio recordings of some of the greatest living Irish traditional music legends, again to save money. But I thought those days were gone and that, in the intense criticism that followed that discovery, lessons had been learned. You'd think if they thought enough about me to give me a six-week series as an Irish artist of some repute they'd value the footage enough to hold onto it as archive? Regrettably not. I think it was an act of artistic and cultural vandalism by the national broadcaster and I'm still not over it yet, I'm afraid.

43

ACCEPTANCE

After *The Paul Brady Songbook* TV series and DVD, I found myself gradually undergoing a fundamental change of attitude in relation to my career. I still wanted to write and to produce new work and to perform live. I still had loads of energy and felt I had more to say. But I was no longer interested in competing in the music business in the way I felt compelled to do throughout the 1980s and 1990s. It was almost like the commercial end of the business was happy to facilitate me in that regard too. The Irish Recorded Music Association (IRMA) bestowed their Lifetime Achievement Award on me in 2002, a sure sign I was expected to move aside. After all, I was now the ripe old age of fifty-five, way past the sell-by date in a world where Westlife ruled the roost. With Reality TV chomping at the bit in the wings even Boyzone were history.

I started touring solo a lot. I was good at it, it was easy, profitable and way less stressful than keeping a five-piece band on the road. Besides, it was increasingly clear to me that a large percentage of my audience actually preferred to see me on my own, feeling that when I performed with a band, a lot of what made me unique as a performer was subsumed, hidden, reduced even. I was never totally sure. I enjoyed and still enjoy the excitement of playing with a bunch of talented musicians and singers. But, career-wise the solo thing made a lot of sense at the time.

In 2003–4 I toured both USA and Australia solo twice. I had started to do individual deals with record labels to get my records out in different territories, licensing deals, where the label would have the right to sell the record for a limited time while I would still own it and the licence would revert to me when the term was up. I put *The Paul Brady Songbook* DVD and CD out in Australia on Little Big Town Records and in Europe on a German label, Hypertension. Both those labels worked hard on the product and sales were reasonably good. Hypertension looked like it would be an effective longer-term outlet for me in Europe. I got on well with them and harboured notions that I could gain more of a foothold in Germany. My profile in Europe had suffered over the past decade, tied as I was to major pop labels, whose only strategy seemed to be 'get day-time radio and aim at the charts'. Further, I had walked away from the folk scene there as 'Irish Music' only meant one thing, traditional music and song. I wasn't doing that anymore and I just didn't fit in, again.

I started talking to a US label based in Nashville called Compass Records. Owned by musicians, Garry West and Alison Brown, they were showing a lot of interest in music from Ireland, both traditional and contemporary, in particular the legendary Mulligan Music catalogue, which they eventually bought. This included the Bothy Band, the by-now legendary *Andy Irvine & Paul Brady* record from 1976 and the *Molloy, Brady, Peoples* album from 1978 featuring Matt Molloy, Tommy Peoples and me. My own record *Welcome Here Kind Stranger* from 1978, while originally on the Mulligan label, had fortunately been acquired by me before the catalogue sale to Compass Records.

On the face of it, it seemed a good move for me to make. While I had a growing fan base in North America, I was not making a breakthrough via the major-label, pop-music route and in truth

I was totally tired of that world. Compass Records had a foot in both the traditional folk-music area and the contemporary 'Americana' singer-songwriter scene. They offered me a deal that would give me good distribution of my records in North America. The only problem was that they were insisting on a worldwide deal that would mean I'd have to end my relationship with Hypertension in Europe and Little Big Town in Australia. I was concerned about this, as with Hypertension in Germany I had an ongoing and effective outlet and I really liked the people there. But Compass head Garry West insisted, saying it wasn't worth his while to put a lot of effort into my career unless he 'had me for the world'. After a couple of weeks agonising I agreed. At the time the American market seemed more attractive to me, more where I should be aiming at than the European market.

Time would tell that was a mistake.

Over the next few years with Compass I made an album in Nashville, 2005's *Say What You Feel* that I felt, and still feel, was a good piece of work. Co-produced by Garry West and me, it was evidence of a good and productive musical relationship between us as individuals and he was very helpful in getting the record made, setting up the studios and booking musicians. But as the relationship with Garry progressed, expanding into personal management, the conflict of interest between the role of a manager and a record company boss became more pronounced. After all, in the music business, it's the manager's job to take the record company to task. Hard for that to happen if they're one and the same. Several times I felt decisions were being made and directions suggested that suited the record company more than the artist. I questioned if the label was more interested in profiting from my existing status in Ireland and the UK than expanding the promised 'world reach' outside North America. I didn't need them in my home territory. The fact that Compass did not have anything like the global reach they talked about in the beginning became more obvious and alarming as time progressed. Tensions increased and the management relationship came to an end, leaving me still with Compass Records for the world.

Other issues had a part to play too. It was getting harder for foreign artists to get to work in the USA. A temporary work permit to cover a short tour was expensive, around $5,000 per individual. Despite Compass' strength in the US market, for a foreign artist like me to make any major waves even in the contemporary/acoustic/folk world, meant spending long periods of time there, which I no longer wanted to do. The usual scenario would be that in the summer festival period gigs would be at weekends, leaving you hanging around the rest of the week, draining the tour's bottom line, or taking on small gigs that weren't enjoyable or financially rewarding.

I gradually realised I'd reached a career ceiling in America as a performing artist and it wasn't going to get any better. The thought of hopping over to France, Holland or Germany for a gig or two on short flights and being back at home the next day became much more appealing than dealing with the vastness of America. But I had neglected the European market for most of my later career and now I was paying the price. To say I don't regret that would be untrue. I could have had a nice career in Germany and France in particular, as I speak the language. But you can't have everything. My career continued to expand in other directions and I'm a guy who doesn't dwell on regrets.

So, yet again I was without professional management. This was a scenario that would have kept me awake at night years previously, but now, operating independently and with success, it didn't seem such a problem. I was drawing away from the mainstream music business and not needing that kind of advice any longer. I was making my own career decisions based on my instincts. What I really needed from management was administration, someone to operate as a buffer between me and the business, a trusted advisor, a sounding board whenever I wanted a second opinion. The last thing I wanted was a 'professional' manager whose income depended on how much I worked and earned, with all the pitfalls that dynamic led to. This was the rant I gave my sound engineer, John Munnis, who was driving us both home from a gig in Ireland one night in early 2009.

I've known John forever. We came of age in the Dublin of the 1970s with all the great music that the city was full of then and over the years he established a reputation as one of the best live gig sound engineers in the country, or, in my opinion, anywhere. I was lucky that he chose to work with me from the late 1990s on.

After about ten minutes of listening to me spluttering and fulminating, amid the laughter that always seemed to accompany conversations with John, he turned to me and said, 'I'll manage you.'

John had recently augmented his role with me to include tour management and that was going very well. He'd budget a tour in advance, do all the travel and accommodation bookings and tot up the figures after tour's end. But overall artist management, involving recording and record distribution, online merchandising, publishing and all that?

'I always seem to fall out with managers, John,' I said, 'I don't want to fall out with you.'

But the seed was planted and after a couple of weeks' thought and discussion, sometime in 2009 we agreed to give it a go and see how it worked out.

It has turned out to be exactly what I need. Thirteen years later we've never had a problem; we're still sucking diesel and laughing a lot.

44

HOOBA DOOBA

When I started off playing music professionally, I laboured under the misapprehension that the listener responded to my music in the same way I felt it. Over time, and with much disillusionment, I came to realise only a small proportion of listeners hear music 'for its own sake', meaning independent of the myriad of contexts in which any music sits: the age, style, image, attitude, identity and of course the politics of the artists who make and perform that music.

Some of these contexts disturbed me more than others. Depending on how liberated or threatened the listener or indeed artist was by modernity, the binary sentiment that 'folk music: old, substantial = good; pop music: young, lightweight = bad' felt too restrictive. True, there was some really bad pop music out there but equally true, there was some ghastly folk music too. As much as I loved playing my native music it no longer interested me as a vehicle for progress, more one of comfort, security and nostalgia and yes, of joy. New music to me (pop or otherwise) *was* progress.

I felt too that the whole business of attributing identity and politics to a certain type of music deterred people from appreciating that music for its own sake. When I started to play traditional music, mainly within the UK folk scene, these tendencies were even more exaggerated. Politics (usually left-wing) often became the central context in which music was experienced, meaning your music was likely to be judged by whatever political stance you adopted – worse was to have no political stance. In Ireland traditional music has always nestled in a political context; that of rebellion, rejection of the old enemy Britain and, to an extent, modernity, with regret for things past-and-gone-forever. Understandably in times of unrest people adopted traditional music like a tribal badge, used it as a common bond of inclusivity, the music itself peripheral to the tribal package. Pre social media, this cohesion gave the folk scene its raison d'être, but it also gave a platform to a host of entertainers whose communication skills enabled them to present themselves as leading lights in folk music. Nothing wrong with that, with tasting success. It was often good entertainment, but how many 'musical artists' came to the fore who were simply political agitators (or comedians) in disguise? How many were performers whose musical 'arsenal' was unimaginative, derivative yet whose agility with the bon mot was finely honed and rewarded?

I'd experienced this in the 1980s around the hunger strikes when my failure to toe the party line was frowned on. Back then the lone wolf in me was already tired of the appropriation of music for ulterior motives. I had ploughed a terminally non-aligned furrow since. Now I was free to make whatever record I liked. My mood was celebratory.

I started making another album. All my recording was now being done in my own studio in Dublin's Sandyford. I began with just a recording engineer, Kieran Lynch, and my longtime drummer Liam Genockey. We worked for five days on some existing basic song structures and started some others from the ground up, me playing acoustic guitar live just with Liam's drums. It might sound a strange way to record but the rhythmic 'feel' of a track is something I have an instinctive grasp of and it's crucial that it's finessed before the harmonic aspects of a song are addressed. Often in the past, with several musicians sitting around in studio at the same time, I would find myself distracted trying to give a role, space and attention to everyone before I had a clear fix on what it was I was looking for myself and often the focus would vanish into the ether. It's taken me a long time to learn that lesson. Nowadays I accept that only I can make my music sound the way I hear it in my head and whatever circumstance allows me to achieve that is the best way to go.

When I was happy with the groove foundations, Jennifer Maidman came in for a couple of days and by the time she had added her bass I knew I had the makings of a good record. I continued on my own for a while, sometimes with Kieran engineering, sometimes recording myself when he had other commitments. Generously he left a lot of his own recording equipment with me while he did other projects and that was a great help in keeping the quality consistent. I recorded guitars, bouzouki, mandolin, piano, keyboards and percussion, even some of my own vocals over the next few weeks. Sarah Siskind, a great singer and songwriter I had met in Nashville when I was making *Say What You Feel* in 2004, was a fan of *Andy & Paul* and came to Dublin for a few days opening for Canadian band Bon Iver. I grabbed her on a day off and she ended up singing on a bunch of songs.

A gracious event, and something I could never have foreseen thirty years ago amid newborn baby anxieties, sleepless nights and career worries was the involvement, before he headed to New Zealand for nine months, of my son Colm. He added harmonica to 'Living the Mystery' which gave it a beautiful colour and more than a touch of personal meaning.

By now into early 2009, Bill Shanley and Anto Drennan (electric guitars), Rod McVey (Hammond organ and accordion) all added some magic. I sent 'Rainbow' to Jerry Douglas in Nashville and there he added some smoking lap steel guitar. Next came a trip to

London for a day to record some backing vocals. Finally, Fiachra Trench came to my studio with an ensemble from the Irish Film Orchestra to add his string arrangements to 'One More Today', 'Mother and Son' and 'The Price of Fame'. Gorgeous stuff. Mixing took place in late spring and summer of 2009 and we eventually decided to avoid the Christmas rush and put the record out in spring 2010. Featuring twelve songs, *Hooba Dooba* is a strikingly varied record in mood, pace and colour. Seven of the songs are my own, both words and music. Four are co-writes and one is a cover of a Lennon/McCartney song from *Rubber Soul*, 'You Won't See Me'.

Why *Hooba Dooba*?

It's a phrase I've used for years to celebrate life. When something difficult works out in the end, when a gig is reaching its climax and you're in full flight. Hey, what else can you shout out but Hooba Dooba! I was pleased with how it turned out; it expressed much of what I was as a singer and musician but because it was unapologetically a demonstration of an ethos I held dear: music for music's sake.

Still, as I set off on a late 2010 tour, I was concerned that the variety on *Hooba Dooba* would be more than the audience could deal with. How wrong I was. A woman I met after the Edinburgh gig who had first seen me twenty odd years before asked me had my song 'The Winners Ball' been influenced by the TV series *The Wire*. Hooba Dooba! She'd got it in one.

John Munnis and I now tried to figure out how we'd release the album. After much research and conversations with many people, the name Malcolm Mills, founder of Proper Records, a UK-based record company and distributor, came to the fore. Malcolm, a former drummer, always felt that the major labels were missing out on so much music that had the potential to be popular with adults, as opposed to kids, that is. He was a fan of jazz, country, blues and contemporary singer-songwriters. It sounded interesting. Indeed, many of my own favourite artists like Jimmy Webb, Jimmy Vaughan, Andy Fairweather-Low, Dr John, Richard Thompson, Gretchen Peters, Bonnie Raitt, Tim O'Brien and Loudon Wainwright were already either signed to the label or had their records licensed to or distributed by them.

John and I went to London in early October, met Malcolm and liked him immediately. Since the Compass Records deal had come to an end, we were also looking for a distributor for my entire back catalogue. Malcolm liked *Hooba Dooba* and after a few weeks back and forth on the phone he came to Dublin to meet us. Later that month we did a licensing *and* distribution deal that has happily remained in place since. In fact, in addition to Proper Record's distributing all my previous recordings, we further licensed to them the 2012 anthology *Dancer in the Fire* and the 2017 *Unfinished Business*.

45

BIG CHANGES

My long relationship with my booking agent, Paul Charles, at Asgard in London, began to get rocky. Ever since our first meeting in Lisdoonvarna back in 1979, Paul had looked after my live performance work. It had been a very successful pairing from my point of view. He was a genuine fan of my music and worked determinedly to bring my profile to a wider world. He interfaced well with Paul Cummins, my then manager, and the various record companies that I had been involved with throughout the 1980s and 1990s. He remained committed to me even after my relationship with Damage Management came to an end in the mid-1990s and was always free with advice from then on, above and beyond the role of booking agent. Over the years through his introductions, I met many new musical friends and future collaborators. It would be fair to say that his input contributed largely to my overall career success. I would certainly not be in the fortunate position I am now without him. So where did it all go wrong, I hear you ask.

It was a question of vision really and the way things developed in the music business. It also had a lot to do with where I saw myself at the time. Paul's musical worldview and booking strategy saw him firmly within the mainstream global, for want of a better word, rock world. And why not? He was very successful, looking after the UK and European live tours of major acts such as Jackson Browne, Crosby, Stills & Nash, Ray Davies, Elvis Costello, Rory Gallagher, Nick Lowe, Ry Cooder, Robert Plant, Tom Waits, Van Morrison and the Undertones to name a few. Ever since we started working together the strategy was to bring me to the same level in that same world. I think he honestly believed, as I did for a long time too, that that was where I was meant to be. God knows, I spent long enough knocking at the door.

But from the dawn of the new century on, I was uncomfortable competing in that 'rock' pool. After the relationship with Rykodisc ended in 2003, I was still touring both solo and with a band, but the venues Paul Charles booked me into, particularly in the UK, were much bigger than I could hope to fill given my current profile there. It was like somehow the strategy of pushing the envelope all the time – bigger venues leading to bigger audiences – wasn't working. The results were that I'd find myself playing to 600 people in a 1,200-seater venue. The sense of disappointment was second only to the reduction in confidence playing these gigs. There was also an economic downside that meant our production costs were much higher than they needed to be. If you're booked into a large hall you need to bring a sound and light system that'll cover the space, with its accompanying cost. To deal with the costs Paul negotiated good fees for me, guaranteed amounts plus percentages over a certain ticket sales figure in the main. But in many cases the guarantees meant the concert promoters either made no money or lost out. Again and again, at this level Paul Brady was beginning to be seen as an unsafe bet and an act whose fees the agency demanded were too high. This, I believe, left me somewhat damaged in the UK.

Part of the booking strategy too, was to apply the 'scarcity value' rule, perfectly logical in the world Asgard operated in and to an extent it worked for me in that, over the previous two decades,

I didn't over-play any territory. In Ireland since 2000 I had been mostly playing only the major cities. But things were changing. Over the 1990s, Ireland had steadily developed a circuit of concert halls nationwide. By the new decade all the major cities had several good venues of differing capacities but most of the bigger towns now had professionally designed and kitted-out theatres of a reasonable size. The population was much younger and growing. There was more disposable income about. My profile was still as high as ever in the country. More and more people outside the major cities wanted to see me play. As my interest in global reach waned, I found myself wanting to play Ireland more. Maybe this was where Paul and I really differed in our vision.

To celebrate and promote the release of *Hooba Dooba* in 2010, Paul booked me and my band into Dublin's new 2,200-capacity Grand Canal theatre, promoted by Darryl Downey of Rag Lane Productions. I felt confident that I would bring in the business there and when the time came, I did. But the one contractual stipulation Rag Lane demanded was that I would agree not to play anywhere on the island of Ireland for, as I recall, seven months before that show and for several months afterwards.

This to me was mad, totally wrong and took the 'scarcity value' rule to an extreme. I felt that Paul, UK-based, was growing out of touch with my situation in Ireland and that the strategy model he was continuing to enact with me no longer met my current reality at home. I also felt it was crazy to continue to, in effect, underplay what was my home market. I told him so. We disagreed. One of Paul's defining characteristics, at least in my experience with him, is that he rarely accepts he's wrong. That became a problem for me, as I felt very strongly that I wanted to stop continuing to be stretched in areas I felt I couldn't reach anymore. The end result was that shortly after the *Hooba Dooba* tour we agreed to end our professional relationship.

We didn't fall out. We still, I would like to think, consider ourselves friends and from time to time we get in touch. I have great regard and respect for Paul Charles. He is a straightforward man with a great sense of humour. We laughed a lot. He was a huge part of my development as an artist. His efforts on my behalf greatly increased my stature and I will always be grateful to him for all he has done for me. I wish him all the best. Of course, like my earlier assessment of my relationship with my former manager Paul Cummins, this is probably a gross over-simplification of what was a very complex thirty-year relationship. There were many highs, definitely some lows. No regrets.

I didn't fully realise it at the time, of course, but this decision finally marked the end of my struggle to attain mainstream global acceptance. As far back as the Johnstons, my drive had seen me reluctant to upset the status quo so long as it held out any hope of improvement, advancement. Several times since, I had come close to walking away from situations that didn't feel right but this little fearful voice always managed to keep me hanging in there, 'The devil you know' kind of thing. Now, no longer imprisoned by the logic of the rock/pop world, I was aware that ending the relationship with Asgard was a seismic shift and I was anxious about what lay ahead.

46

REPRIEVE

I began to look at what I had achieved, as opposed to what I hadn't. At 63 I was fit and healthy. I was financially comfortable, owed no money, owned the house I lived in and had my own studio and could record whatever and whenever I wanted. My kids were raised and 'off the payroll'. Mary and I had come into a purple patch after some rocky periods. We took more breaks, travelled as a couple or with friends. I also rediscovered my love of scuba diving, took up skeet and clay shooting, and fly-fishing became a new passion. I spent as much time as I could on Ireland's lakes and rivers making new friends on the way.

I also seemed to be entering the realm of 'elder statesman' in the Irish cultural and academic fraternity. In a ceremony that would have given Mollie and Sean bragging rights back in the days of my thwarted academic career, I finally graduated with honours; in 2009 I was conferred with an honorary D. Litt from the University of Ulster and later awarded Irish Artist of the Year at The Galway University Foundation dinner in New York. But the undoubted highlight of my forlorn academic career was yet to come. In 2015 I was presented with the National Concert Hall's Lifetime Achievement award by Ireland's President, Michael D. Higgins. What an emotional concert – not least because had my parents still been alive, they would have savoured the accolade, but more because of the delightful irony of location; the NCH is now situated in what was, in 1967, the UCD examination hall where I dramatically ended my academic career by walking out of each exam exactly after the regulation minimum one hour. I was never going to pass those finals. I never even wanted a 'degree'. I just wanted to play music. Now in a bizarre turn of events I was honoured for having espoused that vocation in the very place I had once tasted total disgrace.

Added to this was something I could never have imagined way back as an awkward eleven-year-old 'yap', as we first-years at St Columb's were called. In October 2011, my old school magnanimously presented me with their *Illustrissimus* annual award to a 'distinguished past pupil'. And this despite my bad-mouthing my experience of the school a couple of years previously in a film documentary *The Boys of St Columb's*. There were lessons yet to be learnt from the old *alma mater*; with renewed understanding of the word grace, I now took my place alongside other illustrious past pupils: Seamus Heaney, John Hume, Brian Friel, James Sharkey, Eamonn McCann, Phil Coulter and Martin O'Neill. An honour indeed.

As we headed into the second decade of the century, we had the gift of a beautiful granddaughter, Lyra, from our daughter Sarah who lived in the UK by now. Mary and I travelled over to greet our new family member: so tiny, so determined, and gorgeous. We reminisced about the days Sarah herself was new-born, how out of our depth we were.

Our son Colm became a parent too. A big Neil Young fan, he had gone to see Neil play Roskilde Music festival in 2008 where he met Danielle McCallum, a Kiwi girl working in London. They became an item and Danielle moved to Ireland with Colm. In September 2011 they welcomed Seán, our first grandson and namesake of my own dad, into the world. They set up residence in County

Sligo, my father's ancestral home. Colm, working from home as a software engineer, was a keen surfer and picked a prime spot to live: Ballisodare, midway between Easkey and Strandhill – two popular surfing destinations. In 2012 they moved to New Zealand, to Danielle's hometown Christchurch, where they are still happily ensconced; Colm is now Senior Lead Software Developer with a local company. Since then, two more wonderful grandchildren have arrived, Leo in 2014 and Olive in 2018.

From Sarah and husband Stephen Hamilton, our third grandchild, Finn, arrived in June 2014. Being grandparents, as well as the joy and relief of seeing our family healthy and happy, has many advantages. One of them for Mary and I is an opportunity to travel. As well as the UK, we go to New Zealand every year where we get to do what all grandparents can't do with their own kids – spoil them relentlessly.

I had one scare around this time. It kicked off for real while I was playing a concert in Dublin's St Patrick's Cathedral as part of the annual Temple Bar Folk Festival, 2014. An incipient problem in my right hand flared up badly. I'd been having cortisone injections in the thumb joint for the previous couple of years to alleviate increasing pain but as they'd decreased in effectiveness it became clear I was going to need an operation.

The problem got worse over the next couple of months culminating in a scary episode in London's Royal Albert Hall on the occasion of President Michael D. Higgins' state visit to meet with Queen Elizabeth. *Céiliúradh* (Celebration in Irish) was the title of the evening's entertainment and featured a large selection of prominent Irish singers, musicians, writers and actors of the day.

In the middle of my performance my hand, regularly sore by now, lost grip of the plectrum and it fell to the floor. Lucky I'd a spare one attached to my guitar or I'd have had a problem completing 'Nothing but the Same Old Story'. This was serious now.

It took the rest of that year to figure out the best approach and eventually my good friend Ozzie Kilkenny, through contacts made in the course of his work with the Special Olympics, suggested I go see Dr Tristan Lascar, an eminent surgeon who was a globally renowned pioneer in the invention of new techniques to repair shoulder, knee and hand injuries. The only problem, as it appeared at first, was that his practice was in Monte Carlo, Monaco, at the Princess Grace Hospital where he was Chef de Service!

As luck would have it, my friend Ciaran Tourish, fiddler extra-ordinaire, had introduced me several years previously to Donegal man Pat Doherty, for whom Ciaran's wife Siobhan worked as PA. Pat had a lovely house in Villefranche a few miles from the French border with Monaco and offered the place to me as long as I needed to be there.

Ryanair flights to nearby Nice were plentiful and in the latter half of 2014, I went to see Dr Lascar several times culminating in an operation in November. Ciaran then kindly came to Ville-franche, drove me to and from the hospital and generally looked after me for the extent of my stay. The recuperation period at home was about fourteen weeks, which was an anxious time for me, unsure how things would be when I next wanted to play an instrument.

The operation was a success. Six years later I barely think of what was, potentially, a career-threatening condition. The nice thing about it too was that, in a hospital in Monte Carlo, a place bursting with Russian Oligarchs and Arab Oil Sheiks with proba-bly more money per square inch than any place on earth, the final total cost of the operation and treatment came to about half what it would have cost in Ireland. Go figure, as the Americans say.

Meanwhile, in my studio I continued writing and recording the songs that would eventually come together as the album *Un-finished Business*. In a new departure for me, three songs were co-written with Ireland's much-loved poet, Paul Muldoon ('I Love You but You Love Him', 'Say You Don't Mean', and 'I Like How You Think') taking me into a totally new headspace that became familiar territory surprisingly quickly.

The Muldoon co-writes were a sideways move for me. Paul's poetry interested and excited me. He had co-written songs before with, among others, Warren Zevon, so when he started sending me song lyrics, I was excited to find out what I could bring to them. What was good for me was that he wasn't precious about his input. When I had the musical shape of a song together and it seemed to suggest additional lyrics, or even the need to lose some, he was happy for me to finish things off.

Another co-writer was the much-loved member of the Nashville Songwriters' Hall of Fame, Sharon Vaughn. We enjoyed writing together and always came up with a bunch of 'keepers'. On my 2005 album *Say What You Feel*, Sharon co-wrote 'Don't Try to Please Me', 'Sail Sail On' and 'The You That's Really You'. On this occasion I had a pile of tunes and one or two unfinished lyrics that we now pored over. In two days, we'd written four songs: the titlular 'Unfinished Business', as well as 'Something to Change', 'Oceans of Time' and 'Harvest Time'. A fifth song 'Maybe Tomorrow' came soon after.

Ralph Murphy, whom I'd collaborated with previously on *Hooba Dooba*,* co-wrote 'Once in a Lifetime', which proved a favourite of my granddaughter Lyra who loves singing it.

For the first time since the album *Nobody Knows* back in 1999, I included two traditional folk songs on a record, 'The Cocks Are Crowing' and 'Lord Thomas and Fair Eleanor'.

As we finalised recording in 2016 the creative autonomy that started in *Hooba Dooba* expanded to induce a feeling I

---

* Ralph Murphy and I wrote the ballad 'One More Today' together on *Hooba Dooba*.

hadn't experienced in an entire career spanning nearly fifty years: *Unfinished Business* was the first record I had put out not caring whether it was commercially successful or not. A further indication of how far I had moved outside the music business, how autonomous I had truly become. When it was released in 2017 the leading Irish music paper *Hot Press*, a publication that had regularly championed me in the past, didn't even review the record.

With *Unfinished Business* there was a weight off my back. It was getting about under its own steam. It showed the full breadth of my musical interests and capabilities. I'd made a good record by my own standards. It was a lovely feeling to know that's all that mattered to me right now. I was looking to the future with joy instead of trepidation.

I found myself again and again looking back to the 1970s and my time with Andy Irvine in particular. We were approaching the fortieth anniversary of the release of our 1977 album and thought it would be nice to re-present it live with the other two contributors to that record, Dónal Lunny who produced it and played on several tracks, and fiddler Kevin Burke. In May of 2017 we did a nationwide Irish tour to packed houses everywhere. On first release all those years ago, the record touched a lot of people who now wanted to celebrate and revisit those times. The following year we brought the show to London's Barbican and Prague's Archa Theatre.

47

LOOKING BACK
AND LOOKING FORWARD

It's only now, when I'm finally in the place I'm meant to be, that I can reflect on my long and winding musical journey. From that early feeling at St Columb's of not fitting in, I can see the contradictions and tensions which have whispered in my ear throughout my career.

I chased the major record deals, but they never quite came off and something in the background always held me back anyway – some unwillingness to give up my own artistic vision. I was selling out multiple nights in London venues, raising the roof at the Cambridge Folk Festival and Glastonbury. In Ireland I was still popular, had commercial viability, as evidenced in high volumes of daytime radio play, but the standard model of music success – to have a radio hit in the UK and Europe and on the back of that, build a touring career – didn't follow. My music and my influences were too niche, especially by the mid-1980s. I was a square plug trying to fit into a round hole. I was out of my time.

The musical relationships I built got me huge numbers of opportunities – with Eric Clapton, Dire Straits – but at the same time, they didn't always suit my music or my vision of myself. I'm left wondering the extent to which, for example, Damage Management was an advantage to me or not. And then there was the issue of the way I was being sold and expected to present myself; it made me uncomfortable, though nobody in the music business was to blame. It was a feeling of being out of control of my own life and being dependent on management and record labels for any movement in any direction that was the hardest to bear.

At the time, on some deep subconscious level I had a strong feeling this path wasn't for me, indeed that the appropriate path had yet to appear, but by the mid-1980s I was committed to the status quo in so many ways, aspirationally, contractually, financially, emotionally, professionally that I couldn't let this feeling come to the surface. It created a kind of pressure cooker in me that led to a lot of inner conflict and tensions in my personal life too.

It was probably then that I acquired in some quarters the reputation for being a 'grumpy bollix'. In fact I was just frustrated and deeply unhappy.

I always stayed true to my own creative muse in terms of the songs I wrote but in my willingness to fit in and comply with the dynamic of the mainstream music business in the mid-1980s and be seen to be 'doing my bit', I had to let go of the folk world. This left me exposed and isolated, neither fish nor flesh.

Wisdom now tells me that those years had to unfold as they did to drive me to the point of realisation (not for the first or last time), that it takes time to end a situation that has become limiting so you can reclaim autonomy, start again. And, there's been no shortage of high points along the way.

I am under no illusion about my songwriting success. I was fortunate enough to come in on the tail end of the lyric revolution started by Dylan in the 1960s when songs didn't have to have 'moon' and 'June' in the lyrics to be commercially successful anymore.

But even outside of the industry I have always felt caught, suspended somewhere between music as a serious business that feeds the head, heart and soul and music that's instantly accessible but equally and immediately forgettable; music that's a so-called 'work of art' and music that is disposable entertainment.

I relate to both.

I understand why the two extremes exist.

I see value in both.

But this in the past left me confused as to where to position myself. I once had an idea for a record sleeve that featured a pulldown menu from an app that offered 'pop, rock, jazz, blues, country, folk, classical and other'.

No prizes for guessing which one I ticked.

As 'other', something of this constant push and pull can be seen in the development of my songs. My work has always been quintessentially Irish. Irishness is at the emotional heart of it. My output probably demanded more of the listener than what generally appeared on *Top of the Pops* in the 1980s. But I never thought the answer was to reduce my melodies and narratives to 'simple pop formats' that people could instantly relate to. Time and time again I have found myself in an arena totally unsuited to me, like a show jumper in a steeplechase.

I wanted to be successful. But as I mentioned earlier, there's success and Success (with a capital S). Outside Ireland, the place where my star was still in the ascendancy, there didn't seem to be an arena in which I could show my wares and compete without ceasing to be what I was. I was stuck between the folk and the mainstream pop worlds.

On the one hand I've been courted by academia and given a doctorate for my thoughts and opinions as a 'serious songwriter', while on the other I'm sent fan letters by men and women who are smitten by this or that song; who want to get close to me. Though it's nice to be respected on an intellectual level by educated literary people, I've also always enjoyed meeting fans after a gig and feeling that raw connection based on a shared longing, need, affection and, yes, sexual energy, that the power I'm lucky enough to have coursing through me onstage brings forth. That's what's immediate and real. Maybe that is success – entertaining people, performing. The rest is just 'trying to make sense of it all'.

As the years pass by nice surprises continue to come my way. Out of the blue in late 2018 I got an email from Mark Knopfler saying that his friend, American icon Jimmy Buffett, was coming to Ireland the following year to play a Dublin date and wanted to hook up with me. Mark had introduced Jimmy to my music and he had developed a taste for it. Jimmy and I got in touch and in the course of our communications, I sent him a song I had written with Ralph Murphy called 'Down at the Lah De Dah', a fun little song about a Caribbean beach bar. I never really thought anything would come out of it. The year passed and the following September Jimmy came to Dublin for his show. I was delighted to see he was including both songs in his set list with his ten-piece Coral Reefer Band. I joined him on stage in The Olympia and we duetted on 'The World Is What You Make It' and 'Down at the Lah De Dah'.

Next day we flew to London in his Gulfstream jet and I joined up with them again onstage at the London Palladium. The upshot of all this is that Jimmy has recorded three of my songs on his 2020 album *Life on the Flip Side* – 'The World Is What You Make It', 'Down at the Lah De Dah' and 'Oceans Of Time' from my *Unfinished Business* album.

A further surprise in 2021 was to be gifted with an honorary doctorate by the University of Limerick, whose Irish World Academy of Music and Dance I've been involved in as a patron for several years. Most recently in September 2022 I was granted the Ulysses Medal, University College Dublin's highest honour, for my contribution to Irish music since the 1960s – a further ironic twist on my ignominious failure as a student there all those years ago.

Sad things have happened too. Liam Óg O'Flynn, my musical colleague from our Planxty days, passed on in 2018, as did the master fiddler, Tommy Peoples, with whom I made the record *The High Part of the Road* in the mid-1970s and whose playing was a beautiful addition to *Welcome Here Kind Stranger*.

Arty McGlynn, my old musical sparring partner sadly left us in late 2019. Earlier that year, Ralph Murphy, dear friend and song-writing colleague from Nashville, lost a long fight against illness. He and I had several successes over the years including '21st Century Christmas' that went to No. 2 in the UK for Cliff Richard.

Of course, like everyone in the music fraternity, I was shocked and saddened to hear of the death in 2020 of John Prine from complications after contracting Covid-19. A great loss to his wife Fiona and family and to us all. The deepest loss came when my dear friend and long-time collaborator Shay Healy passed on. In what must have been a prescient mood, he came to me a few years previously with a lyrical concept wherein the narrator/ singer of the song has already left the planet and is assuring loved ones left behind that everything's alright. We called the song 'Just Behind the Veil'. When we'd finished laughing, we made a promise to each other that whoever went first, the other would sing it at his funeral. I did that in April 2021. I know you're still laughing up there, Shay!

As I sit here in Dublin, writing in the middle of a Covid-19 lockdown, although all my concerts for the year have been cancelled, I'm strangely peaceful. I am not unduly concerned, which is unusual for me. It is what it is. And we're all in the same boat. None of us knows what lies ahead.

At the start of the lockdown I released a song I wrote with Sharon Vaughn called 'It's a Beautiful World (Now You Are Here)'. It was initially themed as a love song in a chaotic time. The day I finished the recording coincided with the arrival of a grandson, Lughan, for Philip and Nicola Flynn, dear friends of Mary and me. When Mary heard the song she said, 'This could equally be about the arrival of new life.' I adapted the recording appropriately; it's a song that I hope brings a smile to the face of anyone who hears it.

And so where to now after all these crazy dreams? Right now, I'm recording again. I've just released yet another album … entitled *Maybe So*.

On we go? Maybe so.

ACKNOWLEDGEMENTS

Firstly, I'd like to thank my parents, Sean Brady Sr and Mollie McElholm, for instilling a love of music in me from such an early age.

This book would not have been possible without the loving support of my wife Mary Elliott, and of my two wonderful children, Sarah and Colm.

My thanks to Ferdia MacAnna, Kathy Gilfillan, Antony Farrell and David Dickson for reading the text and providing invaluable feedback. Ferdia was one of the first to read the early draft and his encouragement was much appreciated at that time.

Stephen Rea also read the text at an early stage and I'm extremely grateful for the insights which he provided.

Thanks to Jennifer Brady (no relation), for her expert editorial guidance through the main body of the work. Also, thanks to Heidi Houlihan for her help at the copy-editing stage.

I'd like to thank Conor Graham of Merrion Press for taking on the book and to his staff, Patrick O'Donoghue, Maeve Convery and Wendy Logue, for making the process such an enjoyable experience.

Finally, my thanks, as ever, to my manager and friend John Munnis for all he has done down through the years.

VARIOUS PATS ON THE BACK

1978: *Melody Maker* Folk Album of the Year for *Welcome Here Kind Stranger*

1979: Institute of Creative Advertising and Design 'Best Original Music' award

THE STAG/ HOT PRESS AWARDS (Ireland's leading music paper, critics awards)
1981: Best Single 'Crazy Dreams'
1982: Best Song 'Nothing But The Same Old Story'
1985: Best Songwriter
1986: Best Songwriter and Best Male Singer

1986: 'Opel' National Entertainment Awards 'Best Rock Artist'

1991: Belfast Telegraph Entertainment Media and Arts (EMA) Awards 'Best Solo Rock Artist'

1993: Irish Recorded Music Association (IRMA) Irish Music Awards 'Best Irish Male Artist'

2000: 'Irish Music Magazine' award for Best Contemporary Album *Oh What A World*

2002: IRMA (Irish Recorded Music Association) 'Lifetime Achievement Award'

The ASCAP '#1 Club Award' on Brooks & Dunn reaching No. 1 in the USA with 'The Long Goodbye' written by Paul Brady & Ronan Keating

2004: British Academy of Songwriters and Composers 'Gold Badge Award'

2006: BBC Radio 2 Folk Awards 'Lifetime Achievement Award'

2009: Conferred with Honorary D. Litt at University of Ulster
Chosen as Irish 'artist of the year' by Galway University Foundation

2010: 'Paul Brady Scholarship' announced at University College Limerick
'Tenco Prize' for songwriting at the Rassegna Della Canzone D'Autore, Sanremo, Italy

2011: 'Illustrissimus' Award from my old school St Columb's College, Derry

2013: Inducted to the IMRO Academy

2015: 'Lifetime Achievement Award' from The National Concert Hall, Dublin, Ireland presented by the President of Ireland, Michael D. Higgins

2021: Conferred with Honorary D. Litt at University College Limerick

2022: Awarded the Ulysses Medal by University College Dublin